MATCH

WORLD CUP 2002

ACKNOWLEDGEMENTS

A Last Chance Saloon Production.

Conceived and Edited by:
Chris Hunt and Jon Hayden
Design consultant: Darryl Tooth
Design team: Suzanne Johns and Mark
Church at Richard Rowe and Partners
Contributors: Nick Gibbs and Luke Nicoli

Photographs: supplied by Action Images

Special thanks to:
Tony Warner at Paradigm-ICT and
David Scripps and David Jacobs
at Action Images

A CIP catalogue record for this book is
available from the British Library

The Match logo is a registered trademark
and is used here by kind permission of
EMAP Active Ltd.

First published in Great Britain in 2002 by
Hayden Publishing Limited. Copyright © Hayden Publishing.

Colour Origination by PDQ Digital Media Solutions Ltd.
Printed and bound in Italy by LEGO, Vicenza.
ISBN 1 90363 505 5

NORTH KOREA 🇰🇵

SOUTH KOREA 🇰🇷

INCHEON ⚽ ⚽ SEOUL

⚽ SUWON

DAEJEON ⚽

JEONJU ⚽

⚽ GWANGJU

⚽ DAEGU

⚽ ULSAN

⚽ BUSAN

⚽ SEOGWIPO

S E A   O F

J A P A N

NIIGA

🇯🇵 JA

SAITA

TOKYO

⚽

SHIZUOK

KOBE ⚽

OITA ⚽

OSAKA ⚽

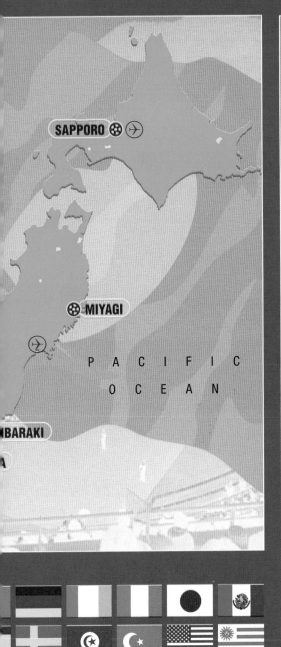

SAPPORO ⊗ ✈

⊗ MIYAGI

✈

P A C I F I C

O C E A N

IBARAKI

MATCH WORLD CUP 2002

A BRIEF HISTORY OF THE WORLD CUP

It all began on July 1930 when France beat Mexico 4-1 in front of just 1000 fans. A succint history of the world's greatest sporting tournament.

6

THE WORLD'S TOP TEN STRIKERS

Who are going to be the Golden Boot contenders at the 2002 World Cup Finals? We pick a likely top ten.

24

DANCING TO GLORY – THE WORLD'S GREAT PLAYMAKERS

David Beckham, Luis Figo and Francesco Totti can class themselves as signed-up members of the footballing superstars club, but until they have made their mark on the biggest stage of all, their life membership remains a tantalising target.

44

WORLD CUP VENUES

All the essential things you need to know about every Korean and Japanese stadium.

54

ON OFFICAL BUSINESS

Who are the thirty six World Cup referees?

63

A GUIDE TO EVERY FINALIST

A country-by-country guide to the squads, likely formations, the men that matter, roads to qualification, every country's low down, and history at the World Cup.

64

1930 Uruguay 4 Argentina 2

Hosts: Uruguay
Final: Uruguay 4 Argentina 2, Estadio Centenario, Montevideo, 93,000
Leading scorer: Guillermo Stabile (Argentina) 8
World Cup weirdness: A different ball was used in each half of the final because the teams couldn't decide which one to use.

It all began on July 13 1930 when France beat Mexico 4-1 in front of just 1,000 fans. Back then, few people could afford to sail abroad to support their team and hardly anyone in Uruguay cared about France. But they did care about Uruguay, and when their heroes played rivals Argentina 93,000 wild fans were there to see it. World Cup fever was born. France were one of only four European teams that could be bothered to go to South America to enter the new competition. The others were Belgium, Romania and Yugoslavia. The Yugoslavs were the only ones to reach the last four as the tone for the winning team coming from the home continent was set. Due to heavy rain, the stadium for the final in Montevideo was only completed five days after the tournament had started. But it was ready for a terrific final in which Uruguay beat Argentina 4-2 amid wild celebrations that continued the following day when a national holiday was called.

1934 Italy 2 Czechoslovakia 1

Hosts: Italy
Final: Italy 2 Czechoslovakia 1 aet, Stadio PNF, Rome, 55,000
Top scorer: Oldrich Nejedly (Czechoslovakia) 5
World Cup weirdness: The Czechoslovakia squad was made up entirely of players from just two clubs.

Because so many European countries snubbed South America four years earlier, the Latinos did the same this time. Even Uruguay didn't show, the only time the winners have failed to defend the trophy. It was left to America, Egypt, Brazil and Argentina to gatecrash the European party. But the event had already grown in popularity: 32 countries wanted to take part and for the first time teams had to qualify. None of them involved England though.

The Football Association still thought they were above such an event. Italy, under the Fascist rule of Benito Mussolini, destroyed the Americans 7-1 in the first round and went on to meet Czechoslovakia in the final. It took 70 minutes for the opening goal and it went to the Czechs. They then hit the post before Italy equalised in the final 10 minutes then went on to win the match in extra time.

ALL TIME TOPSCORERS

14 Gerd Müller (GER)

13 Just Fontaine (FRA)

12 Pelé (BRA)

11 Sandor Kocsis (HUN)

11 Jürgen Klinsmann (GER)

10 Helmut Rahn (GER)

10 Teofilio Cubillas (PER)

10 Gary Lineker (ENG)

10 Grzegorz Lato (POL)

9 Gabriel Batistuta (ARG)

9 Roberto Baggio (ITA)

9 Paolo Rossi (ITA)

9 Uwe Seeler (GER)

9 Jairzinho (BRA)

9 Eusebio (POR)

9 Karl-Heinz Rummenigge (GER)

9 Vava (BRA)

9 Ademir (BRA)

WORLD CUP FACTS

Fastest goal:
Vaclav Masek, Czechoslovakia, 16 seconds v Mexico, 1962

Latest goal:
David Platt, England, 119 minutes v Belgium, 1990

Oldest goalscorer:
Roger Milla, Cameroon v Russia, 1994, age 42 years and 39 days

Youngest goalscorer:
Pelé, Brazil v Wales, 1958, age 17 years and 239 days

Scored in two World Cup finals:
Vava, Brazil 1958 and 1962
Pelé, Brazil, 1958 and 1970
Paul Breitner, West Germany, 1974 and 1982

Portsmouth's **Robert Prosinecki** is the only player to have scored for two countries. He did it for Yugoslavia in 1990 and Croatia in 1998.

Ernie Brandts is the only player to have scored at both ends. He did it playing for Holland v Italy in 1978.

Most goals in one match
5 - Oleg Salenko (RUS) vs Cameroon in 1994.

Scored in most tournaments
4 - **Pelé** (BRA) - 1958, 1962, 1966, 1970
4 - **Uwe Seeler** (GER) - 1958, 1962, 1966, 1970

1938 Italy 4 Hungary 2

Hosts: France
Final: Italy 4 Hungary 2, Stade Colombes, Paris, 55,000
Top scorer: Leonidas (Brazil) 8
World Cup weirdness: Leonidas scored four goals for Brazil in a 6-5 defeat of Poland playing barefoot.

France weren't anything like as good the first time they hosted the World Cup as they were the second time in 1998. After beating Belgium, they ran into the brilliant Italians in the second round where the defending champions beat them 3-1. From then on, Italy were unstoppable but it could have been so different had a late goal against them in the opening round by Norway, with the score level, not been disallowed for offside. For the second tournament running, European teams dominated. Argentina got in a huff for not being chosen as hosts and refused to take part while Uruguay again stayed away. Brazil were the continent's only representative and they provided a taste of what was to come by finishing third and providing the tournament's leading scorer. But it was Italy's year and World War Two meant they held the trophy for 12 years.

1950 Uruguay 2 Brazil 1

Hosts: Brazil
Final: Uruguay 2 Brazil 1, Maracana, Rio de Janeiro, 199,854
Top scorer: Ademir (Brazil) 9
World Cup weirdness: An Italian had hidden the World Cup in a shoebox under his bed during World War II.

Football fever was beginning to build in Brazil and with Europe still in post-war turmoil, they promised to stage a football carnival. For many teams it was just that, but for England 1950 was a nightmare. They arrived for their first World Cup as one of the hot favourites after thrashing a Rest of Europe side 6-1 in 1947. But in one of the biggest shocks in World Cup history they were beaten 1-0 by the United States, a result so unexpected that some newspapers back in England assumed it was a mistake and reported 10-1. With the competition for the first time held in groups, England still had the chance to go through until Spain beat them 1-0. Four teams eventually battled it out in a pool of four as for the only time there was no final. When Brazil met Uruguay they needed only a draw to lift the trophy, but they lost 2-1 in front of the biggest ever crowd for a football match. Uruguay had now won both World Cups they had entered.

1954 West Germany 3 Hungary 2

Hosts: Switzerland
Final: West Germany 3 Hungary 2, Wankdorf Stadion, Berne, 60,000
Top scorer: Sandor Kocsis (Hungary) 11
World Cup weirdness: The quarter-final in Lausanne between Austria and Switzerland produced the most goals in World Cup history. Austria won 7-5.

The first televised World Cup turned out to be the highest-scoring ever, with each match yielding on average 5.38 goals. It also marked the arrival of West Germany as a footballing superpower. It wasn't expected to be that way: Hungary, inspired by Puskas, had emerged as the continent's top team and when they hammered the Germans 8-3 in a group match no-one could possibly imagine the result being reversed. But Germany, showing the kind of resolve for which they would become famous, qualified as group runners-up and began to build momentum. England made it to the Second Round where they lost 4-2 to Uruguay while Scotland, in their first-ever finals, set a standard they have continued to follow by failing to advance beyond the opening round. In a classic final, Hungary raced into a two-goal lead but West Germany equalised in the 18th minute and the game remained deadlocked until the Germans scored an 84th minute winner. A late Puskas equaliser was ruled offside by a Welsh linesman.

1958 Brazil 5 Sweden 2

Hosts: Sweden
Final: Brazil 5 Sweden 2, Rasunda Stadion, Solna, 49,737
Top scorer: Just Fontaine (France) 13
World Cup weirdness: Twenty-eight years after the tournament began, England and Brazil played out the first 0-0 draw in World Cup finals history.

Brazil had been threatening something special for some time and in Sweden they delivered. In their third game they unveiled a 17-year-old striker called Pelé, who would score six goals in the tournament and go on to become the only man to win three World Cups. England began with three draws and faced a play-off for the last eight against the Soviet Union. Again they were found wanting on the big occasion, losing 1-0. But 1958 remains the only time that all four British teams made it to the finals, with Wales and Northern Ireland both reaching the last eight. Brazil edged out Wales 1-0 thanks to a Pelé goal, described by the great man as "the most important of my career", then went on to smash five in the semi-final and another five in the final as their era of dominance began. Just Fontaine's 13-goal haul remains a World Cup record.

1954 and West Germany celebrate winning the World Cup. Wonder what they would have looked like if they'd lost?

Mexico 1970 and the great Pelé goes past a Czechoslovakian defender.

1962 Brazil 3 Czechoslovakia 1

Hosts: Chile
Final: Brazil 3 Czechoslovakia 1, Estadio Nacional, Santiago, 68,679
Top scorer: Garrincha (Brazil), Valentin Ivanov (Soviet Union), Leonel Sanchez (Chile), Vava (Brazil), Florian Albert (Hungary) and Drazan Jerkovic (Yugoslavia) 4 goals
World Cup weirdness: Pelé played most of Brazil's second match with a pulled muscle because no substitutions were allowed. He aggravated the injury and missed the rest of the tournament.

A record 56 teams battled for a place in the finals, which surprisingly were staged in Chile soon after a major earthquake. The grim atmosphere transferred on to the pitch in perhaps the dirtiest and most cynical World Cup in history. One famous match in Santiago between Chile and Italy resulted in fights, a broken nose, spitting and two sendings off. Shortly after the referees were rounded up and told to stamp out the thugs. England scraped through the group stages to face Brazil in the last eight. They lost 3-1 and Brazil, minus the injured 'Black Pearl' Pelé, were on a roll. The Czechs briefly threatened to spoil their party when they took a 1-0 lead in the final. But Brazil fought back to prove beyond question that they were the team of the age by winning the tournament for the second time running, emulating the Italians of the 1930s.

1966 England 4 West Germany 2

Hosts: England
Final: England 4 West Germany 2, Wembley, 96,924
Top scorer: Eusebio (Portugal) 9
World Cup weirdness: The World Cup was lost shortly before the tournament but recovered in bushes in South London by a dog named Pickles.

Could Brazil become the first team to make it three in a row? It didn't take long to discover the answer. Defeats to Hungary and Portugal meant they failed to make it past the group stages as Pelé once again received some brutal treatment by defenders in another rough tournament. Another superpower, Italy, went home early after suffering an amazing 4-3 defeat against North Korea in one of the tournament's most amazing matches ever. Who could fill the void? England hardly looked capable when they kicked off with a dour 0-0 draw against Uruguay. Portugal, spearheaded by the mercurial Eusebio, looked more likely until they were undone by two Bobby Charlton goals in the semi-finals. England had hit form at just the right time and in the final against West Germany looked set for a regulation 2-1 win until the Germans equalised with 15 seconds to go. Then came the Russian linesman, Geoff Hurst's hat-trick – still the only one in a World Cup final – and England's finest hour.

Martin Peters scores for England.

1970 Brazil 4 Italy 1

Hosts: Mexico
Final: Brazil 4 Italy 1, Estadio Azteca, Mexico City, 107,000
Top scorer: Gerd Müller (West Germany) 10
World Cup weirdness: Not a single player was sent off in the 1970 World Cup.

Played in intense heat and at altitude, the 1970 World Cup was one of the best ever. It featured great goals, great players and perhaps the greatest team of all time. After having lumps kicked out of him in the last two World Cups, Pelé vowed not to play in another but he was tempted to make this his swansong. Inspired, Brazil beat defending champions England in the group stages and although Bobby Moore's team still qualified they suffered perhaps their most agonising defeat ever in the quarter-finals when Germany overturned a 2-0 deficit to win 3-2. More classic games followed as Italy beat West Germany 4-3 in the semi-finals only to be on the wrong side of a four-goal hammering in the final against Brazil. In that match, football was played like it had never been played before and Pelé became the only man to win three World Cup winner's medals.

1974 West Germany 2 Holland 1

Hosts: West Germany
Final: West Germany 2 Holland 1, Olympia Stadion, Munich, 77,833
Top scorer: Grzgorz Lato (Poland) 7
World Cup weirdness: Zaire's president awarded each of his players a car, a holiday and a house just for qualifying for the finals.

Holland had never been mentioned as a serious footballing force before the 1970s. They have hardly been described as anything else since. This was where it all began. The orange shirts dominated two consecutive tournaments with their exciting new brand of 'Total Football', yet they never won the World Cup. Twice they fell at the final hurdle. England didn't qualify but Scotland did. They never lost a match but missed out on a place in the Second Round on goal difference to Brazil, who were a shadow of the great team of 1970. Surely Holland's time had come. In Johann Cruyff they had a superstar and he inspired them to victories over Brazil and Argentina. But West Germany had a superstar of their own in Franz Beckenbauer. They made their usual slow start, losing to deadly rivals East Germany in the group stages, but recovered to meet the Dutch in the final. English referee, Jack Taylor, awarded Holland a penalty in the first minute but the Germans fought back to win.

Goalscorer Gerson receives the unwelcome attentions of a Brazilian official.

1978 Argentina 3 Holland 1

Hosts: Argentina
Final: Argentina 3 Holland 1 (aet), Estadio Monumental, Buenos Aires, 77,260
Top scorer: Mario Kempes (Argentina) 6
World Cup weirdness: Peruvian goalkeeper Ramon Quiroga was booked for a foul – committed in the opponent's half.

Holland had emerged as a soccer superpower in '74; in '78 it was Argentina's turn. At home, England's failure to qualify again focused attention on Scotland, who had one of their greatest ever teams. They boasted of winning but learned a painful lesson by losing to Peru and drawing with Iran. An Archie Gemmill wonder goal in the final match, a 3-2 defeat of Holland, couldn't repair the damage and Scotland's best ever chance of advancing beyond the first round had gone. Argentina didn't look too hot in the first group round but in the second group stage Mario Kempes brought them to life. He scored twice against Poland and twice more in the 6-0 rout of Peru, the decisive result that saw Argentina through to the final. Holland beat Italy to reach their second consecutive final, but their worst nightmare was realised when a post denied them victory late in the game before Argentina went on to win by 3-1 and deny them in the final for a second tournament running.

1982 Italy 3 West Germany 1

Hosts: Spain
Final: Italy 3 West Germany 1, Estadio Bernabeu, Madrid, 90,000
Top scorer: Paolo Rossi (Italy) 6
World Cup weirdness: Top scorer Rossi had just served a two-year ban from international football for getting involved in a bribe scandal.

When Italy kicked off the 1982 World Cup with a dire 0-0 draw against Poland, few people thought they had a chance of winning the World Cup. And when striker Paolo Rossi failed to score in the opening four matches, no one could imagine that he would turn into the tournament's superstar. England qualified for the first time since 1974 and never lost in five matches but a lack of goals cost them a semi-final place. Northern Ireland shocked Spain and Algeria stunned West Germany in the early stages, but as always the Germans proved they are a great tournament team by coming strong when it mattered. They beat France on penalties in a dramatic semi-final to meet Italy in the final. Italy had already beaten Brazil 3-2 in a classic match and feared no one. In an eventful final, they proved too good for the Germans to lift the trophy for the third time.

Keegan despairs after missing a chance against spain. Not suprised he missed in those shorts.

1986 Argentina 3 West Germany 2

Hosts: Mexico
Final: Argentina 3 West Germany 2, Estadio Azteca, Mexico City, 114,590
Top scorer: Gary Lineker (England) 6
World Cup weirdness: A foul on Scotland's Gordon Strachan after 56 seconds earned Uruguayan Jose Batista the distinction of fastest ever World Cup dismissal.

World Cups regularly throw up heroes and villains but rarely does one man fill both roles. But Diego Maradona did in 1986 when he scored his 'Hand of God' goal against England then followed it up with probably the greatest goal ever to end Bobby Robson's team's hopes in the quarter-finals. Scotland had been drawn in a Group of Death and fell at the first hurdle. England recovered from a terrible start, losing 1-0 to Portugal, and were hitting top form when they ran into Maradona. At least they had the consolation of boasting the tournament's leading scorer in Gary Lineker. He was to net four more at the next World Cup. England certainly weren't the only team to suffer at the hand, or by the hand, of Maradona: never has one man so dominated a World Cup. He was awesome, making up for the '82 tournament when he was sent off in disgrace by inspiring his side to victory in the final against West Germany.

1990 Germany 1 Argentina 0

Hosts: Italy
Final: Germany 1 Argentina 0, Stadio Olimpico, Rome, 73,603
Top scorer: Salvatore Schillaci (Italy) 6
World Cup weirdness: The United Arab Emirates team were promised a Rolls Royce for every goal scored. They managed two.

Cameroon, who began the tournament with a memorable 1-0 defeat of Argentina, became the first African nation to reach the quarter-finals. When they then went 2-1 up against England, thanks to 38-year-old Roger Milla, anything looked possible but Gary Lineker pulled England through 3-2 in one of the tournament's rare exciting matches. Sadly, the main memories of Italia '90'are of dour draws and penalty shoot-outs. Both semi-finals were settled this way, as no doubt Chris Waddle and Stuart Pearce could tell you. Their misses against Germany cost England their second ever final appearance. Jack Charlton led the Republic of Ireland to the last eight where they were beaten by Italy, who then fell on penalties to Argentina. The final was a repeat of four years earlier with Germany gaining revenge courtesy of a late goal – appropriately enough, it was a penalty. The Germans joined Brazil and Italy as three-time World Cup winners.

Gary Lineker celebrates on his way to the hat-trick that puts England into the second round.

1994 Brazil 0 Italy 0 (Brazil won 3-2 on Penalties)

Hosts: United States of America
Final: Brazil 0 Italy 0 (Brazil won 3-2 on penalties), Rose Bowl, Los Angeles, 94,194
Top scorer: Hristo Stoitchkov (Bulgaria), Oleg Salenko (Russia) 6
World Cup weirdness: Colombian Andres Escobar was murdered on his return home after scoring an own goal against America.

Everyone knows Americans don't like proper sports so the decision to hold the World Cup there was a big gamble. But it paid off as the crowds filled the huge stadia to see some great matches. Sadly, not one British team was there to enjoy it although the Republic of Ireland, managed by England's 1966 hero Jack Charlton, provided plenty of interest. Hosts America made it through the first round only to then have the misfortune of running into Brazil, who beat them 1-0. Argentina made a brilliant start but were rocked by one of the biggest World Cup scandals when Diego Maradona failed a drugs test, his great career ending in shame. It was left to Italy to take on Brazil in a match that would decide which team would be the first to win the competition for a record fourth time. In a match unworthy of what had gone before, the two sides cancelled each other out and penalties followed. Roberto Baggio missed the decisive kick to start the Samba beat long into the night.

1998 France 3 Brazil 0

Hosts: France
Final: France 3 Brazil 0, Stade de France, Paris, 80,000
Top scorer: Davor Suker (Croatia) 6
World Cup weirdness: An estimated one in three people on the planet watched each game of the '98 finals.

By now, the World Cup was massive. Thirty-seven billion people tuned in on telly and few could believe their eyes when they watched the final. Brazil, in their sixth final, were destroyed by France, in their first. Before the match mystery surrounded the fitness of Brazil striker Ronaldo. His name was left off the team sheet only for him to play, but very ineffectively. It sparked all kinds of rumours. Zinedine Zidane inspired France with two goals and the cup was theirs long before Emmanuel Petit added a third in injury time. England were involved in the match of the tournament against Argentina, a 2-2 draw that will forever be remembered for Michael Owen's wonder goal and David Beckham's sending off. Ten-men England played brilliantly only to be undone again on penalties. Roll on the rematch in 2002!

Fabien Barthez famously stops strangely absent Ronaldo.

ENGLAND'S WORLD CUP MATCHES

Year	Opponent		Result	Year	Opponent		Result	Year	Opponent		Result
1950	Chile	W	2-0	1966	Uruguay	D	0-0	1986	Portugal	L	0-1
	United States	L	0-1		Mexico	W	2-0		Morocco	D	0-0
	Spain	L	0-1		France	W	2-0		Poland	W	3-0
1954	Belgium	D	4-4		Argentina	W	1-0		Paraguay	W	3-0
	Switzerland	W	2-0		Portugal	W	2-1		Argentina	L	1-2
	Uruguay	L	2-4		West Germany (a.e.t)	W	4-2	1990	Ireland	D	1-1
1958	Soviet Union	D	2-2	1970	Romania	W	1-0		Holland	D	0-0
	Brazil	D	0-0		Brazil	L	0-1		Egypt	W	1-0
	Austria	D	2-2		Czechoslovakia	W	1-0		Belgium (a.e.t)	W	1-0
	Soviet Union	L	0-1		West Germany (a.e.t)	L	2-3		Cameroon (a.e.t)	W	3-2
1962	Hungary	L	1-2	1982	France	W	3-1		West Germany pens 3-4	D	1-1
	Argentina	W	3-1		Czechoslovakia	W	2-0		Italy	L	1-2
	Bulgaria	D	0-0		Kuwait	W	1-0	1998	Tunisia	W	2-0
	Brazil	L	1-3		West Germany	D	0-0		Romania	L	1-2
					Spain	D	0-0		Colombia	W	2-0
									Argentina pens 3-4	D	2-2

ALL TIME WORLD CUP TABLE

	P	W	D	L	Goals	Pts		P	W	D	L	Goals	Pts
1.Brazil	80	53	14	13	173 -78	120	34.Colombia	13	3	2	8	14 -23	8
2.Germany (West)	78	45	17	16	162 -103	107	35.Norway	8	2	3	3	7 -8	7
3.Italy	66	38	16	12	105 -62	92	36.Ireland	9	1	5	3	4 -7	7
4.Argentina	57	29	10	18	100 -69	68	37.East Germany	6	2	2	2	5 -5	6
5.England	45	20	13	12	62 -42	53	38.Wales	5	1	3	1	4 -4	5
6.France	41	21	6	14	86 -58	48	39.Algeria	6	2	1	3	6 -10	5
7.Spain	40	16	10	14	61 -48	42	40.Saudi Arabia	7	2	1	4	7 -13	5
8.Yugoslavia	37	16	8	13	60 -46	40	41.Tunisia	6	1	2	3	4 -6	4
9.Russia/USSR	34	16	6	12	60 -40	38	42.Costa Rica	4	2	-	2	4 -6	4
10.Uruguay	37	15	8	14	61 -52	38	43.South Korea	14	-	4	10	11 -43	4
11.Holland	32	14	9	9	56 -36	37	44.North Korea	4	1	1	2	5 -9	3
12.Sweden	38	14	9	15	66 -60	37	45.Cuba	3	1	1	1	5 -12	3
13.Hungary	32	15	3	14	87 -57	33	46.Iran	6	1	1	4	4 -12	3
14.Poland	25	13	5	7	39 -29	31	47.Turkey	3	1	-	2	10 -11	2
15.Austria	29	12	4	13	43 -47	28	48.Honduras	3	-	2	1	2 -3	2
16.Czechoslovakia	30	11	5	14	44 -45	27	49.Israel	3	-	2	1	1 -3	2
17.Mexico	37	8	10	19	39 -75	26	50.Egypt	4	-	2	2	3 -6	2
18.Belgium	32	9	7	16	40 -56	25	51.South Africa	3	-	2	1	3 -6	2
19.Romania	21	8	5	8	30 -32	21	52.Jamaica	3	1	-	2	3 -9	2
20.Chile	25	7	6	12	31 -40	20	53.Kuwait	3	-	1	2	2 -6	1
21.Scotland	23	4	7	12	25 -41	15	54.Australia	3	-	1	2	0 -5	1
22.Switzerland	22	6	3	13	33 -51	15	55.Bolivia	6	-	1	5	1 -20	1
23.Paraguay	15	4	6	5	19 -27	14	56.Japan	3	-	-	3	1 -4	0
24.Bulgaria	26	3	8	15	22 -53	14	56.Iraq	3	-	-	3	1 -4	0
25.Portugal	9	6	-	3	19 -12	12	58.Canada	3	-	-	3	0 -5	0
26.Cameroon	14	3	6	5	13 -26	12	59.DutchEastIndies	1	-	-	1	0 -6	0
27.Denmark	9	5	1	3	19 -13	11	60.Utd A. Emirates	3	-	-	3	2 -11	0
28.North. Ireland	13	3	5	5	13 -23	11	61.New Zealand	3	-	-	3	2 -12	0
29.Peru	15	4	3	8	19 -31	11	62.Greece	3	-	-	3	0 -10	0
30.Croatia	7	5	-	2	11 -5	10	63.Haiti	3	-	-	3	2 -14	0
31.United States	17	4	1	12	18 -38	9	64.Zaïre	3	-	-	3	0 -14	0
32.Nigeria	8	4	-	4	13 -13	8	65.El Salvador	6	-	-	6	1 -22	0
33.Morocco	13	2	4	7	12 -18	8							

This table is based on two points for a win and one point for a draw. Only matches in the World Cup Finals are included. Matches decided on penalty shootouts are treated as draws.

ENGLAND'S WORLD CUP RECORDS

Biggest victory:
3-0 v Poland and Paraguay, both 1986

Leading scorer:
Gary Lineker, 10 goals

Biggest defeat:
2-4 v Uruguay, 1954

Most appearances:
Peter Shilton, 17 matches

**NAME: Thierry Henry. AGE: 24.
COUNTRY: France. CLUB: Arsenal.**

SO WHERE'S HE SPRUNG FROM THEN?

Thierry set out on the road to fame and fortune as a winger at the French FA's football academy at Clairefontaine alongside his great friends Nicolas Anelka and David Trezeguet. His tricks and turn of pace prompted the then Monaco coach Arsene Wenger to sign him in 1994, but it wasn't until his £10million switch to Italian giants Juventus four years later that he emerged as a real star in the making. Unfortunately, his dream move turned into a nightmare when he made just 16 appearances and scored three goals in his one season in Turin. He was reunited with Wenger at Arsenal for the start of the 1999-2000 season and he hasn't looked back since.

AND WHAT'S SO GOOD ABOUT HIM?

In a word, it's that pace. Henry would give Atto Bolden a run for his money when it comes to sprinting. Then, when you add skill to the equation and an uncanny knack of scoring breathtaking goals, you have a player who's got the lot. As soon as Tel arrived at the Marble Halls, Wily Ool Wenger took all these ingredients and converted him from winger to striker, instantly transforming him as a player. With almost 60 league goals in three seasons, he is now a Gunners legend.

BUT WOULD YOU SAY HE'S A BORN WINNER?

Well, he picked up a winner's medal at the World Cup four years ago, and repeated the feat two years later at the European Championships in Holland and Belgium, so you'd have to say yes. On the domestic level, Thierry has been top-scorer for The Gunners in each of his three seasons at the club and could well break his duck on the trophy trail too this season as Wenger's side is still in the hunt for FA Cup and Premiership glory.

HAS HE GOT WORLD CUP FEVER YET?

Four years ago, Henry was only a bit-part player in Aimes Jacquet's winning squad, but he is looking forward to more regular action for 'Les Bleus' this time. He says: "I want to contribute more to the side than I did during the last World Cup. A lot has happened to me in the four years since our triumph. I am a better player now and have Arsene Wenger to thank for that. I hope to show to the world that I am justified in my place, should the manager pick me."

FINALLY, A WORLD CUP RATING

With the likes of Zidane and Pires providing the ammunition, there's every chance that Henry will score the goals to fire France to their second successive World Cup Final success. ★ ★ ★ ★

NAME: Michael Owen. AGE: 22.
COUNTRY: England. CLUB: Liverpool.

SO WHERE'S HE SPRUNG FROM THEN?

Michael burst onto the scene at Anfield as a fresh-faced 17-year-old in 1997 and has since emerged as the best striker to wear the England shirt since the halcyon days of Jimmy Greaves and Bobby Charlton. And who are we to argue? Michael's statistics speak for themselves: 63 league goals in just 121 league games for Liverpool has already earnt him God-like status among the Kop faithful, while his wonder goal against Argentina in the 1998 tournament quickly elevated him onto the world stage. Although his career has since been hampered with hamstring problems, Michael remains a feared opponent whenever he slips on the white shirt and he'll be keen to add to his 14 international goals from 32 appearances, which included that hat-trick against Germany in the qualifying campaign.

AND WHAT'S SO GOOD ABOUT HIM?

Again, it's the pace that separates Michael from his striking counterparts. He might not be the strongest of players, but what he lacks in muscle he more than makes up for in speed. In full flow, most defenders are left trailing in his wake and rumours around Anfield suggest that he can run 100 metres in 11 seconds. But we're doing Mike a huge injustice here; he can also score goals, goals, goals from anywhere around the 18-yard box and with either foot, to boot!

BUT WOULD YOU SAY HE'S A BORN WINNER?

Well he hasn't done too badly so far. Michael's goals last season helped Gerard Houllier's side to an unprecedented treble of League Cup, FA Cup and UEFA Cup success, while his goals this season in the Champions League continue to elevate his form to another level. Two late goals in the FA Cup Final success against Arsenal last season also suggest he has the strength of character to perform under the most intense pressure.

HAS HE GOT WORLD CUP FEVER YET?

With The Reds gunning for glory in the Premiership and Champions League, he's had little time to think about this summer's tournament, but believes Sven Goran Eriksson's side has the potential to go much further than the second round England achieved four years ago. "The lads in that squad were inexperienced, but the likes of David Beckham, Paul Scholes and myself have many games under our belts now. When you add names like David Seaman and Teddy Sheringham to the equation, there's a nice balance."

FINALLY, A WORLD CUP RATING

Michael will be a marked man whenever he steps onto the pitch this summer, but much will depend on the supply line to him. If the England midfield create the chances, then you can count on him to finish the job off. ★ ★ ★ ★

**NAME: Raul Gonzalez. AGE: 24.
COUNTRY: Spain. CLUB: Real Madrid.**

SO WHERE'S HE SPRUNG FROM THEN?

Raul Gonzalez Blanco started out as a youth team player with Atletico Madrid but his prolific form soon had the big guns from Real snapping at his heels and he didn't need much persuasion to hot-foot it across the city. Raul was always going to become a star in Spain, having finished top-scorer for his country in the World Youth Championships in Qatar in 1995, and having broken into the Real side as a fresh-faced 17-year-old, he scored a respectable nine league goals in his first 28 appearances. Raul has since bagged well over 100 goals in La Liga, netting 25 goals in 36 appearances last season, but his highlight in the fabled white shirt remains his vital opening goal in the 3-0 Champions League Final victory against Valencia in 2000.

AND WHAT'S SO GOOD ABOUT HIM?

Confident with both feet, Raul's game is about outfoxing his opponents rather than using sheer pace or brute force. He has an uncanny knack of ghosting into the right position at the right time, and can also call on his array of tricks to beat the attention of his markers. Whether it be from 30 centimetres or 30 yards, Raul invariably finds the back of the net.

BUT WOULD YOU SAY HE'S A BORN WINNER?

There's no denying that in the glorious colours of Real Madrid, Raul is a born superstar. He is the golden boy of the side, the goal-getter and the perfect foil for the craftsmanship of Zinedine Zidane. However, his career in a Spain shirt has been chequered to say the least. He failed to make the Euro 96 squad, and never shone at either France '98 or Euro 2000, despite scoring 11 goals in eight qualifying matches on the way to the finals in Holland and Belgium. Having top-scored in qualifying for this tournament, much is expected from Raul's golden boots this time.

HAS HE GOT WORLD CUP FEVER YET?

Raul is certainly aware of the huge expectations that rest on his shoulders, having yet to transfer his club form at the very highest level. He says: "I don't feel that my goalscoring ability has ever been doubted, but there remain question marks surrounding me and the Spanish national team. We have one of the best leagues in the world, now that must be reflected in the success of our team."

FINALLY, A WORLD CUP RATING

There is no doubting Raul's ability inside and outside the box, but much will depend on how well his partnership with Deportivo's Diego Tristan forms. They haven't spent too much time together but if they click, then expect to see goals galore from both players. ★

NAME: Hernan Crespo. **AGE:** 26.
COUNTRY: Argentina. **CLUB:** Lazio.

SO WHERE'S HE SPRUNG FROM THEN?

Hernan started his career back home in Argentina with leading club River Plate and such was his presence, even at the tender age of 18, that he was handed the nickname 'Valdanito' because of his similarities with former superstar Jorge Valdano. With 24 goals to his name in three seasons, he was soon attracting the attention of the big Serie A clubs and it was Parma who took the plunge with a cool £10million bid in 1996. A fee of this size was thought a huge gamble for a club not known for its excessive expenditure, yet he repaid the faith with a goal every two games in his four seasons at the club. As the most wanted man in Italy, the big guns were lining up to sign him, and in 2000 he moved to Lazio on a five-year contract for an initial £80,000 a week in a £20 million deal.

AND WHAT'S SO GOOD ABOUT HIM?

In terms of goalscoring, there's just one word for the guy: prolific. He's in the prime of his career, not only for club but also for country. With 17 goals in 36 appearances for Argentina, Hernan strikes fear into every defender he faces and having coped with the pressures of scoring for Lazio, he's now a stronger player mentally than he was before his arrival at the Stadio Olympico. If he gets a chance, he doesn't need an Andy Cole-number of chances to put the ball away and he's also as good with his head as he is with his feet. In fact, he's the ultimate striker.

BUT WOULD YOU SAY HE'S A BORN WINNER?

Individually, there are few strikers in world football as good, but if we're talking success, then it's only started to fall into place these past couple of years. His 26 goals in 32 league appearances in his first season at Lazio went a long way in making his name, while Argentina are many people's favourites to lift the World Cup this summer. Having played just once in France '98, he is keen to make more of an impact and add to the Olympic silver medal he picked up in Atlanta in 1996.

HAS HE GOT WORLD CUP FEVER YET?

Absolutely. Having top-scored with nine goals in qualification, the country's hopes rest on his shoulders and he is more than aware that he now has to deliver on the biggest stage. "When you're a striker for Argentina, it's a proud position but also one of immense pressure. But that doesn't worry me because I feel good in myself. It's time to put our country back on the map and I want to contribute to that."

FINALLY, A WORLD CUP RATING

Hernan will be a fantastic success, no question, but much depends on Gabriel Batistuta. Coach Marcelo Bielsa feels the pair cannot work together, so if Crespo gets the nod, then the world is his oyster.
★ ★ ★

NAME: Henrik Larsson. AGE: 30.
COUNTRY: Sweden. CLUB: Celtic.

SO WHERE'S HE SPRUNG FROM THEN?

Although a big star back home in Sweden, Henrik really made a name for himself following his £5million arrival at Parkhead in the summer of 1997. In four years with Dutch First Division side Feyenoord, he had netted just 26 league goals, but that was to change in Scotland as he became a one-man goal machine and the scourge of defenders everywhere. His first two seasons were marked with 45 league goals and although his career was interrupted with a double leg fracture at Lyon in October 1999, he bounced back to win the European Golden Boot with 35 league goals as Celtic took the title last season. A host of clubs, including Manchester United, were lining up to sign the star, but he signed a new contract with The Bhoys and his goals this season have again gone a long way in securing Martin O'Neill his second title as Celtic boss.

AND WHAT'S SO GOOD ABOUT HIM?

A very intelligent player, Larsson appears ghost-like in the box and is very difficult to pin down. Although he's not particularly tall, he scores plenty of goals with his head, making him the perfect goalscoring machine.The only criticism that can be levelled at him is that he continues to ply his trade in an inferior league, but he's answered those criticisms by continuing his form for Sweden, where he has scored 21 times in 64 games, including eight in World Cup qualification.

BUT WOULD YOU SAY HE'S A BORN WINNER?

A late winner, more like. Henrik's success has come as he approaches the final furlong of his career and his second successive championship success in Scotland could well be greeted with another European Golden Boot. Although Sweden are highly unlikely to repeat their third-placed finish of 1994, in which Larsson scored once, there are personal goals to reach and he will be keen to show the world that his tag as one of the world's most prolific strikers is justified.

HAS HE GOT WORLD CUP FEVER YET?

He can't wait! Following his broken leg, Larsson was not fully fit as he took his place in Sweden's under-achieving side at Euro 2000. And having been in the shadows of Martin Dahlin and Kennet Andersson for much of his international career, he is aware that this could be his one last chance to make a real name for himself. "I couldn't do myself justice two years ago, it simply wasn't possible," he says. "As a team we were missing key players but we have a fully fit squad to choose from this time. I'm also feeling very good, so let's hope that it will all come together this summer."

FINALLY, A WORLD CUP RATING

Although a star in his own right, Henrik can only be as good as the players around him, namely his strike partner Marcus Allback. And if the Heerenveen man is on top of his game then he'll make the space for Larsson to weave his undoubted magic. ★ ★

NAME: Hakan Sukur. AGE: 30.
COUNTRY: Turkey. CLUB: Parma.

SO WHERE'S HE SPRUNG FROM THEN?

Hakan has almost single-handedly put Turkey on the football map. Once a country of 5-0 hammerings at the hands of England, the Turks have now emerged as a nation to be feared and much of this success can be found at the feet of 'The Bull of the Bosphorus'. With 35 international goals in 70 appearances, he is regarded as the best-ever Turkish striker and his form has also been reflected on the domestic stage where he scored an incredible 103 league goals in 123 games for leading Turkish club Galatasaray. Having helped the club to their greatest triumph, a UEFA Cup final victory against Arsenal in 2000, he joined Serie A giants Inter Milan, but five league goals in his first season saw him shipped off to Parma last August where he has finally found his feet again.

AND WHAT'S SO GOOD ABOUT HIM?

Like an old-fashioned English centre forward, Hakan is a real handful for any defender. Tall, awkward and uncompromising, he also has good touch for a big man and leads the line very well. Yet it would be wrong to label him a targetman; Sukur creates chances too, and there are fewer strikers as good in the air. A danger man in every respect.

BUT WOULD YOU SAY HE'S A BORN WINNER?

Back in Turkey, success is all he knows. A championship winner in all his top-flight seasons with Galatasaray, the hysteria surrounding him remains at David Beckham-sized proportions. However, Hakan has been pilloried following his move to Italy and will be looking to the World Cup to show us all that he still remains a deadly striker.

HAS HE GOT WORLD CUP FEVER YET?

Not just him, but the country as a whole. This is Turkey's first appearance in the finals for 48 years and the expectations are high, particularly for Sukur, who top-scored in qualifying with six goals. He is well aware that a nation's hopes rest on his shoulders. "This could be my first and last appearance at the World Cup, so I will give every drop of sweat for my country. This is our chance to show the world that Turkey are a very good team."

FINALLY, A WORLD CUP RATING

Much of Sukur's goals come from good wing play but, with Sergen Yalcin struggling with a knee injury and Emre Belozoglu stuck on the bench at Inter, there could be a ring-rustiness to his supply line. ★ ★

NAME: Augustine 'Jay-Jay' Okocha. AGE: 28.
COUNTRY: Nigeria. CLUB: Paris St Germain.

SO WHERE'S HE SPRUNG FROM THEN?

Having started his career with Nigerian side Rangers, Jay-Jay's career in Europe started with German Fourth Division side Neunkirchen. By 1992 he had moved to Eintracht Frankfurt where he scored one of the most spectacular goals in Bundesliga history. In the 87th minute of a game against Karlsruhe in 1993, he dribbled through the entire defence before beating goalkeeper Oliver Kahn. At the end of the 1995-6 season, Okocha moved to Turkish club Fenerbahçe for £1 million, where he and his new side immediately won the Turkish league championship. In just two seasons in the Turkish First Division, Okocha's value rocketed. Paris St Germain paid Fenerbahçe an astonishing £10million for his services in the summer of 1998.

AND WHAT'S SO GOOD ABOUT HIM?

You can always expect the unexpected - one minute he'll let fly from 30 yards, the next he'll be dribbling past six players before shooting! Very much like Italy's Totti, Okocha prefers to play behind the front two, where he can let his silky skills and breathtaking juggling confuse even the most hardened of defenders. Sometimes his laidback attitude on the pitch has been interpreted as laziness, but Jay-Jay is adamant that he intends to start chipping in with the goals to help ease the burden on Kanu, who has struggled to find the target for both club and country this season.

BUT WOULD YOU SAY HE'S A BORN WINNER?

Well, success was forthcoming at international level in the early days. Jay-Jay was a member of the side that won the 1994 African Cup of Nations and repeated the feat two years later as a member of the side that won Olympic gold at the Atlanta Games. Only a bit-part player at the 1994 finals, and scoring just the one goal for Nigeria four years later, now is the time for Okocha to start delivering - on the biggest stage of all.

HAS HE GOT WORLD CUP FEVER YET?

Unfortunately for the romantics, Jay-Jay has vowed to cut out the showmanship this summer following stinging criticism from the press in his native Nigeria. They would rather he started scoring goals again, and that is his aim. "You never know what could happen in football, this might be my last chance," he says. "That's why I have to make the most of the opportunity and help the Super Eagles fly once more."

FINALLY, A WORLD CUP RATING

Nigerian fans will expect Jay-Jay to provide that extra touch of magic. He is to his country what Teddy Sheringham is to England - intelligent, has great vision and is often seen with a dodgy barnet! ★

NAME: Nuno Gomes. AGE: 25.
COUNTRY: Portugal. CLUB: Fiorentina.

SO WHERE'S HE SPRUNG FROM THEN?

Nuno started his professional career at Boavista and, alongside Jimmy-Floyd Hasselbaink, he inspired the club to the Portuguese Cup in 1997, having scored 60 goals in three seasons. Naturally, his prolific form attracted the attention of the country's biggest clubs and Benfica soon came calling. He took some time to settle, but regular Champions League football took his career to another level and his potential as an international player was realised at Euro 2000 where he was a star in a Portugal side that reached the semi-finals. With four goals to his credit, including one in the semi-final against France, he joined Fiorentina for £12million, where he has taken over from Argentinean Gabriel Batistuta as the club's superstar.

AND WHAT'S SO GOOD ABOUT HIM?

His skill and agility are just as impressive as his eye for goal. England fans won't need reminding of his ability as he was the man who, having seen his country battle back from 2-0 down, scored the all-important third goal during the first round of Euro 2000. Who could forget the way he outwitted both Tony Adams and Sol Campbell before driving the second-half winner past David Seaman? Not a prolific striker for his country by any means, but certainly a match-winning player for the big occasion.

BUT WOULD YOU SAY HE'S A BORN WINNER?

Not so much a born winner, but a player born with attitude! If you cast your minds back to Euro 2000, Gomes was one of the players who lost his head following Zinedine Zidane's Golden Goal penalty winner at the semi-final stage. Having thrust his shirt at ref Gunter Benko, he was red carded and consequently banned for seven matches so he will want to let his feet do the talking this summer.

HAS HE GOT WORLD CUP FEVER YET?

Anything is a welcome distraction from the turmoil he's facing with his club side Fiorentina. The cash-strapped Italian club has failed to pay their players on occasions this season, so a good tournament should help him move on to new pastures. "My goals at Euro 2000 made my name, hopefully the same can happen to me this time," he has said.

FINALLY, A WORLD CUP RATING

Technically, a superb striker and that is why he makes our top ten. He won't get a hatful of goals, but when he does score it'll turn heads. Again, much depends on the players around him and with Luis Figo providing the ammunition, he should get plenty of chances. ★ ★

NAME: Ronaldinho. AGE: 21.
COUNTRY: Brazil. CLUB: Paris St Germain.

SO WHERE'S HE SPRUNG FROM THEN?

Forget Ronaldo, Ronaldinho Gaucho is the new star of Brazilian football. Having scored 15 goals in 14 matches for his club side Gremio, he burst onto the scene with the national team at the Copa America in 1999 where he scored an amazing goal against Venezuela that was reminiscent of Pelé's wonderful goal in the 1958 World Cup Final. Much to his country's derision, he failed to gain regular international football under former coach Vanderlei Luxemburgo but having joined French side Paris St Germain last year, as a replacement for the out-of-favour Nicolas Anelka, he has been recalled and his ten goals from 22 appearances makes him a star to keep an eye on this summer.

AND WHAT'S SO GOOD ABOUT HIM?

Frightening pace and skill. He admits that he learnt his dribbling skills by running rings around his dog in the back yard of his small wooden home in the run-down town of Oporto Alegre. He would dummy the dog and play one-twos off his legs; to this day Ronaldinho openly admits that he owes much to the small pup! With a build on a par with that of Ronaldo, he is the perfect foil for the less agile but equally skilful Romario and the prospect of the pair of them working in tandem this summer is enough to frighten all their opponents. Still rough around the edges, Ronaldinho is far from the finished article, but when he is bearing down on goal, he needs only a fractional opening to show what he can do.

BUT WOULD YOU SAY HE'S A BORN WINNER?

Well if you're widely regarded as the new Ronaldo, then you can't be doing too badly! So far, he's won the Player of the Tournament award at the World Youth Cup in 1997, finished top scorer at the Confederations Cup in 2000 with six goals and also top scored for his country in qualifying for the Sydney Olympics. However, a tedious transfer wrangle between PSG and his former club dragged on for months, hindering his appearances for the Brazil team in World Cup qualification, and now he's determined to make up for lost time.

HAS HE GOT WORLD CUP FEVER YET?

Ronaldinho believes his time has come. At the age of 21 he feels that he can now be let of the leash, but admits that should he get the nod, it's the experience and presence of Romario that would raise his and the Brazilian team's performance. "Like every Brazilian, I live for the World Cup," he says. "Romario is the player we all look to for inspiration and it would be a dream to play alongside him. Now I have to pray that I have done enough to take my place."

FINALLY, A WORLD CUP RATING

With the likes of Edilson, Elber and Romario also battling for a place, there is still some confusion as to which is coach Scolari's favoured pairing. Still, Ronaldinho is the golden boy of Brazilian football and, when given his chance, is tipped to become the star of the tournament. ★ ★

NAME: Francesco Totti. **AGE:** 25.
COUNTRY: Italy. **CLUB:** Roma.

SO WHERE'S HE SPRUNG FROM THEN?

Francesco is one of that rare breed of footballers who has stayed with the same club, namely AS Roma, for his entire career. He made his Seria A debut at the age of 16 against Brescia, but in his first five seasons in the first-team remained something of a peripheral figure. However, he sprung to life in the 1997–98 season when he scored 13 times in a Roma side that started to show real Scudetta ambitions. His form was rewarded with an international call-up against Switzerland and he is now looked upon as a talismanic figure for both club and country. As captain of Roma, he will forever be remembered as the man that led the club to the title last year.

AND WHAT'S SO GOOD ABOUT HIM?

Totti can best be described as the Italian version of Peter Beardsley, but with much better looks! He is a wizard on the ball and a goalmaker as well as a goaltaker. He seems to prefer playing behind the front two and that is when he is at his most dangerous; a really difficult player for defenders to mark. He finds it hard to fit into the 4-4-2 formation, which Italian sides are always built on, unless he plays alongside his friend Alessandro Del Piero. But wherever he plays, Italy are not the same team unless Totti is in it.

BUT WOULD YOU SAY HE'S A BORN WINNER?

He will always be regarded as a winner following his success at Roma, but Totti is a big name for the big occasion. Like many of the current squad, he was a member of the Italian under-21 side that won the European Championships in 1996 and was widely regarded as Man-of-the-Match during his country's Euro 2000 Final appearance against France. He also scored in the penalty shoot-out against Holland at the semi-final stage, proving his nerve in the most pressured of situations.

HAS HE GOT WORLD CUP FEVER YET?

Having featured in seven of Italy's eight qualifying games, he can't wait for the finals to begin. "I've said it all along, but this could be my year," he says. "Having had a good Euro 2000 did my morale a lot of good but the result was horrible for the team. Now we have a chance to put that right."

FINALLY, A WORLD CUP RATING

He might not grab the headlines like Del Piero, but Totti can hold the key to Italy's success. Now in the peak of form, much will be expected from his magical feet.
★ ★ ★ ★

★	All the ability in the world, but still to do it at World Cup level
★ ★	Goals galore – if the service is supplied
★ ★ ★	World beater – if he gets on the pitch
★ ★ ★ ★	Tournament winner if the service is supplied

David Beckham, Luis Figo and Francesco Totti can class themselves as signed-up members of the footballing superstars club, but until they have made their mark on the biggest stage of all, the World Cup Finals, their life membership remains a tantalising target.

Those already enshrined in the history of the beautiful game, thanks to their historic contributions to the Finals of yesteryear, include the greats Pelé and Maradona, Dutch master Johan Cruyff, England's Geoff Hurst and the Italian Paolo Rossi, but as this summer's finals approach on the horizon, who will be the next name to join such esteemed company?

Of all the runners and riders, our very own Becks was hotly tipped to take the tournament by storm following a bitter-sweet induction four years ago. His omission from England's starting line-up for the opening two games at France '98 caused more of a stir than the actual results, yet when he was finally unleashed by Glenn Hoddle, Becks delivered in the grandest manner. A trademark free-kick against Colombia booked a place in the second round as his star began to rise to the very top. The media lavished the pin-up with praise, while his critics were told 'do believe the hype'. Yet he would soon discover that every silver lining has a cloud.

As England squared up against old foes Argentina in what was one of the best matches of the tournament, a petulant flick on the calf of Diego Simeone signalled Becks's premature exit from the game. Just four days after his national hero status had been projected, he was a traitor who had cost his nation the chance of further progress.

To suggest back then that England would plan to go into their next World Cup mission with Beckham as captain would have brought cries of derision, but he has done so much more than merely rebuild a reputation that had been so savagely shattered.

As runner-up in FIFA's World Player of the Year award this year, he has won every honour possible with Manchester United and risen to the challenge as England captain. "I've enjoyed the responsibility of the job," says the quietly spoken Londoner, whose dramatic late goal against Greece booked his country's passage to the finals.

"When I was asked to be England captain I didn't have to think twice about accepting it and I have been pleased with the way it's gone since I've had the arm band."

"The team has picked up well and after a bad start to our qualifying campaign, we did well to come back and finish top of our group. I have had so much success with United over the years, but what is missing is to win something with England. Hopefully that can happen at this World Cup."

Then an incident in Manchester United's April quarter-final clash with Deportivo La Coruña changed everything.

Already bruised by Diago Tristam's tackle a week earlier, a 16th minute late lunge by Pedro Duscher seems to have destroyed Beckham's (and possibly England's) World Cup dreams. It's a strange and bitter irony that the blow, which has broken a bone in Beck's left foot, should have been delivered by an Argentine boot.

Beckham had every hope of avenging England's defeat to Argentina at France 98 and take his place among the pantheon of footballing World Cup greats. Everything now depends on whether he recovers full fitness in time for the Finals and, at the time of writing, that's reckoned to be no more than a 50/50 possibilty.

He may not be fit enough to play, but Captain Beckham will still lift his team-mates in Japan/Korea.

Fit or not, Beckham will almost certainly travel to Japan/Korea, where is presence will act as a considerable boost to his team-mates. England fans can only wait and hope.

Nothing less than brilliance will do for masterly Portuguese midfielder Luis Figo, the man who claimed that same World Player of the Year award a couple of months back. At £37.5m, he was the world's costliest player when he made a highly controversial move from Barcelona to Real Madrid in 2000, but what a bargain he has proved to be.

Whether it's from the right flank or in the centre of midfield, Figo is one of the greatest players to have pulled on that colourful Portugal shirt, yet still has some way to go to eclipse the best.

That mantle is still held by the great Eusebio and the reason why he is held in such esteem is the fact that his finest hour occurred in a World Cup finals. The 1966 tournament in England may have been won by the hosts, yet Eusebio was its greatest star.

After failing to qualify in 1994 and 1998, this is Figo's first chance to show his worth on the highest stage and there is every reason to believe he can deliver. Captain of a national team whose inconsistency is as bewildering as their brilliance on the ball, they have been handed an enticing opening group and that should ensure their brilliant No.10 has plenty of time to pull the strings as he makes his mark.

"I have done so much in the game, but playing in a World Cup is the ultimate achievement for any player,"

says Figo. "I go there believing Portugal can win the tournament. We have the players to beat anyone in the world and now we have to go out and prove it. I know there is high expectation on me, but that is what I like."

Figo has replaced Zinedine Zidane as the

world's number one player. For the mercurial Frenchman, who shone like a beacon as his country won the World Cup four years ago, this tournament will be all about confirming that he has it all.

Unlike Beckham, the balding Real Madrid playmaker doesn't have the looks to go with his genius, but Zidane is the best all-round midfielder and has the one medal they all want safely packed into his overflowing trophy cabinet. "Both personally and as a team, it's going to be harder for us this time," he warns.

"The emotion of winning the World Cup in front of our own fans is something that can never be beaten, but the team has the ability in every area, so we can do it again."

"But to reach such peaks fills you with the desire to do it again. You don't get many chances, maybe just two if you are lucky, so I know this could be my last chance on such a platform."

Zidane scored twice in that 1998 World Cup Final against Brazil, which was billed as a duo between himself and Brazilian superstar Ronaldo. Unfortunately, the Inter Milan striker's knee injury scuppered his performance that day and he's been suffering ever since. However, it appears the greatest non-playing footballer the game has ever seen may be on the verge of making a dramatic return in time for this summer's tournament.

After playing his first game for Brazil in some two-and-a-half years a few weeks ago, coach Luis Felipe Scolari will doubtless be under pressure to include him if he can get anywhere close to full fitness. Yet even a half-fit Ronaldo is worth a gamble. He possesses such grace and skill on the ball that when he is running at goal, there is not a single defender in the world who can stop him within the laws of the game.

He did enough in the game against Yugoslavia to suggest that he can still sparkle at the highest level and prove to the world that he has the ability to fill the legendary number 10 shirt. Certainly it remains his dream to board a plane to Japan and Korea this summer.

"I have learnt not to take anything for granted, but I believe the World Cup is my destiny," he says. "The team has done very well without me but I deserve some good fortune. Of course the final decision rests with the coach, but I would like to declare myself ready for the greatest show on earth."

Certainly, success in the number ten shirt goes hand-in-glove with the World Cup and the task for Ronaldo and company must be to match the achievements of Maradona, the greatest World Cup hero of them all. He is the only player who can claim to have single-handedly won the trophy as he danced his way to glory with Argentina in Mexico 86. And as his nation has been installed as tournament favourites this time, the footy-mad Argentine fans will be looking for another hero to take on the baton.

Whether that will be Lazio striker Hernan Crespo or Manchester United midfielder Juan Sebastian Veron remains to be seen. Both have the ability to make this tournament their own and for Veron, it will be the chance to prove his doubters wrong after a difficult first – and possibly last – season at Old Trafford.

At £28m, he became English football's most expensive signing by some distance last summer, but the towering playmaker has struggled to find his feet in the

Premiership and fit into United's system this season. Indeed, the likes of Beckham, Ryan Giggs and Ruud Van Nistelrooy have comfortably overshadowed a player who rarely has a bad game for his country and the talk remains strong that he may return to Lazio after the World Cup.

Yet his importance to Argentina cannot be underestimated and although Crespo and Gabriel Batistuta remain the golden boys who score all the goals, the supply line always harps back to Veron, and success this summer is largely dependent on a series of stunning displays from the United man. If he pulls it off, those tough times in his club career will be quickly forgotten and his transfer value will no doubt hit new heights, so his club cannot really lose.

Crespo, incidentally, is joint-favourite with Thierry Henry to join the esteemed company of Frenchman Just Fontaine, Germany's Gerd Muller, Mario Kempes of Argentina and England's Gary Lineker to finish as a World Cup Finals top-scorer and when the winners medals are handed out in Yokohama on June 30, it's a safe bet that the side with the most potent goalscorer in the tournament will be on hand.

Italy boasted such a player when Paolo Rossi shot the Azzurri to success in 1982 and for history to repeat that triumph of 20 years ago, they will

need one of their potent strikers to come to the fore this time.

That man is likely to be Roma's Francesco Totti. A scorer of brilliant goals each week in Serie A, he also has the brains to go with his ability. As an out-and-out striker or a player that drops deep, he can unlock the most miserly of defences and with a team that thinks defence before attack, the hopes of a nation will rest on his shoulders this summer. "I can deal with the pressure," he said prior to his country's friendly victory against England recently.

"To play for Italy you need to be more than just a footballer because the expectations are so high. If people see me as a major player, then I see that as an honour rather than a problem. There is still bitterness of losing the Euro 2000 final to France, so if I can play my part in helping Italy do better this time, then I will be a very happy man."

Whatever happens this summer, the World Cup Finals will become a tournament of star players rather than star teams. Those who shine brightest will play a big part in shaping their country's destiny while at the same time etching their own place in football folklore. Now, let the fun begin.

SOUTH KOREA FACTFILE

Association: South Korea Football Association
Joined FIFA: 1948
Honours: Asian Cup 1956, 1960; Asian Cup runners-up 1972, 1980, 1988; Asian Games 1978, 1986
Players: 736,000
Website: www.kfa.or.kr
Coach: Guus Hiddink
Hiddink was appointed in Nov. 2000 and his contract runs until June 30. South Korea hope he will have just as much success in this World Cup as the last, where he led Holland to the semi-finals.
Capital: Seoul
Population: 46.9 million
Leader: President Kim Dae-jung
Main industries: Shipbuilding & consumer electronics

INFO ON SOUTH KOREA

Historians believe that football was introduced to the area around 1880 by British marines. There are, however, no records of football being played until the country was annexed by Japan in 1910. The South Korean FA was closed down in 1938 when Japan ruled the country as a colony, and from 1936 the best Korean players were even allowed to play for the Japanese national side – until the country was liberated in 1945. Out of all the Asian countries, South Korea holds the record for qualifying for the most World Cup Finals. Neighbouring North Korea is the most successful Asian nation to date though – having reached the quarter-final stages in 1966.

NORTH KOREA

SOUTH KOREA

INCHEON
SEOUL
SUWON
DAEJEON
JEONJU
DAEGU
GWANGJU
ULSAN
BUSAN
SEOGWIPO

S E
J A

KOBE
OITA
OSAK.

JAPAN FACTFILE

Association: Football Association of Japan
Joined FIFA: 1929
Honours: 1968 Olympics bronze medal & 1992 Asian Cup
Players: 796,873
Website: www.jfa.or.jp
Coach: Philippe Troussier
The Frenchman managed South Africa at the 1998 World Cup, where they drew with Denmark and Saudi Arabia but lost to France.

Troussier was chosen to coach the Japanese national side this. His contract with Japan runs out at the end of June 2 the World Cup Finals end.
Capital: Tokyo
Population: 126.5 million
Leader: Yoshiro Mori
Main industries: Construction & industry

SAPPORO ⚽

MIYAGI ⚽

NIIGATA ⚽

🔴 **JAPAN**

SAITAMA ⚽

TOKYO ⚽ ⚽ **IBARAKI**

⚽ **YOKOHAMA**

⚽ **SHIZUOKA**

P A C I F I C

O C E A N

FO ON JAPAN

...all is believed to have been brought to Japanese shores by ...shman, Lieutenant Commander Douglas of the Royal Navy ...He was a teacher at the naval academy in Tokyo and ...ootball in his spare time.

...st ever game in Japan's professional league, the J-League, ...ff on May 15, 1993 when a full house of 59,626 fans saw ...awasaki play Yokohama Marinos. The league became an ...t sensation and has drawn big crowds ever since.

• You won't find normal football fare on sale at Japan's national football stadium in Tokyo. Rather than snacking on a meat pie or hamburger, you can treat yourself to some fried noodles or octopus dumplings instead. You first then!

• Japan became the first ever Asian side to play at Wembley when they took on England in a friendly tournament, the Umbro International Trophy, in June 1995. Japan lost 2-1, with Ihara scoring for Japan and Anderton and Platt on the scoresheet for England.

ASIA

Incheon Munhak Stadium

Venue Incheon

Capacity 50,300

Games played here
June 11 Denmark v France
June 9 Costa Rica v Turkey
June 14 Portugal v South Korea
June 16 Second Round tie.

Stadium fact
Incheon is the last stadium to be completed. With a new international airport also being constructed for the finals, cash rewards are on offer for the first utility to be finished.

What's so good about it?
Wherever you sit in the stadium, you are assured of stunning views of the nearby mountains.

What does it compare to?
It looks frighteningly similar to the new stadium being built by Arsenal at Ashburton Grove.

If I'm visiting, what else can I see?
Located about 30 kilometres west of Seoul, Incheon is famous as the site for MacArthur's strategic landing during the Korean War. Off the coast are numerous islands, some still uninhabited, and they make the perfect venue to get away from it all.

Sangam Mapo-Ku

Venue Seoul

Capacity 63,930

Games played here
May 31 France v Senegal
June 13 Turkey v China
June 25 Semi-Final

Stadium fact
This stadium is the oldest of all 25 venues, having been built for the 1988 Olympic Games. Holders France will kick off the tournament here on May 31.

What's so good about it?
The breathtaking shape of the stands which represent the traditional Korean sailboats which can be found in the neighbouring Han River.

What does it compare to?
It's a flash version of the Millennium Stadium in Cardiff, but with fewer seats and less Welshmen.

If I'm visiting, what else can I see?
As Seoul is the capital of South Korea, there are numerous museums, palaces and parks. Take a ride up Namsan (South Mountain) to get the best views of the city.

Suwon Stadium

Venue Suwon

Capacity 43,200

Games played here
June 11 Senegal v Uruguay
June 13 Costa Rica v Brazil
June 5 USA v Portugal

Stadium fact
After the tournament, Suwon will be used by the Samsung Blue Wings, a local team that won back-to-back titles in the late 1990s.

What's so good about it?
It's not the biggest venue but Suwon boasts an auxiliary stadium and two practice pitches, as well as swimming pools, tennis courts, cinemas and concert halls.

What does it compare to?
At first glance, it looks very similar to the Olympic Stadium in Barcelona, but on closer inspection, the unique wing-style design on one side makes it one of the most unusual stadiums in the world.

If I'm visiting, what else can I see?
The Gyeonggi Province, where Suwon is located, boasts ski resorts, hot springs, and other natural resources for those who want to get away from the bustling city. The village of Panmunjeom is also worth a look as it rests in the middle of the Demilitarized Zone that divides Korea.

Daejeon World Cup Stadium

Venue Daejeon

Capacity 40,400

Games played here
June 12 South Africa
June 14 Poland v USA
June 18 Second Round tie

Stadium fact
After the World Cup, the stadium will be used exclusively by the Daejoen Citizen football team.

What's so good about it?
Based at the heart of Korea's Silicon Valley, Daejon has a high-tech stadium to match its surroundings. Not only does it feature a semi-closed roof but other facilities include a shopping mall and swimming pool which are already in operation.

What does it compare to?
It compares very favourably to the Bernabeu Stadium, home of the mighty Real Madrid.

If I'm visiting, what else can I see?
Located in the heart of the Korean Peninsula, the Gyeryong-san, Sogni-san and Daedun-san national parks are worth a peak; likewise the temples of Beopju-sa, Donghak-sa, and Gap-sa.

Jeonju World Cup Stadium

Venue Jeonju

Capacity 42,400

Games played here
June 7 Spain v Paraguay
June 10 Portugal v Poland
June 17 Second Round tie

Stadium facts
Jeonju portrays an image of Chonju (the traditional foldable fan made of thin bamboo sticks and paper or cloth). The fan represents an openness to the world.

What's so good about it?
Well the architects of this stadium like to think it is the most beautiful of the Korean venues. Cables suspended from the roof represent the 12 strings of a Gaya Harp – a local Korean instrument – while an existing river that winds its way around the stadium has been purified for the tournament.

What does it compare to?
From the outside it looks like Bolton's Reebok Stadium but don't tell them that!

If I'm visiting, what else can I see?
The region maintains much of its agricultural heritage and boasts the country's best cuisine, so visit the first restaurant you see!

Daegu World Cup Stadium

Venue Daegu

Capacity 70,100

Games played here
June 6 Denmark v Senegal
June 8 South Africa v Slovenia
June 10 South Korea v USA

Stadium fact
The globe shape of the stadium symbolises harmony and world peace.

What's so good about it?
The Teflon roof – which reflects the curves of a traditional thatched Korean house. Visiting fans are encouraged to collect their own litter to take home after the games, particularly those hot-dog loving Americans!

What does it compare to?
The Olympic Stadium in Sydney but with more parks and gardens.

If I'm visiting, what else can I see?
Daegu is a major textile centre for Korea, so if it's fake Lacoste you're after, then you're in the right place.

Gwangju World Cup Stadium

Venue Gwangju

Capacity 42,900

Games played here
June 2 Spain v Slovenia
June 4 China v Costa Rica
June 22 Quarter-Final tie

Stadium fact
Gwangju reflects the artistic nature of the area, hence its distinctive oval-shaped stands.

What's so good about it?
Well if China v Costa Rica does nothing for you, why not venture onto the concourse at half-time for the fourth annual Biennale arts festival, which will run for the duration of the tournament.

What does it compare to?
The only comparison in this country is the McAlpine Stadium but on a much bigger scale. And unlike Huddersfield's home, we're guaranteed crowds at this venue!

If I'm visiting, what else can I see?
Many of the nation's democratic movements had their roots in the area, including the March 1 Independence Movement (1919) and the May 18 Democratic Uprising – both are commemorated in monument form.

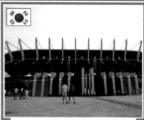

Ulsan Munsu Football Stadium

Venue Ulsan

Capacity 54,500

Games played here
June 1 Uruguay v Denmark
June 3 Brazil v Turkey
June 21 Quarter Final tie

Stadium fact
One of the venues for the Fifa Confederations Cup, the design resembles a crane – the bird which is the symbol of Ulsan – in crouching position ready for flight.

What's so good about it?
You can drink the water out of the bogs, honest! Although Ulsan is a huge industrial city, the stadium – which lies next to a huge reservoir – has been passed as economically clean in compliance with the FIFA World Cup Spirit of Natural Environment Preservation!

What does it compare to?
It wouldn't look out of place in the Premiership and is a cross between Old Trafford and St James' Park.

If I'm visiting, what else can I see?
The South Gyeongsang Province, where Ulsan is located, contains some of Korea's most spectacular scenery and houses the Hallyeo Haesang National Park.

Busan Sports Arena

Venue Busan

Capacity 43,500

Games played here
June 6 France v Uruguay
June 2 Paraguay v South Africa
June 4 South Korea v Poland

Stadium fact
After the World Cup, the 14th Asian Games will be held here.

What's so good about it?
It's different to any stadium you're going to see this summer. From above, it looks like a giant goldfish bowl and the pitch itself stands four storeys above ground level.

What does it compare to?
The Amsterdam Arena must have been built by the same construction company – it's identical.

If I'm visiting, what else can I see?
The city is famous for its seafood and beaches, as well as the Hallyosudo Waterway with its picturesque islands. Also check out the Busan fish market which has a huge selection of fresh seafood in the early morning.

Jeju World Cup Stadium

Venue Seogwipo

Capacity 42,300

Games played here
June 12 Slovenia v Paraguay
June 8 Brazil v China
June 15 Second Round tie

Stadium fact
Jeju remains one of the top honeymoon destinations for Korean newlyweds and the stadium's adjoining hotel has been flooded with couples wanting a room for the finals.

What's so good about it?
Seogwipo has a stadium to match the local breathtaking landscape. The futuristic design is complemented by a water park and market place, likewise a host of restaurants on the stadium's walk-way.

What does it compare to?
It looks very similar to the Olympic Stadium in Munich, with a half-built roof.

If I'm visiting, what else can I see?
The island offers visitors a wide range of activities: hiking on Halla-san (South Korea's highest peak), viewing majestic waterfalls, riding horses, or simply lying around on the many sandy beaches.

Sapporo Dome

Venue Sapporo

Capacity 43,000

Games played here
June 1 Germany v Saudi Arabia
June 7 Argentina v England
June 3 Italy v Ecuador

Stadium fact
Sapporo is the first dome stadium to possess a grass conversion system (artificial grass for baseball that is switched to real grass for football).

What's so good about it?
It's been dubbed the most futuristic stadium on the planet and when the football pitch is needed, it is rolled inside the stadium on a cushion of air, while the seating system moves aside to allow it in. The process takes about two hours.

What does it compare to?
A cross between the Houston Astrodome and the Millennium Stadium.

If I'm visiting, what else can I see?
Sapporo is a centre for politics, culture and economics but forget all that – the Dome is the city's showpiece.

Miyagi Stadium

Venue Miyagi

Capacity 49,300

Games played here
June 12 Sweden v Argentina
June 9 Mexico v Ecuador
June 18 Second Round tie

Stadium fact
The stadium's crescent-shaped roof is intended to replicate the battle helmet of the powerful Date clan who ruled during Japan's feudal period.

What's so good about it?
The fantastic facilities for the disabled. Multipurpose rest areas, seats, multiple hearing equipment and elevators are installed in careful consideration for the 3,500 spaces available for the disabled.

What does it compare to?
With its amazing boomerang-style roof, there's nothing quite like it on earth. Simply breathtaking!

If I'm visiting, what else can I see?
The Mats Sima is a famous mountain worth visiting, likewise the Rikunagaikan National Park.

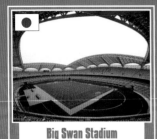

Big Swan Stadium

Venue Niigata

Capacity 42,000

Games played here
June 1 Ireland v Cameroon
June 3 Croatia v Mexico
June 15 Second Round tie

Stadium fact
Officially Japan's least accessible stadium because of the surrounding mountains, Niigata will host the first World Cup finals match to be played in Japan.

What's so good about it?
The translucent white Teflon roof will no doubt make for one of the best atmospheres of all the stadiums. The roof itself represents the swans on the nearby Doyano Lake and covers 90% of the seating area should it rain.

What does it compare to?
A more enclosed version of the Stadio Olympico in Rome.

If I'm visiting, what else can I see?
The Zoshines, Jubusangaku and Nicko national parks are the biggest pull but it would be rude not to visit Doyano and feed the swans!

Ibaraki Prefectural Kashima Stadium

Venue Ibaraki

Capacity 43,000

Games played here
June 5 Germany v Ireland
June 2 Argentina v Nigeria
June 8 Italy v Croatia

Stadium fact
As home to the Kashima Antlers, a statue of Brazilian great Zico, who has played and managed the club, meets visitors.

What's so good about it?
Despite Zico's South American entrance this stadium has a distinctly European design, which lends itself to an intimate feel. Built in 1993, it originally housed just 15,000 fans but the capacity has been increased for this summer's finals and two giant video screens have been added to show replays of Ireland's goals against the Germans!

What does it compare to?
It has a Nou Camp feel, but with three fewer tiers.

If I'm visiting, what else can I see?
Ibraki is home to Hitachi, so get your bargain DVD players here. However, steer clear of the nearby nuclear power plant.

Saitama Prefectural Soccer Stadium

Venue Saitama

Capacity 63,700

Games played here
June 6 Cameroon v Saudi Arabia
June 2 England v Sweden
June 4 Japan v Belgium
June 26 Semi Final

Stadium fact
The stadium developers have created state-of-the-art acoustics and lighting, not that they'll be needed when Sven's Army comes to town.

What's so good about it?
By all accounts, the high-tech facilities makes it possible for spectators to hear the players breathing as a result of the seat design in relation to the pitch. Female Beckham fans, you have been warned!

What does it compare to?
Very much like Stamford Bridge but with two arrow- like roofs on either side of the stadium.

If I'm visiting, what else can I see?
The nearby Piedmont district was the home of ancient Koryo and there are many historical sites and burial mounds remaining today.

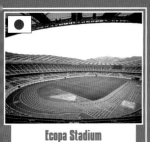

Ecopa Stadium

Venue Shizuoka

Capacity 50,000

Games played here
June 11 Cameroon v Germany
June 14 Belgium v Russia
June 21 Quarter-Final

Stadium fact
The Ecopa is dubbed 'The Mecca of Japanese Soccer' as it houses Asian Champions Jubilo Iwata and 40% of Japan's players at France 98 hailed from the area.

So what's so good about it?
There is an ambience that remains unique at the quiet, out-of-town location of Shizuoka. The exterior is designed to incorporate the image of the beautiful nearby Ogasayama Mountains and the design reflects a variety of environment-friendly features. There are 5,500 mobile seats which will be installed for the quarter-final.

What does it compare to?
It looks very similar to the new Wembley, except this stadium was built on time last year.

If I'm visiting, what else can I see?
The famous Mount Fuji is just a stone's throw away.

Nagai Stadium

Venue Osaka

Capacity 50,000

Games played here
June 12 Nigeria v England
June 14 Tunisia v Japan
June 22 Quarter-Final

Stadium fact
The locals have immense pride in Nagai, hence its bid to host the 2008 Olympics, too.

What's so good about it?
The high-speed rail link that connects the stadium to the nearby city. For the duration of the tournament, all rail services will be free to fans, leaving Sven's Army to splash the cash in the beer tents.

What does it compare to?
It does look more like an athletics stadium than football ground, and is identical to the revamped Olympic Stadium in Athen.

If I'm visiting, what else can I see?
The Shitennosa temple is worth a look, likewise the Osaka harbour which is famed for its freshwater fish.

Kobe Wing Stadium

Venue Kobe

Capacity 42,000

Games played here
June 7 Sweden v Nigeria
June 5 Russia v Tunisia
June 17 Second Round tie

Stadium fact
Kobe is best known for its great earthquake of 1995 and this stadium is constructed with special steel which can endure 7.2 on the Richter Scale. It will also be used as an emergency shelter if and when another serious tremor does occur.

What's so good about it?
Fans can sit in comfort thanks to the heated and air conditioned environment, but the focal point remains the wing design, which represents a city rising from the ashes.

What does it compare to?
Both main stands look very similar to the new structure built at Villa Park.

If I'm visiting, what else can I see?
Kobe City has a fine harbour, while views from the Rokko mountains overlooking the city are breathtaking.

Big Eye Stadium

Venue Oita

Capacity 43,300

Games played here
June 13 Mexico v Italy
June 10 Tunisia v Belgium
June 16 Second Round tie

Stadium fact
The name of this impressive domed stadium is explained by the retractable roof which, when opened and closed, represents a giant winking eye.

What's so good about it?
For the first time ever, cameras have been installed in the roof. The entire stadium is the shape of the globe promoting the 'Protect Earth's Environment' message.

What does it compare to?
Very much like the Sapporo Dome, but its retractable roof makes it unique.

If I'm visiting, what else can I see?
The Beppu hot springs are the ideal place to get away for those suffering World Cup overkill.

Yokohama International Stadium

Venue Yokohama

Capacity 70,000

Games played here
June 11 Saudi Arabia v Ireland
June 13 Ecuador v Croatia
June 9   Japan v Russia
June 30 World Cup Final

Stadium fact
The venue for the final, Yokohama boasts the first two-tiered stand in Japan and remains the biggest venue in the country.

So what's so good about it?
In terms of looks and technology it's not the best stadium at the finals, but it remains Japan's showpiece stadium, simply for its sheer size. Keep an eye out for an air driven automatic mobile camera, which reaches speeds of 100m per 7 seconds, which will feature heavily on the giants screens at each end of the stadium.

What does it compare to?
It looks like the Nou Camp from the outside and the Bernebeu from inside. Good job Spain are not playing here then!

If I'm visiting, what else can I see?
Check out the Sports Science Centre at the stadium.

It won't just be 32 teams bidding for a place in the World Cup Final in Yokohama on June 30. A serious-looking group of 36 men in black (or green or yellow) will be seeking a once in a lifetime experience as they contest the opportunity to referee the world's most important soccer match. Interestingly though, the final choice of the big day's official has less to do with who is considered to be the world's best referee, but rather will depend on how the ref's own national team has progressed in the tournament.

To start with, this entire bunch of referees is already thought to be the best in the world (hard to believe sometimes isn't it!) and now they have just a couple of games to impress the World Cup Referees Committee. A self-effacing, consistent and controlling performance with obvious implementation of FIFA's latest crackdown on diving (and no dodgy decisions) will catch the committee's eye. With 20 of 36 referees on duty in Japan and Korea from countries in the Finals, a number can expect to be sent home after the group stage, so Graham Poll's hopes of becoming the fourth Englishman to referee a World Cup Final – after Reader (1950), Ling (1954) and Taylor (1974) – will depend on how badly Sven's men do!

With a one referee per country rule, the early departure of some of world's best officials could lead to a worrying lack of refereeing talent in the latter stages of the tournament. Still, FIFA rightly wants to be seen to be scrupulously fair and nobody has come up with a better suggestion yet!

Italy's Pierluigi Collina would be everyone's choice to referee this summer's Final, but with Italy one of the leading contenders that's not likely. Scotland's Hugh Dallas and Switzerland's Urs Meier are realistic European contenders for the top job, although there is a feeling that the first Asian World Cup will also see the first Asian World Cup Final Referee. The experienced Ali Bujsaim, at his third World Cup, is likely to figure, although Final-hosting Japan would like to see the honour go to Toru Kamikawa.

2002 WORLD CUP **REFEREES**	
Ubaldo AQUINO	Paraguay
Carlos BATRES	Guatemala
+ Ali BUJSAIM	United Arab Emirates
Cofi CODIJA	Benin
▲ Pierlugui COLLINA	Italy
Mourad DAAMI	Tunisia
▲ Hugh DALLAS	Scotland
Ndoye FALLA	Senegal
▲ Anders FRISK	Sweden
▲ Gamal GHANDOUR	Egypt
Mohamed GUEZZAZ	Morocco
Brian HALL	USA
Terje HAUGE	Norway
Toru KAMIKAWA	Japan
KIM Young Joo	South Korea
Antonio LOPEZ NIETO	Spain
Jun LU	China
Saaed Kamel MANE	Kuwait
William MATTUS VEGA	Costa Rica
▲ Urs MEIER	Switzerland
Markus MERK	Germany
Lubos MICHEL	Slovakia
▲ Vitor MILO PEREIRA	Portugal
Byron MORENO	Ecuador
▲ Kim Milton NIELSEN	Denmark
Rene ORTUBE	Bolivia
Graham POLL	England
Peter PRENDERGAST	Jamaica
Felipe RAMOS RIZO	Mexico
Oscar Julian RUIZ	Colombia
Angel SANCHEZ	Argentina
Mark SHIELD	Australia
Carlos Eugenio SIMON	Brazil
Kyros VASSARAS	Greece
Gilles VEISSIERE	France
Jan WEGEREEF	Holland

▲ Referee at France 98
+ Referee at USA 94 & France 98

GROUP F

OPPONENT	DATE	UK TIME	VENUE
Nigeria	**2 June**	06.30	**Ibaraki, Japan**
England	**7 June**	12.30	**Sapporo, Japan**
Sweden	**12 June**	07.30	**Miyagi, Japan**

"the tournament's hot favourites"

ARGENTINA

★ THE LOWDOWN

Population: 37.3 million

Capital: Buenos Aires

Leader: Fernando De La Rua

Life Expectancy: Male: 72 yrs Female: 79 yrs

>> Warning for vegetarians visiting Argentina; beef dominates the restaurant menus and every part of the animal is eaten, including the intestines and udders!

>> Argentina leads the world in setting voluntary greenhouse gas targets.

>> In 1995 the Argentine Foreign Minister offered to buy the Falkland Islands from the Islanders; 2000 islanders were offered 800 dollars each, it was not successful.

Argentina are the red-hot favourites to win the first World Cup of the new millennium with a team oozing world-class quality in not only their first choice players, but in an outstanding squad. A quick look at their awe-inspiring attacking force demonstrates just what the rest of the finalists are up against. Hernan Crespo topped the South American goalscoring charts with nine goals in 12 appearances establishing him as first choice striker since replacing Gabriel Batistuta as sub in the 3-1 win away to Colombia. It's not certain that Batistuta, Argentina's all-time top goalscorer with 55 goals – his 55th netted in the 2-2 draw in Paraguay – will be selected for the finals, but in pairing Crespo with Claudio Lopez, Argentina has a formidable striking partnership. Waiting in the wings is Javier Saviola who helped Argentina win the 2001 World Youth Cup. Saviola was the tournament's leading scorer with 11 goals and voted the competition's Most Valuable Player. This led the youngster to a £19 million move from River Plate to Barcelona – making him the world's most expensive teenager in the process.

Even the loss of Diego Simeone, their captain and most capped player – with 104 international appearances – failed to undermine Argentina's faultless path through the qualifiers. Simeone suffered a cruciate ligament injury and is not certain to be fit for the Finals. His last appearance for Argentina was the 2-0 victory in Ecuador that clinched Argentina's place in the Finals – with four games to spare! Argentina dominated the South American group from the kick off. An opening 4-1 win over Chile put them to the top of the table and thereafter they never relinquished pole position. Coach Marcelo Bielsa used only 28 players during qualifying (compared to Brazil's staggering 62!), most of whom play club football with top European sides. Only Ariel Ortega and Juan Roman Riquelme play in Argentina's debt-ridden domestic league, while the tenacious Juan Pablo Sorin plays across the border in the bizarre world of Brazilian soccer.

Argentina, up to the end of qualification, had suffered just one defeat in their previous 24 games (away to Brazil) and in that time failed to score just once, against Kevin Keegan's England side at Wembley in February 2000. England will face Argentina in Japan with still painful memories of their last World Cup encounter, which ended in an Argentine victory after a dramatic second-round penalty shoot out.

Twelve years earlier England and Argentina had met in the quarter-finals of the Mexico World Cup when Diego Maradona scored his infamous "hand of god" goal, following it a few minutes later with a moment of sublime footballing genius, scoring, arguably, one of the competition's best ever goals. England were beaten 2-1 and Argentina marched on to win the World Cup. In recognition of Maradona's contribution to the national team, the country has retired his number 10 shirt, so no Argentine player at the 2002 tournament will be allocated that squad number.

Frankly, it won't matter what shirt numbers Argentina's quality side wear. They are the favourites – the team that everyone must beat to win the World Cup.

★ **ASSOCIATION:** Asociaion de Futbol Argentino
★ **JOINED FIFA:** 1912
★ **JOINED CONMEBOL:** 1916
★ **PLAYERS:** 306,400

★ **CLUBS:** 3,035
★ **WEBSITE:** www.afa.org.ar
★ **HONOURS:** World Cup – 1978, 1986; Copa America
  – 1910/21/25/27/29/37/41/45/46/47/55/57/59/91/93.

Argentina's all-time top goalscorer.

★ ROAD TO QUALIFICATION

Mar 00 Chile (h) > (w) **4**-1
Batistuta 10, Veron 34, 71 pen, Lopez,C 88

Apr 00 Venezuela (a) > (w) 0-**4**
Crespo 1, Ortega 4, 76, Ayala 8

Jun 00 Bolivia (h) > (w) **1**-0 Lopez,C 82

Jun 00 Colombia (a) > (w) 1-**3**
Batistuta 24, 45, Crespo 75

Jul 00 Ecuador (h) > (w) **2**-0
Crespo 24, Lopez,C 51

Jul 00 Brazil (a) > (l) 3-**1** Almeyda 45

Aug 00 Paraguay (h) > (d) **1**-1 Aimar 67

Sep 00 Peru (a) > (w) 1-**2**
Crespo 27, Veron 38

Oct 00 Uruguay (h) > (w) **2**-1
Gallardo 28, Batistuta 42

Nov 00 Chile (a) > (w) 0-**2**
Ortega 26, Husain 90

Mar 01 Venezuela (h) > (w) **5**-0
Crespo 13, Sorin 31, Veron 51, Gallardo 60,
Samuel 85

Apr 01 Bolivia (a) > (d) 3-3
Crespo 43, 88, Sorin 89

Jun 01 Colombia (h) > (w) **3**-0
Kily Gonzalez 22, Lopez,C 35, Crespo 38

Aug 01 Ecuador (a) > (w) 0-**2**
Veron 19, Crespo 34 pen

Sep 01 Brazil (h) > (w) **2**-1
Gallardo 76, Cris 84 og

Oct 01 Paraguay (a) > (d) 2-2
Pocchettino 67, Batistuta 73

Nov 01 Peru (h) > (w) **2**-0
Samuel 46, Lopez,C 85

Nov 01 Uruguay (a) > (d) 1-**1** Lopez,C 44

★ FINAL GROUP TABLE

Team	P	W	D	L	F	A	Pts
Argentina	18	13	4	1	42	15	43
Ecuador	18	9	4	5	23	20	31
Brazil	18	9	3	6	31	17	30
Paraguay	18	9	3	6	29	23	30
Uruguay	18	7	6	5	19	13	27
Colombia	18	7	6	5	20	15	27
Bolivia	18	4	6	8	21	33	18
Peru	18	4	4	10	14	25	16
Venezuela	18	5	1	12	18	44	16
Chile	18	3	3	12	15	27	12

★ RECENT RESULTS

Feb 02 Wales (a) > 1-**1** (d) Cruz 62

Mar 02 Cameroon (n) > 2-2 (d)
Veron 18 pen, Aimar 62

DID YOU KNOW?

An Englishman, Alexander Hutton, the Director of English high schools in Buenos Aires, formed the Argentine FA in 1891

Coach Marcelo Bielsa's 3-3-1-3 formation is designed to be adaptable and allows Argentina's flair players to shine. German Burgos has established himself as the number one goalkeeper behind a three-man defence of the experienced Nestor Sensini, Roberto Ayala and Walter Samuel. If injuries should rule out any of the trio, Argentina can call on Mauricio Pochettino, Nelson Vivas or even Javier Zanetti. Under Bielsa's system Zanetti is pushed forward on the right of a three-man midfield with either Juan Pablo Sorin or Kily Gonzalez on the left. The crucial central role is held by Matias Almeyda alongside pivotal playmaker Juan Sebastian Veron, who has a free role linking midfield to a three-man attack. Up front Hernan Crespo and Claudio Lopez combines well with Gabriel Batistuta, Argentina's top scorer, adding to their firepower.

PROBABLE FORMATION 3-3-1-3

BURGOS

SENSINI — SAMUEL

AYALA

ZANETTI — ALMEYDA — SORIN

VERON

BATISTUTA — C LOPEZ — CRESPO

★ MEN THAT MATTER!

HERNAN CRESPO

Age>> 26

Club>> Lazio

Crespo scored nine goals in 12 appearances during the qualifiers where he linked well with Gabriel Batistuta and Claudio Lopez. Cost Lazio £37 million in 2000 and playing his second World Cup.

ARIEL ORTEGA

Age>> 28

Club>> River Plate

Finished the last World Cup in shame with a red card for head-butting an opponent. Influential midfielder playing his third World Cup and was also a silver medallist at the 1996 Olympics.

JUAN SEBASTIAN VERON

Age>> 27

Club>> Man U.

The pulse of the Argentine midfield and likewise with Lazio until passport scandal opened the way for a move to England. Playing in his second World Cup and only missed two qualifiers.

★ PROBABLE SQUAD   ★ QUALIFICATION RECORD

NAME	POSITION	CLUB	APS/GOALS	GAMES	MINS	Y/C	R/C	GOALS
Roberto Bonano	Goalkeeper	Barcelona, Spain	12/0	9	736	2	0	0
German Burgos	Goalkeeper	Atletico Madrid, Spain	34/0	8	704	2	0	0
Pablo Cavallero	Goalkeeper	Celta Vigo, Spain	6/0	2	180	1	0	0
Roberto Ayala	Defender	Valencia, Spain	74/3	17	1530	2	0	1
Mauricio Pochettino	Defender	Paris Saint-Germain, France	15/2	6	540	3	0	1
Walter Samuel	Defender	Roma, Italy	31/3	17	1530	4	0	2
Roberto Sensini	Defender	Parma, Italy	60/0	8	636	1	0	0
Nelson Vivas	Defender	Internazionale, Italy	37/1	9	664	2	0	0
Pablo Aimar	Midfielder	Valencia, Spain	18/1	12	587	2	0	1
Matias Almeyda	Midfielder	Parma, Italy	31/1	8	439	3	0	1
Marcelo Gallardo	Midfielder	Monaco, France	41/14	6	233	0	0	3
Kily Gonzalez	Midfielder	Valencia, Spain	30/4	13	1014	1	0	1
Claudio Husain	Midfielder	Napoli, Italy	12/1	3	198	0	0	1
Gustavo Lopez	Midfielder	Celta Vigo, Spain	29/4	10	246	0	0	0
Ariel Ortega	Midfielder	River Plate, Argentina	81/17	16	1113	1	0	3
Diego Simeone	Midfielder	Lazio, Italy	104/11	14	1203	3	0	0
Juan Sorin	Midfielder	Cruzeiro, Brazil	33/5	14	971	1	0	2
Juan Sebastian Veron	Midfielder	Manchester United, England	46/7	16	1372	2	0	5
Javier Zanetti	Midfielder	Internazionale, Italy	64/3	14	1101	1	0	0
Gabriel Batistuta	Forward	Roma, Italy	75/55	5	427	0	0	5
Claudio Lopez	Forward	Lazio, Italy	47/10	16	1063	3	0	6
Hernan Crespo	Forward	Lazio, Italy	33/17	12	839	0	0	9
Javier Saviola	Forward	Barcelona, Spain	1/0	1	15	0	0	0

KEY: APPS/GOALS = International Appearances/Goals; GAMES=Qualification Games played; MINS=Minutes played; Y/C= Yellow cards R/C=Red cards

HISTORY AT THE WORLD CUP

1930 1934 1938 1950 1954 1958 1962 1966 1970 1974 1978 1982 1986 1990 1994 1998

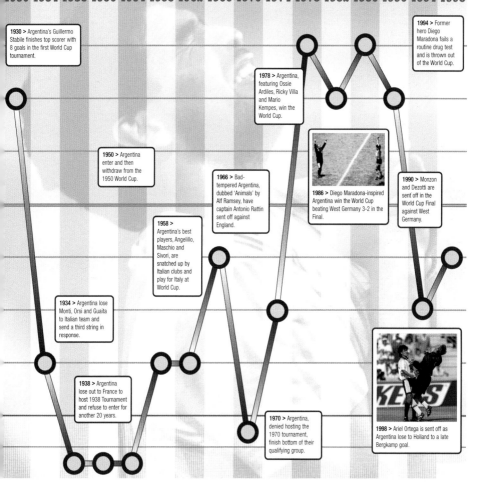

1930 > Argentina's Guillermo Stabile finishes top scorer with 8 goals in the first World Cup tournament.

1994 > Former hero Diego Maradona fails a routine drug test and is thrown out of the World Cup.

1978 > Argentina, featuring Ossie Ardiles, Ricky Villa and Mario Kempes, win the World Cup.

1950 > Argentina enter and then withdraw from the 1950 World Cup.

1966 > Bad-tempered Argentina, dubbed 'Animals' by Alf Ramsey, have captain Antonio Rattin sent off against England.

1986 > Diego Maradona-inspired Argentina win the World Cup beating West Germany 3-2 in the Final.

1990 > Monzon and Dezotti are sent off in the World Cup Final against West Germany.

1958 > Argentina's best players, Angelillo, Maschio and Sivori, are snatched up by Italian clubs and play for Italy at World Cup.

1934 > Argentina lose Monti, Orsi and Guaita to Italian team and send a third string in response.

1938 > Argentina lose out to France to host 1938 Tournament and refuse to enter for another 20 years.

1970 > Argentina, denied hosting the 1970 tournament, finish bottom of their qualifying group.

1998 > Ariel Ortega is sent off as Argentina lose to Holland to a late Bergkamp goal.

★ WORLD CUP HISTORY

1930 >> Runners-Up		1970 >> Did Not Qualify	
1934 >> First Round		1974 >> Second Round	
1938 >> Did Not Enter		1978 >> Winners	
1950 >> Withdrew		1982 >> Second Round	
1954 >> Did Not Enter		1986 >> Winners	
1958 >> First Round		1990 >> Runners-Up	
1962 >> First Round		1994 >> Second Round	
1966 >> Quarter-Final		1998 >> Quarter-Finals	

★ WORLD CUP RECORDS, STORIES AND WEIRDNESS

MOST GOALS IN A TOURNAMENT >> Guillermo Stábile scored 8 in the 1930 tournament.

GREATEST WORLD CUP GOAL >> Diego Maradona unquestionably scored the greatest ever goal seen at a World Cup Finals. Against England in 1986, and just minutes after the infamous ''Hand of God'' goal, Maradona ran from his own half beating English player after player then slipped it past a bemused and helpless Peter Shilton. Argentina won 2-0.

GROUP H

OPPONENT	DATE	UK TIME	VENUE
Japan	4 June	10.00	Saitama, Japan
Tunisia	10 June	10.00	Oita, Japan
Russia	14 June	07.30	Shizuoka, Japan

"will it be an early bath for the Belgiques?"

BELGIUM

★ THE LOWDOWN

Population: 10.2 million

Capital: Brussels

Leader: Guy Verhofstadt

Life Expectancy: Male: 74 yrs Female: 81 yrs

>> Belgium only became independent from the Netherlands in 1830.

>> Besides being famous for sprouts, chocolate and good lager, the Belgians also claim to have "invented" fish & chips. Mmm, what a healthy, well-balanced diet!

>> Brussels is the seat of both the European Union and NATO.

Six successive successful qualifications for the Finals (without hosting the tournament along the way) make Belgium something of a World Cup fixture. But they rarely cut the mustard, departing on the early flight home. In France, they drew all three of their group games against Holland (0-0), Mexico (2-2) and South Korea (1-1) and that was that.

Their best performance was at Mexico 86 where, defying the form book, they reached the semi-finals only to be beaten by Argentina and then lose a thrilling third place play-off to France, 4-2 after extra-time.

Nobody would accuse the current Belgium side of possessing abundant flair, but they are a solid, reliable outfit who know their capabilities and play to them. Belgium finished second in their qualifying group with an impressive tally of 25 goals in eight games. However, 14 of those were against minnows San Marino including a 10-1 thrashing in which 59th minute substitute Bob Peeters scored the 8th, 9th and 10th goal for an unlikely hat-trick.

Crucially in the group, they got the better of Scotland over two matches. In Glasgow, the Belgians salvaged a point after trailing 2-0 and having right-back Eric Deflandre sent off. Marc Wilmots halved the deficit in the 58th minute and Daniel Van Buyten scored the crucial equaliser in stoppage time. Van Buyten, incidentally, has not played for Belgium since that game.

The return fixture in Brussels saw Belgium go ahead after 28 minutes. Playmaker Johan Walem hit a superb measured pass for Wesley Sonck to set up left back Nico Van Kerckhoven, as he ran unmarked into the box. A Bart Goor goal in the last minute saw Belgium run out 2-0 winners.

Against Croatia however, a goalless draw at home in their opening game and a 1-0 defeat away sent Belgium to the play-offs against the Czech Republic.

Striker Gert Verheyen proved crucial to the outcome of both games. In Brussels, Verheyen scored his eighth international goal giving Belgium a 1-0 victory. In Prague Belgium had to do some solid defending to hold on to their slender aggregate lead, but in the 85th minute Verheyen was fouled in the area. Up stepped captain Marc Wilmots to convert the penalty for his eighth goal of the qualifiers and book Belgium's place in the Finals.

What Belgium will achieve in Japan and Korea is difficult to assess. They are capable of finishing in the top half of their Group, but they're just as likely to all fall down. They begin against a much-improved Japanese side then face tough African outfit Tunisia. However, the crucial match will be the last group outing in Shizuoka against Russia, a European team of equal ability.

★ **ASSOCIATION:** Union Royale des Societes de
Football Association
★ **JOINED FIFA:** 1904
★ **JOINED UEFA:** 1954

★ **PLAYERS:** 390,500
★ **CLUBS:** 2,120
★ **WEBSITE:** www.footbel.com
★ **HONOURS:** Olympics – 1920.

Glen De Boeck auditions for Riverdance during a quiet moment in a match.

★ ROAD TO QUALIFICATION

Sep 00 **Croatia** (h) > (d) **0**-0

Oct 00 **Latvia** (a) > (w) 0-**4**
Wilmots 4, Peeters 12, Cavens 81,
Verheyen 90

Feb 01 **San Marino** (h) > (w) **10**-1
Vanderhaeghe 10, 50, Mpenza, E 13, Goor
25, 62, Baseggio 65, Wilmots 71, Peeters,
B 75, 83, 88

Mar 01 **Scotland** (a) > (d) 2-**2**
Wilmots 58, Van Buyton 90

Jun 01 **Latvia** (h) > (w) **3**-1
Wilmots 2, Mpenza, E 12, Zemlinskis 50 og

Jun 01 **San Marino** (a) > (w) 1-**4**
Wilmots 10, 89 pen, Verheyen 60,
Sonck 68

Sep 01 **Scotland** (h) > (w) **2**-0
Van Kerckhoven 28, Goor 90

Oct 01 **Croatia** (a) > (l) 1-**0**

★ FINAL GROUP TABLE

Team	P	W	D	L	F	A	Pts
Croatia	8	5	3	0	15	2	18
Belgium	8	5	2	1	25	6	17
Scotland	8	4	3	1	12	6	15
Latvia	8	1	1	6	5	16	4
San Marino	8	0	1	7	3	30	1

★ RECENT RESULTS

Feb 02 **Norway** (h) > (w) **1**-0 Tanghe 82

Mar 02 **Greece** (a) > (l) 3-**2**
Goor 28, Sonck 54

69

DID YOU KNOW?

Midfielder Sven Vermant made his international debut against Armenia in October 1995 but had to wait a further three years for his second appearance.

While Robert Waseige remains a steadfast advocate of the 4-4-2 system, his rigid approach has made Belgium a team less than exciting to watch. Waseige believes in attacking football but the current side lacks any real flair. Defensively, keeper Geert De Vlieger plays behind a central partnership of Glen De Boeck and Joos Valgaeren with Eric Van Meir an alternative. Right back Eric Deflandre and Nico Van Kerckhoven on the left are encouraged to get forwards. Johan Walem has developed into a playmaker and should perfectly complement the hard-working team captain, Marc Wilmots, who sits alongside him. Bart Goor is firmly established on the left of midfield although the right side is still a problem – Sven Vermant will probably get the nod ahead of Timmy Simons. In attack, Wesley Sonck has been a revelation alongside the in form Gert Verheyen. The tall Bob Peeters and the tenacious Emile Mpenza provide attacking alternatives.

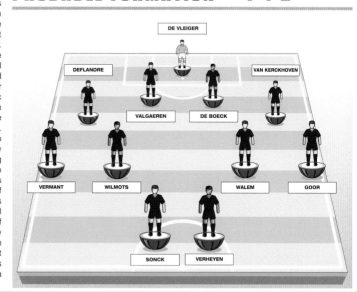

PROBABLE FORMATION 4-4-2

DE VLEIGER

DEFLANDRE — VAN KERCKHOVEN

VALGAEREN — DE BOECK

VERMANT — WILMOTS — WALEM — GOOR

SONCK — VERHEYEN

★ MEN THAT MATTER!

WESLEY SONCK

Age>> 23

Club>> Genk

This young striker, blessed with extraordinary pace, was the discovery of the qualifiers for Belgium. He has the makings of becoming Belgian's Michael Owen injecting creativity into a side that needs it.

MARC WILMOTS

Age>> 33

Club>> Schalke

Influential captain travelling to his fourth World Cup. He scored eight goals in qualifying including the decisive penalty in the play off against the Czech Republic. Takes penalties and free kicks.

BART GOOR

Age>> 29

Club>> Hertha Berlin

Ever-present on the left of midfield throughout the qualifiers who will be making his World Cup debut. He scored twice in Belgium's 10-1 thrashing of San Marino. Played at Euro 2000.

★ PROBABLE SQUAD ★ QUALIFICATION RECORD

NAME	POSITION	CLUB	APS/GOALS	GAMES	MINS	Y/C	R/C	GOALS
Geert De Vlieger	Goalkeeper	Willem II, Holland	21 /0	10	900	0	0	0
Ronny Gaspercic	Goalkeeper	Real Betis, Spain	8 /0	0	0	0	0	0
Frederic Herpoel	Goalkeeper	Ghent, Belgium	2 /0	0	0	0	0	0
Philippe Clement	Defender	Brugge, Belgium	14 /0	2	180	1	0	0
Bertrand Crasson	Defender	Anderlecht, Belgium	26 /1	2	114	1	0	0
Glen De Boeck	Defender	Anderlecht, Belgium	30 /0	5	404	0	0	0
Eric Deflandre	Defender	Lyon, France	36 /0	9	786	1	1	0
Marc Hendrikx	Defender	Anderlecht, Belgium	15 /0	3	57	0	0	0
Joos Valgaeren	Defender	Celtic, Scotland	13 /0	5	418	1	0	0
Daniel Van Buyton	Defender	Marseille, France	3/1	2	122	0	0	1
Nico Van Kerckhoven	Defender	Schalke, Germany	35 /3	6	529	0	0	1
Eric Van Meir	Defender	Standard Liege, Belgium	28 /1	8	676	2	0	0
Walter Baseggio	Midfielder	Anderlecht, Belgium	8 /1	3	246	1	0	1
Danny Boffin	Midfielder	St Truiden, Belgium	49 /1	3	38	0	0	0
Bart Goor	Midfielder	Hertha Berlin, Germany	32 /7	10	852	0	0	3
Timmy Simons	Midfielder	Brugge, Belgium	6 /0	4	273	0	0	0
Sven Vermant	Midfielder	Schalke, Germany	9 /0	6	225	0	0	0
Johan Walem	Midfielder	Standard Liege, Belgium	29 /1	6	525	2	0	0
Marc Wilmots	Midfielder	Schalke, Germany	62 /24	9	719	0	0	7
Emile Mpenza	Forward	Schalke, Germany	35 /12	5	424	1	0	2
Bob Peeters	Forward	Vitesse Arnhem, Holland	12 /4	7	247	1	0	3
Wesley Sonck	Forward	Genk, Belgium	7 /1	6	291	1	0	1
Gert Verheyen	Forward	Brugge, Belgium	42 /10	8	720	0	0	3

KEY: APPS/GOALS = International Appearances/Goals; GAMES=Qualification Games played; MINS=Minutes played; Y/C = Yellow cards R/C=Red cards

HISTORY AT THE WORLD CUP

1930 1934 1938 1950 1954 1958 1962 1966 1970 1974 1978 1982 1986 1990 1994 1998

1986 > Jan Ceulemans-inspired Belgium reach the semis and finish in fourth place.

1994 > Philippe Albert scores the decisive goal that beats arch rivals Holland in the Citrus Bowl.

1934 > Belgium lose 5-2 to Germany in Florence in the first round.

1930 > Belgium lose both of their games against the USA and Paraguay in Uruguay.

1938 > Belgium lose 3-1 to hosts France in Paris.

1954 > Belgium draw 4-4 with England.

1990 > Belgium is beaten by a dramatic last-minute extra-time goal scored by England's David Platt.

1998 > Goalkeeper Filip De Wilde inflicts some severe hair cutting on his fellow squad members.

1950 > Belgium, preoccupied with rebuilding after the war, withdraw from a group including Switzerland and Luxembourg.

1966 > Belgium lose to Bulgaria in qualification play-off decider.

★ WORLD CUP HISTORY

1930 >> First Round		**1970** >> First Round	
1934 >> First Round		**1974** >> Did Not Qualify	
1938 >> First Round		**1978** >> Did Not Qualify	
1950 >> Withdrew		**1982** >> Second Round	
1954 >> First Round		**1986** >> Fourth Place	
1958 >> Did Not Qualify		**1990** >> Second Round	
1962 >> Did Not Qualify		**1994** >> Second Round	
1966 >> Did Not Qualify		**1998** >> First Round	

★ WORLD CUP RECORDS, STORIES AND WEIRDNESS

LATEST GOAL >> England's David Platt put the winning goal past Belgium in the 119th minute of a second round match at Italy '90.

GROUP C

OPPONENT	DATE	UK TIME	VENUE
Turkey	**3 June**	10.00	**Ulsan, Japan**
China	**8 June**	12.30	**Seogwipo, Korea**
Costa Rica	**13 June**	07.30	**Suwon, Korea**

"they put the 'beautiful' into the beautiful game"

BRAZIL

Historically speaking, Brazil are the World Cup's most successful team. They've won the competition on an unprecedented four occasions and are the only team to have appeared in every tournament since 1930. In the past their glorious one touch passing game put the 'beautiful' into the beautiful game.

But that was then and this is now. The Brazilian national side is currently in a mess. From the start of the South American qualifying tournament in March 2000 to the time they finally booked their place in the Finals, with their last match at home to Venezuela in November 2001, Brazil suffered no fewer than six defeats. An amazing record when you realise Brazil had only previously suffered one defeat in qualifying throughout their entire history!

During qualifying Brazil had four (yes four!) different coaches, none of whom had any real affinity for the beautiful game. Wanderley Luxemburgo had been in charge since France 98 and, to his credit, masterminded a 3-1 victory over South American rivals Argentina, but that was sandwiched between defeats by Paraguay (2-1) and Chile (3-0). He met his personal Waterloo at the Sydney Olympics. Brazil, hot favourites to win gold, were knocked out at the quarter-final stage by a nine-man Cameroon. Before he boarded the plane home Luxemburgo was told he was sacked.

Candido was put in caretaker charge for a trip to Venezuela, arguably South America's worst team. Candido selected Romario – who had been recalled by Luxemburgo and had

scored a hat-trick against Bolivia who again responded with a four-goal haul in a 6-0 win.

Emerson Leon took over for the next ten games during which he used a staggering 62 players. He presided over a 1-0 World Cup qualifying defeat by Ecuador and a disastrous Confederations Cup. Although sanctioned by the Brazilian FA to take an experimental squad to the Cup they were less than happy when Brazil drew games with Canada and Japan and were ignominiously defeated by Australia.

Luiz Felipe Scolari was the choice of both fans and media alike, but he too didn't start well, suffering a 1-0 defeat in Uruguay. Another experimental Brazil squad suffered defeats by Mexico and Honduras at the Copa America. Back on the World Cup trail home wins over Paraguay and Chile were offset by away defeats in Argentina and Bolivia.

Brazil, Uruguay and Colombia were by now vying for the fourth automatic qualifying place and the play-off spot in the last round of matches. Fortunately, Brazil had the easier task – at home to Venezuela, against whom they had never lost. This time they didn't fail and picked up the points for qualification.

Scolari's Brazil had done what they needed to do. The World Cup is Brazil's favourite arena. And with their glorious history and a squad of experienced players, it's not too much to hope that, once the horrors of the last couple of years are forgotten, Brazil will once more be the football masters everyone longs to see....

★ **ASSOCIATION:** Confederacao Brasileira de Futebol
★ **JOINED FIFA:** 1923
★ **JOINED CONMEBOL:** 1916
★ **PLAYERS:** 552,000

★ **CLUBS:** 13,987
★ **WEBSITE:** www.brasilfutebol.com
★ **HONOURS:** World Cup – 1958, 1962, 1970, 1994; Copa America – 1919, 1922, 1949, 1989, 1997, 1999.

Roberto Carlos, all poise and skill.

★ ROAD TO QUALIFICATION

Mar 00 **Colombia** (a) > (d) 0-**0**

Apr 00 **Ecuador** (h) > (w) **3**-2
Rivaldo 17, 52, Roberto Carlos 43

Jun 00 **Peru** (a) > (w) 0-**1** Carlos, A 35

Jun 00 **Uruguay** (h) > (d) **1**-1
Rivaldo 85 pen

Jul 00 **Paraguay** (a) > (l) 2-**1** Rivaldo 74

Jul 00 **Argentina** (h) > (w) **3**-1
Alex 5, Vampeta 45, 51

Aug 00 **Chile** (a) > (l) 3-0

Sep 00 **Bolivia** (h) > (w) **5**-0
Romario 12, 77, 81, Rivaldo 47 Marques 88

Oct 00 **Venezuela** (a) > (w) 0-**6**
Euller 21, Juninho 29, Romario 31, 36, 39 pen, 64

Nov 00 **Colombia** (h) > (w) **1**-0
Roque Junior 90

Mar 01 **Ecuador** (a) > (l) **1**-0

Apr 01 **Peru** (h) > (d) **1**-1 Romario 65

Jun 01 **Uruguay** (a) > (l) **1**-0

Aug 01 **Paraguay** (h) > (w) **2**-0
Marcelinho 4, Rivaldo 69

Sep 01 **Argentina** (a) > (l) 2-**1** Ayala 2 og

Oct 01 **Chile** (h) > (w) **2**-0
Edilson 52, Rivaldo 63

Nov 01 **Bolivia** (a) > (l) 3-**1** Edilson 26

Nov 01 **Venezuela** (h) > (w) **3**-0
Luizao 12, 19, Rivaldo 34

★ FINAL GROUP TABLE

Team	P	W	D	L	F	A	Pts
Argentina	18	13	4	1	42	15	43
Ecuador	18	9	4	5	23	20	31
Brazil	18	9	3	6	31	17	30
Paraguay	18	9	3	6	29	23	30
Uruguay	18	7	6	5	19	13	27
Colombia	18	7	6	5	20	15	27
Bolivia	18	4	6	8	21	33	18
Peru	18	4	4	10	14	25	16
Venezuela	18	5	1	12	18	44	16
Chile	18	3	3	12	15	27	12

★ RECENT RESULTS

Feb 02 **Saudi Arabia** (a) > (w) 0-**1**
Djalminha 72

Mar 02 **Iceland** (h) > (w) **6**-1
Anderson Polga 4, 73, Kleberson 19, Kaka 46, Gilberto Silva 51, Edilson 63

Mar 02 **Yugoslavia** (h) > (w) **1**-0 Luizao 71

DID YOU KNOW?

Garrincha scored and was sent-off in the 1962 semi-final agains Chile but FIFA gave him the all-clear to play in the Final.

Brazil's summer line-up is still unpredictable and will depend on the recovery of Ronaldo and whether Romario, at 36, is even selected for the squad. Brazil have played so many games and used so many players (62 in the qualifiers) in the last eighteen months that there has been no settled line-up from one match to the next. In defence, Cafu and Roberto Carlos are certain to play with Antonio Carlos and Roque Junior probably the centre backs in front of goalkeeper Marcos. Juninho Paulista is a major creative force in midfield, although Rivaldo, alongside him, should be too – but seems to lack that spark that would take him from reliable to the special. Vampeta and Ze Roberto should play the wide midfield roles, but coach Scolari may opt for the destructive (and cynical) prowess of Emerson Ferreira. The attack, if Romario or Ronaldo are not immediately available, will fall to Flamengo's controversial Edilson alongside Bayern Munich's Giovane Elber. Luizao and Marcelinho are also front men contenders.

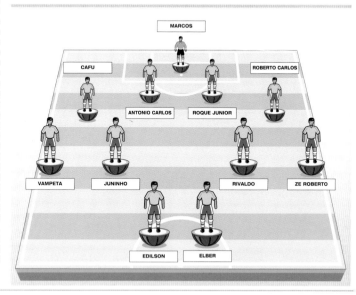

PROBABLE FORMATION 4-4-2

★ MEN THAT MATTER!

RIVALDO

Age>> 30
Club>> Barcelona

A virtual ever-present in midfield from where he has averaged a goal every two games including eight in the qualifiers. His popularity is on the wane with the fans demanding better performances.

JUNINHO PAULISTA

Age>> 28
Club>> Vasco Da Gama/Atletico Madrid (loan)

Injury ruled him out of France 98 but he is currently in excellent form for both club and country. Made his debut in February 1995 and later had spells with Middlesbrough and Atletico Madrid.

ROMARIO

Age>> 36
Club>> Vasco Da Gama

FIFA Golden Ball winner as the tournament's best player in Brazil's 1994 World Cup-winning team. This is his fourth World Cup, recalled during the qualifiers and continues to show sharp form inside the box.

★ PROBABLE SQUAD　　　　　　　　★ QUALIFICATION RECORD

NAME	POSITION	CLUB	APS/GOALS	GAMES	MINS	Y/C	R/C	GOALS
Dida	Goalkeeper	Corinthians, Brazil	40/0	7	630	0	0	0
Marcos	Goalkeeper	Palmeiras, Brazil	11/0	6	540	0	0	0
Rogerio Ceni	Goalkeeper	Sao Paulo, Brazil	13/0	5	450	0	0	0
Antonio Carlos	Defender	Roma, Italy	10/1	9	794	3	0	1
Cafu	Defender	Roma, Italy	102/5	11	990	3	1	0
Cris	Defender	Cruzeiro, Brazil	8/0	3	270	0	0	0
Edmilson	Defender	Lyon, France	12/0	8	675	3	0	0
Juan	Defender	Flamengo, Brazil	7/0	3	254	0	0	0
Lucio	Defender	Bayer Leverkusen, Germany	13/0	7	630	1	0	0
Roberto Carlos	Defender	Real Madrid, Spain	83/6	12	1050	1	0	1
Roque Junior	Defender	Milan, Italy	9/1	8	720	4	0	1
Denilson	Midfielder	Real Betis, Spain	51/7	6	165	0	0	0
Djalminha	Midfielder	Deportivo Coruna, Spain	4/0	2	100	0	0	0
Emerson Ferreira	Midfielder	Roma, Italy	41/5	10	900	5	0	0
Juninho Paulista	Midfielder	Vasco da Gama, Brazil	32/4	11	595	0	0	2
Rivaldo	Midfielder	Barcelona, Spain	57/28	15	1319	1	0	8
Vampeta	Midfielder	Corinthians, Brazil	40/2	15	972	2	0	2
Ze Roberto	Midfielder	Bayer Leverkusen, Germany	42/3	8	386	0	0	0
Edilson	Forward	Flamengo, Brazil	11/4	4	321	1	0	2
Luizao	Forward	Corinthians, Brazil	5/3	3	125	0	0	2
Romario	Forward	Vasco da Gama, Brazil	69/54	5	450	0	0	8
Ronaldinho Gaucho	Forward	Paris Saint-Germain, France	23/10	6	308	2	0	0
Ronaldo	Forward	Internazionale, Italy	54/36	0	0	0	0	0

KEY: APPS/GOALS = International Appearances/Goals; GAMES=Qualification Games played; MINS=Minutes played; Y/C= Yellow cards R/C=Red cards

HISTORY AT THE WORLD CUP

1930 1934 1938 1950 1954 1958 1962 1966 1970 1974 1978 1982 1986 1990 1994 1998

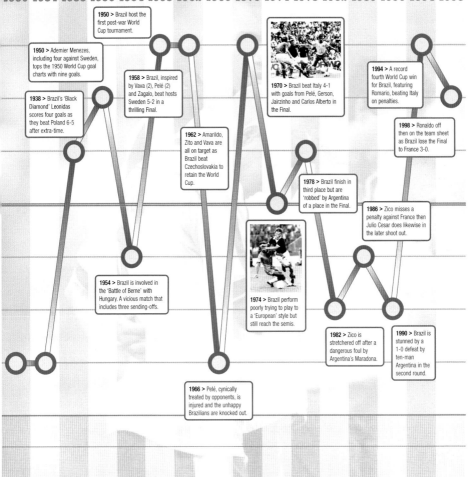

1950 > Brazil host the first post-war World Cup tournament.

1950 > Ademier Menezes, including four against Sweden, tops the 1950 World Cup goal charts with nine goals.

1958 > Brazil, inspired by Vava (2), Pelé (2) and Zagalo, beat hosts Sweden 5-2 in a thrilling Final.

1938 > Brazil's 'Black Diamond' Leonidas scores four goals as they beat Poland 6-5 after extra-time.

1962 > Amarildo, Zito and Vava are all on target as Brazil beat Czechoslovakia to retain the World Cup.

1970 > Brazil beat Italy 4-1 with goals from Pelé, Gerson, Jairzinho and Carlos Alberto in the Final.

1994 > A record fourth World Cup win for Brazil, featuring Romario, beating Italy on penalties.

1998 > Ronaldo off then on the team sheet as Brazil lose the Final to France 3-0.

1978 > Brazil finish in third place but are 'robbed' by Argentina of a place in the Final.

1986 > Zico misses a penalty against France then Julio Cesar does likewise in the later shoot out.

1954 > Brazil is involved in the 'Battle of Berne' with Hungary. A vicious match that includes three sending-offs.

1974 > Brazil perform poorly trying to play to a 'European' style but still reach the semis.

1982 > Zico is stretchered off after a dangerous foul by Argentina's Maradona.

1990 > Brazil is stunned by a 1-0 defeat by ten-man Argentina in the second round.

1966 > Pelé, cynically treated by opponents, is injured and the unhappy Brazilians are knocked out.

★ WORLD CUP HISTORY

1930 >> First Round		1970 >> Winners	
1934 >> First Round		1974 >> Fourth Place	
1938 >> Third Place		1978 >> Third Place	
1950 >> Runners-Up		1982 >> Second Round	
1954 >> Quarter-Final		1986 >> Quarter-Final	
1958 >> Winners		1990 >> Second Round	
1962 >> Winners		1994 >> Winners	
1966 >> First Round		1998 >> Runners-Up	

★ WORLD CUP RECORDS, STORIES AND WEIRDNESS

MOST GOALS >> Pele has achieved more than any other player in World Cup history. Surprisingly, he hasn't topscored in any of the four World Cups in which he's appeared, but he occupies third place on the all-time topscorers table with 12 goals. He is, however, the only player to have won three World Cups.

MOST GOALS IN A TOURNAMENT >> Ademir totalled 9 for Brazil in Brazil in 1950, including 4 against Sweden.

GREATEST TEAM EVER >> The World Cup Brazilian side of 1970 has often been described as the best football team of all time. Its list of world class players included Pelé, Jairzinho, Tostao and Rivelino. They won all six games in the 1970 competition.

OPPONENT	DATE	UK TIME	VENUE
Ireland	1 June	07.30	Niigata, Japan
Saudi Arabia	6 June	10.00	Saitama, Japan
Germany	11 June	12.30	Shizuoka, Japan

"Indomitable Lions carry African hopes"

CAMEROON

★ THE LOWDOWN

Population: 15.8 million

Capital: Yaounde

Leader: Peter Musonge

Life Expectancy: Male: 53 yrs Female: 55 yrs

>> There are four times as many radios as TVs in Cameroon, which will account for the immense popularity of the BBC's World Service during the World Cup.

>> Cameroon has the highest mountain in sub-Saharan West Africa, and yes, it's called Mount Cameroon!

>> The modern state was formed in 1961 from French Cameroon and part of British Cameroon.

Cameroon, reigning African champions, have qualified for a fifth World Cup Finals, a record number of appearances in the Finals for an African country. The whole world still remembers how at Italia 90 Roger Milla, with his exuberant goal celebrations and his charismatic Cameroon team mates, endeared themselves to a worldwide football-loving audience. Now, with their fourth successive appearance at the Finals, there is every hope and expectation that while carrying the hopes of African football they will better their previous quarter-final appearance, which is the furthest any African nation has progressed at the tournament.

A somewhat unanticipated success at the Sydney Olympics, where the Cameroon Under-23s took the gold medal, has meant that a good number of the current squad has already tasted international success and we can expect that several of the Cameroon players, including current African Footballer of the Year Patrick Mboma, his strike partner Samuel Eto'o and winger Lauren Etame Mayer, will be found among the real entertainers in Japan/Korea.

Qualification for the Finals proved to be relatively painless. 50 teams entered the Confederation Africaine de Football (CAF) competition; all teams playing a knock-out preliminary round with home/away legs. The 25 winners of the preliminary round then went through to the second phase, which contained five groups with five teams in each group. The five group winners would qualify for the World Cup Finals.

After seeing off Somalia in the preliminary round, Cameroon dominated Group 1, a group that also included Angola, Zambia, Togo and Libya – none of whom had ever reached the Finals – winning six of their eight matches and losing only one, away to nearest rivals Angola. Cameroon took 19 points; Angola finished runner up on 13.

Patrick Mboma finished top scorer on 6, including a hat-trick at the away leg against Libya, and Samuel Eto'o and Marc-Vivien Foe chipped in with three each. A 2-2 draw away to World Cup favourites Argentina in a friendly in March this year has set them up nicely for Japan/Korea.

The Indomitable Lions they may be on the pitch, but off it they've done well not to be utterly subdued by last year's coaching turmoil. With only months to go to the start of the tournament, German-born coach Winfried Schäfer has taken on the managerial role after Frenchman Pierre Lechantre had given way to Olympic coach Paul Akono and then returned, following Akono's resignation, only to lead the team to a disappointing Confederations Cup where he became a managerial casualty yet again.

★ **ASSOCIATION:** Federation Camerounaise de Football
★ **JOINED FIFA:** 1962
★ **JOINED CAF:** 1963
★ **PLAYERS:** 9,400

★ **CLUBS:** 200
★ **WEBSITE:** None.
★ **HONOURS:** African Nations Cup – 1984, 1988, 2000, 2002; Olympics – 2000.

ques Songo'o gives crystal clear instructions to Cameroon's three-man defence.

★ ROAD TO QUALIFICATION

Apr 00 **Somalia** (a) > (w) 0-**3**
Mboma 26, Foe 31, Eto'o 37

Apr 00 **Somalia** (h) > (w) **3**-0 (agg **6**-0)
Jama 15, 27, Olembe 48

Jun 00 **Libya** (a) > (w) 0-**3**
Mboma 35, 67, 88 pen

Jul 00 **Angola** (h) > (w) **3**-0
Abanda 20, Tchoutang 68, 74

Jan 01 **Togo** (a) > (w) 0-**2**
Eto'o 57, Mboma 75

Feb 01 **Zambia** (h) > (w) **1**-0 Mboma 22

Apr 01 **Libya** (h) > (w) **1**-0 Lauren 78

May 01 **Angola** (a) > (l) 2-0

Jul 01 **Togo** (h) > (w) **2**-0 Eto'o 27, Foe 49

Jul 01 **Zambia** (a) > (d) 2-**2**
Foe 52, N'diefi 64

★ FINAL GROUP TABLE

Team	P	W	D	L	F	A	Pts
Cameroon	8	6	1	1	14	4	19
Angola	8	3	4	1	11	9	13
Zambia	8	3	2	3	14	11	11
Togo	8	2	3	3	10	13	9
Libya	8	0	2	6	7	19	2

★ RECENT RESULTS

Mar 02 **Argentina** (a) > (d) 2-2
Eto'o 19, Suffo 86

DID YOU KNOW?

Roger Milla, who changed his name from Miller to sound more African, is the oldest man to score in the final stages of a World Cup. He was 42 when he scored against Russia in the 1994 World Cup.

Cameroon's fourth coach in a year, Winfried Schafer, has stuck with the familiar 3-5-2 formation which has served the Indomitable Lions so well in recent years. Raymond Kalla, Rigobert Song, the captain, and Bill Tchato form a formidable back three in front of goalkeeper Boukar Alioum and have been automatic choices for much of the last two years. The five-man midfield is given width by Geremi Njitap and Pierre Wome on the right and left respectively. In midfield, Marc-Vivien Foe is the central playmaker with Lauren Etame-Mayer to his right and the impressive Salomon Olembe on his left. All in all, an attack minded midfield that has no cause to fear anyone. The striking partnership pitches together the goal machine and star of African football Patrick Mboma with the young and pacy Samuel Eto'o. Nicolas Alnoudji could earn a place in midfield while Pius N'Diefi is a likely alternative up front.

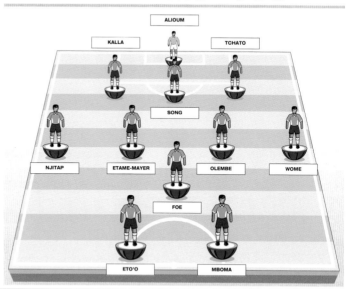

PROBABLE FORMATION 3-5-2

ALIOUM

KALLA   TCHATO

SONG

NJITAP   ETAME-MAYER   OLEMBE   WOME

FOE

ETO'O   MBOMA

★ MEN THAT MATTER!

PATRICK MBOMA

Age>> 31
Club>> Parma
Missed the 2002 African Nations Cup Final through injury but won it in 2000 along with the Olympic Gold. Turned down Cameroon at USA 94 but played at France 98. He is the team's top scorer.

SAMUEL ETO'O

Age>> 21
Club>> Mallorca
Only 21 but already a medal winner at the African Nations Cup and the Olympics. He made a brief 24-minute appearance against Italy at France 98 for only his fourth cap.

RIGOBERT SONG

Age>> 25
Club>> Koln
Cameroon's captain with four African Nations Cup and two World Cups under his belt. Regarded as one of Africa's best defenders with club experience in France, Italy, England and Germany.

★ PROBABLE SQUAD   ★ QUALIFICATION RECORD

NAME	POSITION	CLUB	APS/GOALS	GAMES	MINS	Y/C	R/C	GOALS
Boukar Alioum	Goalkeeper	Samsunspor, Turkey	38/0	7	630	0	0	0
Idriss Carlos Kameni	Goalkeeper	Le Havre, France	1/0	0	0	0	0	0
Jacques Songo'o	Goalkeeper	Metz, France	66/0	0	0	0	0	0
Raymond Kalla	Defender	Extremadura, Spain	47/2	5	450	0	0	0
Pierre Njanka	Defender	Strasbourg, France	12/0	7	629	2	1	0
Geremi Njitap	Defender	Real Madrid, Spain	38/0	6	540	0	0	0
Rigobert Song	Defender	Koln, Germany	59/2	6	540	0	0	0
Bill Tchato	Defender	Montpellier, France	12/1	7	485	0	0	0
Jerry-C'tn Tchuisse	Defender	Moscow Spartak, Russia	2/0	2	118	0	0	0
Pierre Wome	Defender	Bologna, Italy	46/1	2	160	0	0	0
Nicolas Alnoudji	Midfielder	Caykur Rizespor, Turkey	15/0	7	474	1	0	0
Serge Branco	Midfielder	Eintracht Frankfurt, Germany	1/0	1	1	0	0	0
Jean Dika	Midfielder	Uniao Lamas, Portugal	4/0	2	180	0	0	0
Joel Epalle	Midfielder	Panahaiki, Greece	22/2	6	420	0	0	0
Lauren Etame-Mayer	Midfielder	Arsenal, England	15/1	3	270	2	0	1
Marc-Vivien Foe	Midfielder	Lyon, France	47/6	5	411	1	0	2
Salomon Olembe	Midfielder	Nantes, France	39/3	5	379	0	0	0
Bernard Tchoutang	Midfielder	Roda JC, Holland	35/6	4	222	0	0	2
Samuel Eto'o	Forward	Mallorca, Spain	27/7	4	339	0	0	2
Joseph-Desire Job	Forward	Middlesbrough, England	34/5	3	133	0	0	0
Patrick Mboma	Forward	Sunderland, England	42/23	5	424	0	0	2
Pius N'diefi	Forward	Sedan, France	13/3	4	198	0	0	1
Patrick Suffo	Forward	Sheffield United, England	18/2	3	69	0	0	0

KEY: APPS/GOALS = International Appearances/Goals; GAMES=Qualification Games played; MINS=Minutes played; Y/C= Yellow cards R/C=Red cards

HISTORY AT THE WORLD CUP

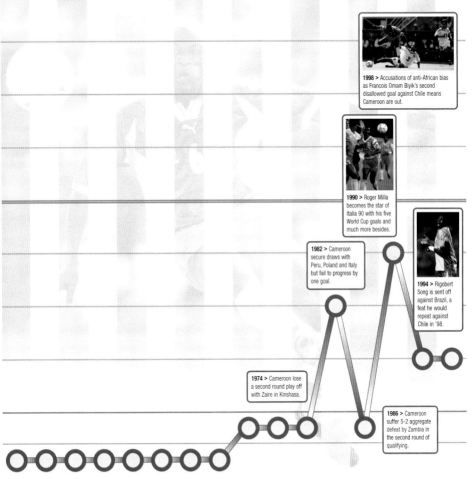

1998 > Accusations of anti-African bias as Francois Omam Biyik's second disallowed goal against Chile means Cameroon are out.

1990 > Roger Milla becomes the star of Italia 90 with his five World Cup goals and much more besides.

1982 > Cameroon secure draws with Peru, Poland and Italy but fail to progress by one goal.

1994 > Rigobert Song is sent off against Brazil, a feat he would repeat against Chile in '98.

1974 > Cameroon lose a second round play off with Zaire in Kinshasa.

1986 > Cameroon suffer 5-2 aggregate defeat by Zambia in the second round of qualifying.

★ WORLD CUP HISTORY

1930 >> Did Not Enter		**1970** >> Did Not Qualify	
1934 >> Did Not Enter		**1974** >> Did Not Qualify	
1938 >> Did Not Enter		**1978** >> Did Not Qualify	
1950 >> Did Not Enter		**1982** >> Second Round	
1954 >> Did Not Enter		**1986** >> Did Not Qualify	
1958 >> Did Not Enter		**1990** >> Quarter-Final	
1962 >> Did Not Enter		**1994** >> First Round	
1966 >> Did Not Enter		**1998** >> First Round	

★ WORLD CUP RECORDS, STORIES AND WEIRDNESS

RED CARDS >> Cameroon share second place with Uruguay, after Brazil and Argentina, for being shown the most red cards (6) in all World Cup Finals.

BEST MATCH >> Cameroon against Argentina 1990 ended this match with nine men and managed to keep the defending champions at bay, securing a famous victory in the opening game of the 1990 World Cup.

GROUP C

OPPONENT	DATE	UK TIME	VENUE
Costa Rica	**4 June**	**07.30**	**Gwangiu, Korea**
Brazil	**8 June**	**12.30**	**Seogwipo, Korea**
Turkey	**13 June**	**07.30**	**Seoul, Korea**

"oriental debutantes"

CHINA

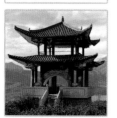

Yu Genwei made history with his first international goal against Oman in Shenyang, scoring the goal that takes China to their first ever World Cup Finals. The midfielder normally sits on the substitutes' bench and is called on late in the game to replace the established players Yang Cheng or Ma Mingyu. In the absence of creative Qi Hong, who scored the winner for a massively pressurised China in the previous game against the United Arab Emirates, Yu Genwei started a World Cup qualifier for the first time. After 36 minutes he scored the goal Chinese soccer had been waiting for, for 40 years.

China has been attempting to qualify for the Finals since 1982 despite having 7.5 million registered footballers, although its professional league, dominated by the Dalian Shide club, only came into existence in 1994.

Progress has been made at junior levels and in women's football as the respective sides have all qualified for international tournaments.

The appointment of Serb coach Bora Milutinovic, combined with a modicum of good luck plus undoubted determination, has been responsible for China booking their place in Japan/Korea. A more open Chinese society has meant that Chinese players have also benefited from overseas experience. Defenders Fan Zhiyi, Sun Jihai and midfielder Zhang Enhua have played in Britain, while forwards Xie Hui and Yang Chen play in Germany. Sun Jihai is reputed to be under scrutiny by several Italian sides and the influential Li Tie of Liaoning, China's Player of the Year, is in line for a move to Holland.

The qualifying journey began with the easiest of first round groups where they collected maximum points, scoring 25 goals including a 10-1 thrashing of the Maldives in their opening match (a hat-trick for Xie Hui). The team's first piece of good fortune came with the news that the Asian Confederation decided to seed the United Arab Emirates instead of the in form Iran. The subsequent draw meant China would avoid the main Asian football powerhouses of Iran and Saudi Arabia.

Luck stayed with them when the loss of key midfielder Zhang Enhua through injury led to the unearthing of a bright new talent in Li Weifeng, who combined superbly with the driving Li Tie, to dominate games from midfield. After opening with a 3-0 home win over the seeded United Arab Emirates, they faced a testing tie away to Oman. The Chinese survived a first-half missed penalty, then broke the deadlock in the 70th minute through Qi Hong. Fan Zhiyi's penalty six minutes from time sealed the victory.

A trip to Qatar nearly undid the good work done. With defeat looming, Li Weifeng's scored a dramatic last minute equaliser. Uzbekistan were despatched 2-0 despite China losing Wu Chengying, sent off in the 74th minute. The United Arab Emirates presented them with a must win tie, but China produced a resolute winning performance which left a celebratory victory over Oman taking China to the first Asian World Cup Finals.

China's aims will be modest in South Korea and, if their luck continues, hope to reach the second round, which means defeating Costa Rica – a former Milutinovic team.

★ THE LOWDOWN

Population: 1.3 billion

Capital: Beijing

Leader: Zhu Rongji

Life Expectancy: Male: 69 yrs Female: 73 yrs

>> China is the third largest country in the world after Canada and Russia, but contains the highest population

>> It has 52.5 million students in junior middle schools, the same number of people as the entire population of England.

>> China has over 5000 family names, the most common are Zhang, Wang, Li and Zhao.

>> 2002 is the Chinese year of the horse.

★ **ASSOCIATION:** Football Association of the People's Republic of China
★ **JOINED FIFA:** 1979
★ **JOINED AFC:** 1974

★ **PLAYERS:** 2,250,000
★ **CLUBS:** 1,045
★ **WEBSITE:** www.fa.org.cn
★ **HONOURS:** None.

It maybe the year of the horse, but Wu Chengying takes things a bit far trying to climb on his invisible dobbin.

★ ROAD TO QUALIFICATION

Apr 01 **Maldives** (h) > (w) **10**-1
Xu Yan 13, 45, Wu 17, Xie 42, 49, 62, Zhiyi 51, 75, Yeng 59, Lin 90

Apr 01 **Maldives** (a) > (w) 0-**1** Xie 44

May 01 **Cambodia** (a) > (w) 0-**4**
Li, J 5, 63, Qu 43, Ma 58

May 01 **Indonesia** (h) > (w) **5**-1
Li, W 51, Yeng 60, Xie 70, 90, Qi 79

May 01 **Cambodia** (h) > (w) **3**-1
Ma 6, Xu Yan 21, Li, B 87

May 01 **Indonesia** (a) > (w) 0-**2**
Xie 44, Wu 70

Aug 01 **UAE** (h) > (w) **3**-0
Li Xiao 3, Qi 20, Hao 34

Aug 01 **Oman** (a) > (w) 0-**2** Qi 71, Zhiyi 84

Sep 01 **Qatar** (h) > (d) **1**-1 Li, W 89

Sep 01 **Uzbekistan** (h) > (w) **2**-0
Li, W 63, Zhiyi 75

Sep 01 **UAE** (a) > (w) 0-**1** Qi 43

Oct 01 **Oman** (h) > (w) **1**-0 Yu 36

Oct 01 **Qatar** (h) > (w) **3**-0
Su 11, Qu 29, Hao 56

Oct 01 **Uzbekistan** (a) > (l) 1-**0**

★ 2ND RND GROUP TABLE

Team	P	W	D	L	F	A	Pts
China PR	8	6	1	1	13	2	19
UAE	8	3	2	3	10	11	11
Uzbekistan	8	3	1	4	13	14	10
Qatar	8	2	3	3	10	10	9
Oman	8	1	3	4	7	16	6

★ 1ST RND GROUP TABLE

Team	P	W	D	L	F	A	Pts
China PR	6	6	0	0	25	3	18
Indonesia	6	4	0	2	16	7	12
Maldives Rep.	6	1	1	4	8	19	4
Cambodia	6	0	1	5	2	22	1

★ RECENT RESULTS

Feb 02 **Hong Kong** (a) > (d) 1-**1** Yu 64
(Hong Kong won 5-4 on pens)

Feb 02 **Slovenia** (n) > (d) **0**-0
(Slovenia won 4-3 on pens)

DID YOU KNOW?

In the mid-seventies China played a friendly against West Bromwich Albion, the second half of which was televised live on BBC2.

China will have the tallest goalkeeper at the World Cup in the 6ft 7in and agile Jiang Jin – something of a comfort to their back four led by Fan Zhiyi. Li Weifeng, who replaced the established Zhang Enhua in qualification, has formed a useful defensive partnership with Fan Zhiyi and both are dangerous at set pieces. In attack, China has one of Asia's finest strikers in Hao Haidong who is partnered by the tall Su Maozhen. However, midfield is China's real problem. Qi Hong is the creative force while Li Tie provides the drive, but overall China's midfield is too lightweight and will soon be overrun, especially by top class European opposition. In Ma Minygu China have a useful free kick specialist and a player who likes to shoot from distance, while Li Ming on the right is another positive-minded player.

PROBABLE FORMATION 4-4-2

JIANG JIN

SUN JIHAI | WU CHENGYING

LI WEIFENG | FAN ZHIYI

LI MING | LI TIE | MA MINGYU | QI HONG

HAO HAIDONG | SU MAOZHEN

★ MEN THAT MATTER!

FAN ZHIYI

Age >> 32
Club >> Dundee
Defender/ midfielder who has been the star of Chinese football in recent years largely thanks to his exploits abroad. He will captain China at their first World Cup.

QI HONG

Age >> 25
Club >> Shanghai Shenhua
China's most important midfield player. Creative and robust, he has the spark to make surprising things happen as well as scoring the occasional goal himself.

SU MAOZHEN

Age >> 29
Club >> Shandong
Su Maozhen is China's big target man who regularly scored goals for China under Milutinovic. Injury ruled him out for all but three qualifiers but is likely to return to the team for the World Cup.

★ PROBABLE SQUAD ★ QUALIFICATION RECORD

NAME	POSITION	CLUB	APS/GOALS	GAMES	MINS	Y/C	R/C	GOALS
Jiang Jin	Goalkeeper	Tianjin Taida, China	34/0	10	879	0	0	0
Ou Chuliang	Goalkeeper	Yunnan Hongta, China	3/0	1	70	0	0	0
Qi An	Goalkeeper	Dalian Shide, China	5/0	4	282	0	0	0
Du Wei	Defender	Shanghai Shenhua SVA, China	3/0	2	180	0	0	0
Fan Zhiyi	Defender	Dundee, Scotland	25/6	12	1061	1	0	4
Gang Chen Jin	Defender	Qingdao Yizhong, China	2/0	1	9	0	0	0
Li Weifeng	Defender	Shenzhen Ping'an, China	41/9	12	1080	0	0	3
Pu Yang	Defender	Beijing Guo'an, China	9/0	6	229	1	0	0
Sun Jihai	Defender	Manchester City, England	14/0	9	645	2	0	0
Wu Chengying	Defender	Shanghai Shenhua SVA, China	40/4	6	525	3	1	0
Zhang Enhua	Defender	Dalian Shide, China	6/0	2	100	0	0	0
Li Ming	Midfielder	Dalian Shide, China	18/2	8	523	0	0	0
Li Tie	Midfielder	Liaoning Bird, China	40/3	12	1080	1	0	0
Li Xiaopeng	Midfielder	Shandong Luneng, China	22/1	10	813	1	0	1
Ma Mingyu	Midfielder	Sichuan Dahe, China	31/7	13	966	0	0	0
Shao Yi Jia	Midfielder	Beijing Guo'an, China	10/9	4	63	0	0	0
Shen Si	Midfielder	Shanghai Zhongyuan Huili, China	31/4	9	667	0	0	0
Qi Hong	Midfielder	Shanghai Shenhua SVA, China	28/10	9	710	0	0	4
Hao Haidong	Forward	Dalian Shide, China	12/9	6	453	1	0	2
Qu Bo	Forward	Qingdao Yizhong, China	13/4	5	341	1	0	2
Su Maozhen	Forward	Shandong Luneng, China	22/13	3	181	0	0	1
Xie Hui	Forward	Shanghai Shenhua SVA, China	15/14	2	119	0	0	0
Yu Genwei	Forward	Tianjin Taida, China	9/1	5	169	1	0	0

KEY: APPS/GOALS = International Appearances/Goals; GAMES=Qualification Games played; MINS=Minutes played; Y/C= Yellow cards R/C=Red cards

HISTORY AT THE WORLD CUP

1930 1934 1938 1950 1954 1958 1962 1966 1970 1974 1978 1982 1986 1990 1994 1998

1986 > China score 23 goals in six games in qualifying but still manage to finish behind Hong Kong.

1990 > China finish fourth in the six-team World Cup Asian Qualifying Tournament in Singapore.

1994 > Finish second to Iraq by a point in Asian Group A.

1998 > Finish third behind Saudi Arabi and Iran in Asian Second Qualifying Round.

1982 > China lose 2-1 to New Zealand in Asia/Oceania play-off in Singapore.

★ WORLD CUP HISTORY

1930 >> Did Not Enter		1970 >> Did Not Enter	
1934 >> Did Not Enter		1974 >> Did Not Enter	
1938 >> Did Not Enter		1978 >> Did Not Enter	
1950 >> Did Not Enter		1982 >> Did Not Qualify	
1954 >> Did Not Enter		1986 >> Did Not Qualify	
1958 >> Did Not Enter		1990 >> Did Not Qualify	
1962 >> Did Not Enter		1994 >> Did Not Qualify	
1966 >> Did Not Enter		1998 >> Did Not Qualify	

★ WORLD CUP RECORDS, STORIES AND WEIRDNESS

FIRST SPONSOR >> The first sponsor of the Chinese national team was the Qixin pharmaceutical factory in Guangzhou in 1989.

SMALLEST CROWD >> In the 1988 Asia Cup Finals, China played Bahrain in front of a crowd of just 200 in Qatar.

GROUP C

OPPONENT	DATE	UK TIME	VENUE
China	**4 June**	07.30	**Gwangiu, Korea**
Turkey	**9 June**	10.00	**Incheon, Korea**
Brazil	**13 June**	07.30	**Suwon, Korea**

"the 'Ticos' will test even the best"

COSTA RICA

Costa Rica qualified for the World Cup Finals as North/ Central American group winners – a successful qualification programme that owed much to their tenacity and a disconcerting habit of snatching results from the jaws of defeat in the dying seconds of games.

It had not started well with the appointment of new Brazilian coach Gilson Nunez, who admitted he knew nothing about Costa Rican football. And it showed. Costa Rica were beaten in their opening semi-final group game by Barbados. They recovered to beat the USA 2-1 in controversial circumstances when they were awarded a penalty, which Hernan Medford converted, four minutes into injury time.

Home wins over Guatemala and Barbados followed plus a draw in the USA. Next up Guatemala, and they were within two minutes of qualifying for the next stage when Guatemala's Carlos Ruiz scored to make it 2-1, forcing not only a play-off but the resignation of Nunez. Nunez's assistant Alexandre Guimaraes took over and in the play-off (held in neutral Miami) Costa Rica thrashed Guatemala 5-2 with Manchester City's Paulo Wanchope and Rolando Fonseca among the scorers.

The final group of six teams now competed for three World Cup Final places. Once again Costa Rica started poorly, struggling to salvage a point from their home tie with Honduras. Twice Costa Rica had to come back from behind before the determined Rodrigo Cordero finally netted the second equaliser in injury time.

The turning point in the campaign came at the Guillermo Caneda stadium in Mexico City with an astonishing 2-1 victory over Mexico. Mexico had never been beaten in a competitive game in the stadium that in 30 years had witnessed 54 World Cup games. Fonseca cancelled out Mexico's seventh minute lead with a stunning 25-yard free kick and the winner came just three minutes from time from Hernan Medford, who played in Costa Rica's only previous World Cup appearance in 1990. Wins over Jamaica, Honduras, Trinidad & Tobago and the USA followed, but it was a goalless home draw with Mexico that clinched Costa Rica's place in the Finals.

They will be considered one of the outsiders at the Finals – as they were at Italia 90. But then Costa Rica, featuring Alexandre Guimares, surprised everyone by beating both Scotland and Sweden to reach the Second Round. In Paulo Wanchope they have a regular goalscorer who last year scored five goals in four Copa America ties and another seven in the qualifiers. And then there is the "Ticos" main striker Rolando Fonseca, who at 27 is the country's all-time top goalscorer with 39 goals (in 75 games) including ten during qualifying.

Costa Rica can draw on plenty of recent tournament experience. Apart from the 2001 Copa America, Costa Rica were runners-up at both the 2001 UNCAF Cup and the 2002 Gold Cup.

★ THE LOWDOWN

Population: 3.7 million

Capital: San Jose

Leader: Miguel Rodriguez

Life Expectancy: Male: 73 yrs
Female: 78 yrs

>> Tourism is the main industry in Costa Rica.

>> There is no summer or winter as such, just a rainy season from May to November and a dry season from December to April.

>> Costa Rica is part of the Pacific "Rim of Fire", which is not what the male botty region feels like after 14 pints and a vindaloo, but has 7 of the area's 42 active volcanoes and is prone to large and unexpected eruptions. Actually, it sounds exactly like a man's pant area after a good night out!

★ **ASSOCIATION:** Federacion Costarricense de Futbol
★ **JOINED FIFA:** 1921
★ **JOINED FOOTBALL CONFEDERATION:** 1962
★ **PLAYERS:** 12,500

★ **CLUBS:** 431
★ **WEBSITE:** www.intnet.co.cr/sports/fedefutbol/fede.html
★ HONOURS: CCCF/CONCACAF Gold Cup – 1941, 1946, 1948, 1953, 1955, 1960, 1961, 1963, 1969, 1989.

High scoring Paulo Wanchope.

★ ROAD TO QUALIFICATION

Jul 00 **Barbados** (a) > (l) **2-1** Madrigal 47

Jul 00 **United States** (h) > (w) **2-1**
Fonseca, R 10, Medford 90 pen

Aug 00 **Guatemala** (a) > (w) **2-1**
Wanchope 33, 58

Sep 00 **Barbados** (h) > (w) **3-0**
Soto 36, Fonseca, R 41, Meford 54

Oct 00 **United States** (a) > (d) **0-0**

Nov 00 **Guatemala** (a) > (l) **2-1**
Fonseca, R 71

Jan 01 **Guatemala** (n) > (w) **5-2**
Wanchope 6, Fonseca, R 43, 59, Parks 58, Soto 87

Feb 01 **Honduras** (h) > (d) **2-2**
Fonseca, R 65, Lopez 90

Mar 01 **Trinidad & Tobago** (h) > (w) **3-0**
Bryce 46, Wanchope 80, 89

Apr 01 **United States** (a) > (l) **1-0**

Jun 01 **Mexico** (a) > (w) **1-2**
Fonseca, R 72, Medford 86

Jun 01 **Jamaica** (h) > (w) **2-1**
Marin 4, Wanchope 38

Jun 01 **Honduras** (a) > (w) **2-3**
Wanchope 9, Fonseca, R 13, Solis 83

Sep 01 **Trinidad & Tobago** (a) > (w) **0-2**
Gomez 4, 35

Sep 01 **United States** (h) > (w) **2-0**
Fonseca, R 39, 68

Oct 01   **Mexico** (h) > (d) **0-0**

Nov 01 **Jamaica** (a) > (w) **0-1** Sunsing 5

★ FINAL GROUP TABLE

Team	P	W	D	L	F	A	Pts
Costa Rica	10	7	2	1	17	7	23
Mexico	10	5	2	3	16	9	17
United States	10	5	2	3	11	8	17
Honduras	10	4	2	4	17	17	14
Jamaica	10	2	2	6	7	14	8
Trinidad & Tob	10	1	2	7	5	18	5

★ SEMI-FINAL GROUP TABLE

Team	P	W	D	L	F	A	Pts
United States	6	3	2	1	14	3	11
Costa Rica	6	3	1	2	9	6	10
Guatemala	6	3	1	2	9	6	10
Barbados	6	1	0	5	3	20	3

★ RECENT RESULTS

Jan 02 **South Korea** (a) > (w) **1-3**
Gomez 44, Wanchope 77, 82

Feb 02 **United States** (a) > (l) **2-0**

Mar 02 **Morocco** (h) > (l) **0-1**

DID YOU KNOW?

Coach Alexandre Guimaraes was a member of Costa Rica's 1990 World Cup Squad making three substitute appearances against Brazil, Sweden and Czechoslovakia.

Club football in Costa Rica is usually played to 3-5-2 and so will the national team. At the back Luis Marin is first choice sweeper alongside Saprissa team players Reynaldo Parks, an excellent man-marker, and the hard-working Gilberto Martinez. In midfield, Mauricio Solis handles the defensive duties while possession-loving Walter Centeno is the playmaker. Jervis Drummond, a former track athlete, provides blistering pace on the right with, at left wing back, Carlos Castro in a role suited to his close control skills. Rolando Fonseca, Costa Rica's all-time top goalscorer, is allowed to roam just behind the front two and link up play down the middle. Veteran Hernan Medford and Costa Rica's best known player Paulo Wanchope are the two-pronged attack. The three – Fonseca, Medford and Wanchope – can all switch their roles in the attack. Wilmer Lopez can provide another creative outlet in midfield, but any further changes to the side and the quality will evaporate.

PROBABLE FORMATION 3-5-2

LONNIS

PARKS — MARTINEZ

MARIN

DRUMMOND — CENTENO — M SOLIS — C CASTRO

FONSECA

MEDFORD — WANCHOPE

★ MEN THAT MATTER!

ROLANDO FONSECA

Age>> 27
Club>> La Piedad
Costa Rica's all-time top goalscorer
with an increasing tally to his name. He scored ten goals during qualification from open play and directly from free kicks. A real danger to defences.

PAULO WANCHOPE

Age>> 25
Club>> Manchester City
Hot on the heels of Fonseca in the all-time goal stakes with a vastly superior scoring rate. Despite their rivalry, the high-profile Wanchope combines well with Fonseca.

HERNAN MEDFORD

Age>> 34
Club>> Saprissa
A survivor from Italia 90 where he scored the winner against Sweden that took Costa Rica into the Second Round. Medford played in all 17 qualifiers including six as a sub.

★ PROBABLE SQUAD   ★ QUALIFICATION RECORD

NAME	POSITION	CLUB	APS/GOALS	GAMES	MINS	Y/C	R/C	GOALS
Ricardo Gonzalez	Goalkeeper	Alajuelense, Costa Rica	5/0	0	0	0	0	0
Erick Lonnis	Goalkeeper	Saprissa, Costa Rica	71/0	9	810	0	0	0
Alvaro Mesen	Goalkeeper	Alajuelense, Costa Rica	13/0	8	720	0	0	0
Juan B Esquivel	Defender	Saprissa, Costa Rica	2/0	0	0	0	0	0
Austin Berry	Defender	Herediano, Costa Rica	65/6	6	464	3	0	0
Carlos Castro	Defender	Alajuelense, Costa Rica	16/0	10	788	1	0	0
Jervis Drummond	Defender	Saprissa, Costa Rica	36/1	12	1066	3	0	0
Alexander Madrigal	Defender	La Piedad, Mexico	9/1	6	530	0	0	1
Luis Marin	Defender	Alajuelense, Costa Rica	71/3	6	540	2	0	1
Gilberto Martinez	Defender	Saprissa, Costa Rica	18/0	10	900	2	0	0
Reynaldo Parks	Defender	Saprissa, Costa Rica	47/1	17	1513	1	0	1
Harrold Wallace	Defender	Alajuelense, Costa Rica	53/1	10	764	0	0	0
Steven Bryce	Midfielder	Alajuelense, Costa Rica	24/4	11	581	1	0	1
Walter Centeno	Midfielder	Saprissa, Costa Rica	45/6	10	741	1	0	0
Rodrigo Cordero	Midfielder	Herediano, Costa Rica	24/1	15	1037	2	0	0
Ronald Gomez	Midfielder	OFI Crete, Greece	50/17	6	390	1	0	2
Wilmer Lopez	Midfielder	Alajuelense, Costa Rica	63/6	10	641	0	1	1
Mauricio Solis	Midfielder	Alajuelense, Costa Rica	80/5	12	655	1	0	1
William Sunsing	Midfielder	New England Revolution, USA	17/1	10	236	0	0	1
Rolando Fonseca	Forward	La Piedad, Mexico	75/38	16	1150	2	0	8
Hernan Medford	Forward	Saprissa, Costa Rica	86/19	17	966	1	0	3
Paulo Wanchope	Forward	Manchester City, England	47/34	13	1080	4	0	7
Oscar Rojas	Forward	La Piedad, Mexico	3/0	1	90	0	0	0

KEY: APPS/GOALS = International Appearances/Goals; GAMES=Qualification Games played; MINS=Minutes played; Y/C= Yellow cards R/C=Red cards

HISTORY AT THE WORLD CUP

1930 1934 1938 1950 1954 1958 1962 1966 1970 1974 1978 1982 1986 1990 1994 1998

1958 > Costa Rica lose 3-1 on aggregate to Mexico in deciding fixtures for place in Finals.

1990 > Juan Arnoldo Cayasso scores the goal that beats Scotland in Costa Rica's first World Cup match.

1962 > Costa Rica play first qualifier beating Guatemala in San Jose.

1954 > Costa Rica refused entry into the World Cup because their application was on the wrong form.

★ WORLD CUP HISTORY

1930 >> Did Not Enter	1970 >> Did Not Qualify
1934 >> Did Not Enter	1974 >> Did Not Qualify
1938 >> Did Not Enter	1978 >> Did Not Qualify
1950 >> Did Not Enter	1982 >> Did Not Qualify
1954 >> Did Not Enter	1986 >> Did Not Qualify
1958 >> Did Not Qualify	1990 >> Second Round
1962 >> Did Not Qualify	1994 >> Did Not Qualify
1966 >> Did Not Qualify	1998 >> Did Not Qualify

★ WORLD CUP RECORDS, STORIES AND WEIRDNESS

MOST GOALS >> Yugoslavian Bora Milutinovic has coached a World Cup record number (4) of teams, including Costa Rica, taking all of them past the first round.

OPPONENT	DATE	UK TIME	VENUE
Mexico	**3 June**	07.30	**Niigata, Japan**
Italy	**8 June**	10.00	**Ibaraki, Japan**
Ecuador	**13 June**	12.30	**Yokohama, Japan**

"old hands bolster a struggling side"

CROATIA

★ THE LOWDOWN

Population: 4.3 million

Capital: Zagreb

Leader: Ivica Racan

Life Expectancy: Male: 70 yrs Female: 78 yrs

›› Croatia declared its independence in 1991 following the break-up of Yugoslavia.

·· The Croatian territory encompasses 1,185 islands, islets and reefs, including 67 inhabited islands.

·· Croatia controls most land routes from Western Europe to the Aegean Sea and Turkish Straits.

Four years ago Croatia made a sensational World Cup debut, reaching the semi-finals before losing to eventual winners France. After qualifying via the play-offs, they beat Jamaica and Japan to finish as group runners-up to Argentina. That earned them a second-round clash with Romania, which was decided by a Davor Suker penalty.

In the last eight, Croatia gave a magnificent performance defeating Germany 3-0. The Croatians' aggressive approach rattled the Germans who had Christian Worns sent off five minutes before the break. Robert Jarni put Croatia ahead on the stroke of half time with Vlaovic and Davor Suker scoring late on for a comprehensive victory.

Croatia's World Cup fairy tale ended when they came up against the superior French side who had a player sent off and had to come from behind to win 2-1. As consolation Croatia won the third place play-off beating Holland 2-1 with the winning goal scored by Suker – his sixth of the tournament – making him top scorer at France 98.

Croatia will have to do well if they are to come close to equalling their performance of four years ago. They missed out on Euro 2000 and have been trying to rebuild their ageing team ever since. Even so, coach Mirko Jozic has had to lure back several long-serving players who had opted for international retirement. Alen Boksic, Robert Prosinecki and Igor Stimac have all

been persuaded to put back on the red and white checked shirt and add their experience to a team in the midst of a tough qualifying campaign.

Croatia were drawn in a tight group alongside Belgium and Scotland, with Latvia and San Marino making up the numbers. A 0-0 draw in Belgium was an ideal start to their campaign, but the 1-1 home draw against Scotland was not. Coach Miroslav Blazevic stood down and in came Jozic to try and rectify a run of one win in the previous nine games.

Jozic did get Croatia winning again. A first half Bosko Balaban hat-trick helped Croatia to a 4-1 home win against Latvia. Four more goals were netted against San Marino while Balaban scored the only goal in a 1-0 victory in Riga over Latvia.

A goalless draw away to Scotland, combined with their superior goal difference, put Croatia within touching distance of qualification and, boosted by another four-goal haul in San Marino, Croatia knew all they had to do was to beat Belgium in their last game to book their place at the World Cup Finals.

Two years earlier Croatia had failed to qualify for Euro 2000, and it looked, for a while, as if it was going to be *déjà vu* all over again. A lacklustre performance was looking far worse after Prosinecki missed a first half penalty, but with 15 minutes remaining, the deadlock was broken as Boksic swept in Balaban's cross for the winning goal.

★ **ASSOCIATION:** Croatian Football Association
★ **JOINED FIFA:** 1992
★ **JOINED UEFA:** 1992
★ **PLAYERS:** 78,200

★ **CLUBS:** 1,221
★ **WEBSITE:** www.hns-cff.hr
★ **HONOURS:** None

Astute midfielder Zvonimir Soldo.

★ ROAD TO QUALIFICATION

Sep 00 **Belgium** (a) > (d) 0-**0**

Oct 00 **Scotland** (h) > (d) **1**-1 Boksic 15

Mar 01 **Latvia** (h) > (w) 4-1
Balaban 8, 42, 45, Vuguric 89

Jun 01 **San Marino** (h) > (w) 4-0
Vlaovic 3, Balaban 30, Suker 55 pen, Vugrinec 61

Jun 01 **Latvia** (a) > (w) 0-**1** Balaban 39

Sep 01 **Scotland** (a) > (d) 0-**0**

Sep 01 **San Marino** (a) > (w) 0-**4**
Kovac, N 40, Prosinecki 48, 90, Soldo 77

Oct 01 **Belgium** (h) > (w) **1**-0 Boksic 75

★ FINAL GROUP TABLE

Team	P	W	D	L	F	A	Pts
Croatia	8	5	3	0	15	2	18
Belgium	8	5	2	1	25	6	17
Scotland	8	4	3	1	12	6	15
Latvia	8	1	1	6	5	16	4
San Marino	8	0	1	7	3	30	1

★ RECENT RESULTS

Feb 02 **Bulgaria** (h) > (d) 0-**0**

Mar 02 **Slovenia** (h) > (d) 0-**0**

DID YOU KNOW?

Coach Mirko Jozic has already guided a team to World Cup success at Under-20 level when Yugoslavia won the World Youth Cup in 1987.

Croatia's 3-5-2 formation is organised, primarily, for defence. In front of keeper Stipe Pletikosa are a back three of man-marker Dario Simic, the uncompromising Robert Kovac and sweeper Igor Tudor – widely regarded as one of Croatia's best players, The five-man midfield is geared to stifling their opponents' play. Stjepan Tomas is a sweeper turned defensive midfielder and is anchored alongside the astute Zvonimir Soldo. Boris Zivkovic is another defender converted into a right (or left) wing-back position, while Robert Jarni, at 33, usually provides crosses and long passes from the left, although he's sometimes invited to play as a third forward. Croatia's most talented and experienced player, Robert Prosinecki, is their only genuinely attacking midfielder providing the link to the England-based pair of Bosko Balaban and Alen Boksic. The old guard of Davor Suker and Goran Vlaovic will act as cover for the striker's slot.

PROBABLE FORMATION 3-5-2

PLETIKOSA

D SIMIC — R KOVAC

TUDOR

ZIVKOVIC — TOMAS — SOLDO — JARNI

PROSINECKI

BALABAN — BOKSIC

★ MEN THAT MATTER!

BOSKO BALABAN

Age >> 23
Club >> A. Villa
Balaban came to the fore during qualifying scoring five of Croatia's 15 goals including a hat-trick against Latvia. It was his cross that set up the decisive goal against Belgium.

IGOR TUDOR

Age >> 24
Club >> Juventus
Outstanding in qualifying, Tudor is an excellent defender. He causes opponents real problems at corners and free kicks. Played just 13 minutes in three sub appearances at France 98.

ROBERT PROSINECKI

Age >> 31
Club >> Portsmouth
Has the distinction of scoring at two World Cups with different countries – Yugoslavia in 1990 and Croatia in 1998. Attacking midfielder who can still turn a game at international level.

★ PROBABLE SQUAD ★ QUALIFICATION RECORD

NAME	POSITION	CLUB	APS/GOALS	GAMES	MINS	Y/C	R/C	GOALS
Tomislav Butina	Goalkeeper	Dinamo Zagreb, Croatia	3/0	1	90	0	0	0
Stipe Pletikosa	Goalkeeper	Hajduk Split, Croatia	16/0	6	540	0	0	0
Zeljko Pavlovic	Goalkeeper	Anderlecht Belgium	7/0	1	90	0	0	0
Mario Cvitanovic	Defender	Venezia, Italy	27/4	1	44	1	0	0
Robert Kovac	Defender	Bayern Munich, Germany	17/0	6	528	2	0	0
Dario Simic	Defender	Internazionale, Italy	47/1	7	630	1	0	0
Igor Stimac	Defender	Hajduk Split, Croatia	53/2	4	360	0	0	0
Stjepan Tomas	Defender	Vicenza, Italy	15/1	3	267	0	0	0
Igor Tudor	Defender	Juventus, Italy	25/0	6	450	2	0	0
Boris Zivkovic	Defender	Bayer Leverkusen, Germany	13/1	5	405	0	0	0
Igor Biscan	Midfielder	Liverpool, England	15/1	4	104	1	0	0
Robert Jarni	Midfielder	Las Palmas, Spain	75/1	8	675	0	0	0
Niko Kovac	Midfielder	Bayern Munich, Germany	18/2	5	424	3	0	1
Robert Prosinecki	Midfielder	Portsmouth, England	45/10	7	578	1	0	2
Milan Rapajic	Midfielder	Fenerbahce, Turkey	20/1	2	94	0	0	0
Danijel Seric	Midfielder	Panathinaikos, Greece	24/0	2	115	0	0	0
Zvonimir Soldo	Midfielder	Stuttgart, Germany	58/3	5	386	1	0	1
Mario Stanic	Midfielder	Chelsea, England	42/7	3	195	1	0	0
Bosko Balaban	Forward	Aston Villa, England	13/6	8	523	1	0	5
Alen Boksic	Forward	Middlesbrough, England	35/10	2	165	0	0	2
Davor Suker	Forward	1860 Munich, Germany	66/44	5	333	1	0	1
Goran Vlaovic	Forward	Panathinaikos, Greece	49/15	4	243	0	0	1
Davor Vugrinec	Forward	Lecce, Italy	18/7	7	320	1	0	2

KEY: APPS/GOALS = International Appearances/Goals; GAMES=Qualification Games played; MINS=Minutes played; Y/C= Yellow cards R/C=Red cards

HISTORY AT THE WORLD CUP

1930 1934 1938 1950 1954 1958 1962 1966 1970 1974 1978 1982 1986 1990 1994 1998

1998 > Robert Prosinecki scores a World Cup goal for Croatia against Jamaica on the way to the semis.

1990 > Robert Prosinecki scores a World Cup goal for Yugoslavia against the United Arab Emirates.

★ WORLD CUP HISTORY

1930	>> Did Not Enter	1970	>> Did Not Enter
1934	>> Did Not Enter	1974	>> Did Not Enter
1938	>> Did Not Enter	1978	>> Did Not Enter
1950	>> Did Not Enter	1982	>> Did Not Enter
1954	>> Did Not Enter	1986	>> Did Not Enter
1958	>> Did Not Enter	1990	>> Did Not Enter
1962	>> Did Not Enter	1994	>> Did Not Enter
1966	>> Did Not Enter	1998	>> Third Place

★ WORLD CUP RECORDS, STORIES AND WEIRDNESS

MOST GOALS IN A TOURNAMENT >> Davor Suker in France 98 with 6.

UNIQUE SCORING RECORD >> Robert Prosinecki is the only player to have scored for two different countries. He represented Yugoslavia in 1990, scoring against the United Arab Emirates and then Croatia in 1998, scoring against Jamaica.

OPPONENT	DATE	UK TIME	VENUE
Uruguay	1 June	10.00	Ulsan, Korea
Senegal	6 June	07.30	Daegu, Korea
France	11 June	07.30	Incheon, Korea

"will they bring home the bacon?"

DENMARK

★ THE LOWDOWN

Population: 5.3 million

Capital: Copenhagen

Leader: Poul Rasmussen

Life Expectancy: Male: 74 yrs
Female: 79 yrs

>> Until 1976 the Danish Football Rulers, the DFU, banned professional footballers from playing in the national team.

>> Danes are renowned for their good environmental attitude; the Danish countryside is full of wind turbines, providing clean energy.

>> They are less inventive when it comes to surnames; nearly 8% of the population is called Jensen. Who'd be a Danish postman??!!

Denmark reached the 1998 World Cup quarter-finals before bowing out to Brazil 3-2 in one of the tournament's most thrilling games. An exciting and positive Danish side almost forced extra-time when Marc Reiper's header crashed against the crossbar in the 89th minute. That slender defeat marked the international retirement of Michael Laudrup, who is now assistant coach of the national side. Two years later at Euro 2000 Denmark looked a pale shadow of their World Cup team. No goals, no wins, no draws and no points.

New coach, and former Danish player, Morten Olsen had to make changes after the Euro 2000 debacle, promoting youngsters such as Claus Jensen and Dennis Rommedahl. Even so, Denmark did not make a promising start to their World Cup qualifying group. Although a 2-1 win over Iceland in Reykjavik was a welcome opening result, successive 1-1 draws with Northern Ireland – where Rommedahl scored his first goal – and Bulgaria weakened the Danes' chances of qualifying.

Added to Danish woes was the retirement from international football of legendary goalkeeper Peter Schmeichel after 128 appearances (he later earned a 129th in a friendly against Slovenia). His successor was Sunderland goalkeeper Thomas Sorenson who had previously made just one appearance for the national side.

The morale boosting 2-1 win over Germany in a friendly proved a turning point for Olsen. It was the Danes' first victory over the Germans since the 1992 European Championship Final and Rommedahl's two goals was the first time a Dane had scored twice against the Germans since 1930. Confidence boosted, the Danes blasted Malta 5-0 (including a hat-trick from Denmark's leading marksman Ebbe Sand). A magnificent goalless draw against the Czech Republic, in which goalkeeper Sorenson was excellent, put their qualification efforts back on track.

Two late goals in successive matches against the Czech Republic and Malta put by now unbeaten Denmark at the top of the table. With three games left, it was a three-horse race between Bulgaria, the Czech Republic and Denmark for the automatic and play-off qualification places. It was going to go down to the wire.

A Danish win over Iceland in their last game would assure qualification irrespective of the outcome between Bulgaria and the Czech Republic. Olsen's men were up for it and stormed to a 4-0 lead by the 35th minute with Rommedahl, Sand and Thomas Gravesen (twice) scoring. Sand and Jan Michaelsen added further goals for a 6-0 win. Denmark were going to the World Cup Finals for only the third time in their history.

Morten Olsen's Denmark will be realistically looking to progress beyond the group stage. The side is studded with top internationals, most of whom play outside Denmark. The British-based contingent includes Thomas Gravesen of Everton and Thomas Sorensen, who has performed well in goal and has comfortably emerged from the enormous shadow cast by the legendary Peter Schmeichel. Thomas Gravesen and Stig Tofting have developed a good partnership with Jesper Gronkjaer, Martin Jorgensen or Dennis Rommedahl providing the width. Ebbe Sand is the team's main striker, his nine goals in ten qualifying appearances justifying his selection, with Jon Dahl Tomasson in the withdrawn striker's role.

★ **ASSOCIATION:** Dansk Boldspil Union
★ **JOINED FIFA:** 1904
★ **JOINED UEFA:** 1954
★ **PLAYERS:** 268,600

★ **CLUBS:** 1,555
★ **WEBSITE:** www.vbu.dk
★ **HONOURS:** European Championship – 1992.

Martin Laursen is surprised by the sudden appearance of a round white thing.

★ ROAD TO QUALIFICATION

Sep 00 **Iceland** (a) > (w) 1-**2**
Tomasson 26, Bisgaard 48

Oct 00 **Northern Ireland** (a) > (d) 1-1
Rommedahl 60

Oct 00 **Bulgaria** (h) > (d) **1**-1 Sand 72

Mar 01 **Malta** (a) > (w) 0-**5**
Sand 8, 63, 79, Heitz 51, Jensen 76

Mar 01 **Czech Republic** (a) > (d) 0-0

Jun 01 **Czech Republic** (a) > (w) **2**-1
Sand 5, Tomasson 81

Jun 01 **Malta** (h) > (w) **2**-1 Sand 43, 83

Sep 01 **Northern Ireland** (h) > (d) **1**-1
Rommedahl 3

Sep 01 **Bulgaria** (a) > (w) 0-**2**
Tomasson 47, 90

Oct 01 **Iceland** (h) > (w) **6**-0
Rommedahl 12, Sand 14, 65, Gravesen 31, 35, Michaelsen 90

★ FINAL GROUP TABLE

Team	P	W	D	L	F	A	Pts
Denmark	10	6	4	0	22	6	22
Czech Republic	10	6	2	2	20	8	20
Bulgaria	10	5	2	3	14	15	17
Iceland	10	4	1	5	14	20	13
N. Ireland	10	3	2	5	11	12	11
Malta	10	0	1	9	4	24	1

★ RECENT RESULTS

Feb 02 **Saudi Arabia** (a) > (w) 0-**1** Sand 17

Mar 02 **Rep of Ireland** (a) > (l) 3-**0**

DID YOU KNOW?

It was not until 1976 that the Danish national team allowed professional players to be considered for the team.

Denmark, undefeated throughout the World Cup qualifiers, scored goals freely and conceded few. This owes much to Morten Olsen's adaptable 4-4-1-1 formation that can quickly pack the defence or flow forward in numbers in attack. Goalkeeper Thomas Sorenson is well protected by the superb central defensive partnership of Rene Henriksen and Martin Laursen. In Thomas Helveg and Jan Heintze Denmark have two of the most experienced full backs in the game. There is a no-nonsense feel about the midfield with Thomas Gravesen and Stig Tofting providing a presence that would make any international midfielder wary of bothering them. In Martin Jorgensen and Dennis Rommedahl, or alternatively Jesper Gronkjaer, Denmark have wing players who can weave their way to the byline with skill and pace. Jon Dahl Tomasson is a key player for Denmark playing in a withdrawn striker's role where he quickly becomes a partner and an option for the main striker Ebbe Sand.

PROBABLE FORMATION 4-4-1-1

★ MEN THAT MATTER!

EBBE SAND

Age>> 29
Club>> Schalke
Ever present (10 games) and top scorer (9 goals) during Denmark's qualification. Joined Schalke from Brondby in 2000 and became 2001 Bundesliga top scorer. Will be playing in his second World Cup.

RENE HENRIKSEN

Age>> 31
Club>> Panathinaikos
Centre-back who is more than a stopper, with excellent pace and vision allows him to instigate and negate for Denmark. Overlooked for France 98 but played at Euro 2000.

THOMAS SORENSON

Age>> 25
Club>> Sunderland
Emerged as Denmark's number one following retirement of Peter Schmeichel with some outstanding performances. He was third choice keeper at Euro 2000 and served plenty of bench time before getting his deserved chance.

★ PROBABLE SQUAD | ★ QUALIFICATION RECORD

NAME	POSITION	CLUB	APS/GOALS	GAMES	MINS	Y/C	R/C	GOALS
Jan Hoffmann	Goalkeeper	AB, Denmark	0/0	0	0	0	0	0
Peter Kjaer	Goalkeeper	Aberdeen, Scotland	3/0	2	169	0	0	0
Thomas Sorensen	Goalkeeper	Sunderland, England	10/0	6	461	0	0	0
Jan Heintze	Defender	PSV Eindhoven, Holland	79/3	10	900	1	0	1
Thomas Helveg	Defender	Milan, Italy	65/2	10	880	1	0	0
Rene Henriksen	Defender	Panathinaikos, Greece	35/0	10	900	0	0	0
Niclas Jensen	Defender	Copenhagen, Denmark	4/0	0	0	0	0	0
Martin Laursen	Defender	Milan, Italy	12/0	6	540	1	0	0
Steven Lustu	Defender	AB, Denmark	3/0	0	0	0	0	0
Jan Michaelsen	Defender	Panathinaikos, Greece	8/1	4	91	0	0	1
Per Frandsen	Midfielder	Bolton, England	21/0	1	21	0	0	0
Thomas Gravesen	Midfielder	Everton, England	19/2	7	605	2	0	2
Claus Jensen	Midfielder	Charlton, England	12/1	7	222	1	0	1
Mads Jorgensen	Midfielder	Brondby, Denmark	1/0	1	10	0	0	0
Christian Poulsen	Midfielder	Schalke, Germany	2/0	0	0	0	0	0
Brian Steen Nielsen	Midfielder	Malmo, Sweden	61/3	6	320	1	0	0
Peter Nielsen	Midfielder	B Munnchengladbach, Germany	9/0	2	115	0	0	0
Stig Tofting	Midfielder	Bolton Wanderers, England	34/2	9	795	1	0	0
Jesper Gronkjaer	Forward	Chelsea, England	22/1	8	471	1	0	0
Ebbe Sand	Forward	Schalke, Germany	41/17	0	0	0	0	0
Peter Madsen	Forward	Brondby, Denmark	2/0	1	21	0	0	0
Dennis Rommedahl	Forward	PSV Eindhoven, Holland	15/5	10	796	1	0	3
Jon Dahl Tomasson	Forward	Feyenoord, Holland	35/13	9	766	2	0	4

KEY: APPS/GOALS = International Appearances/Goals; GAMES=Qualification Games played; MINS=Minutes played; Y/C= Yellow cards R/C=Red cards

HISTORY AT THE WORLD CUP

1930 1934 1938 1950 1954 1958 1962 1966 1970 1974 1978 1982 1986 1990 1994 1998

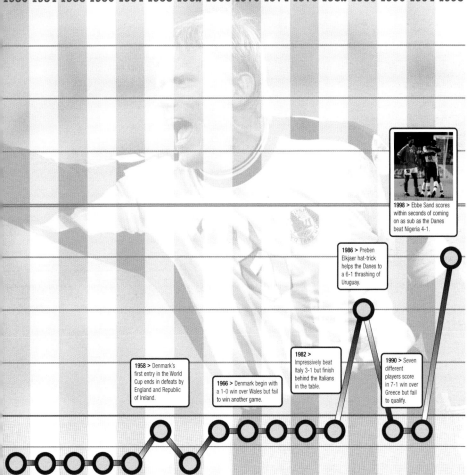

1998 > Ebbe Sand scores within seconds of coming on as sub as the Danes beat Nigeria 4-1.

1986 > Preben Elkjaer hat-trick helps the Danes to a 6-1 thrashing of Uruguay.

1982 > Impressively beat Italy 3-1 but finish behind the Italians in the table.

1990 > Seven different players score in 7-1 win over Greece but fail to qualify.

1958 > Denmark's first entry in the World Cup ends in defeats by England and Republic of Ireland.

1966 > Denmark begin with a 1-0 win over Wales but fail to win another game.

★ WORLD CUP HISTORY

1930 >> Did Not Enter		**1970** >> Did Not Qualify	
1934 >> Did Not Enter		**1974** >> Did Not Qualify	
1938 >> Did Not Enter		**1978** >> Did Not Qualify	
1950 >> Did Not Enter		**1982** >> Did Not Qualify	
1954 >> Did Not Enter		**1986** >> Second Round	
1958 >> Did Not Qualify		**1990** >> Did Not Qualify	
1962 >> Did Not Enter		**1994** >> Did Not Qualify	
1966 >> Did Not Qualify		**1998** >> Quarter-Finals	

★ WORLD CUP RECORDS, STORIES AND WEIRDNESS

SUBSTITUTION >> Ebbe Sand scored the fastest ever goal by a substitute – only 16 seconds after getting on the pitch. It was against Nigeria in 1998. Denmark won 4-1.

OPPONENT	DATE	UK TIME	VENUE
Italy	**3 June**	**12.30**	**Sapporo, Japan**
Mexico	**9 June**	**07.30**	**Miyagi, Japan**
Croatia	**13 June**	**12.30**	**Yokohama, Japan**

"at least they'll be acclimatised"

ECUADOR

Ecuador is a republic on the Equator, hence its name, on the Pacific coast of South America, big on bananas, cocoa and coffee, but not much cop at football – until now. Ecuador has finally qualified for the World Cup Finals at the 11th time of asking. The Galapagos Islands, now a national park, belong to Ecuador and that's where Charles Darwin found much evidence for his theory of evolution. Colombian coach Hernan Dario Gomez has had to introduce an evolutionary managerial policy of his own, inculcating much-needed discipline into the side.

At the halfway stage of qualifying Ecuador were in sixth place – an average side that had won four and lost four of their first nine games.

Then came the first sensation: a shock 1-0 win over Brazil at the Atalhualpa Stadium in Quito. It was Ecuador's first ever win over the Brazilians in 22 attempts. So well did Ecuador control the game that during long sequences of possession, every Ecuadorian pass was greeted with cries of 'Ole!' by the crowd. The magical party was almost spoiled by Brazil's Romario who goaded keeper Jose Francisco Cevallos into a magnificent double-save in the last minute, blocking Romario's header and the subsequent follow up.

Delgado was the goalscoring hero in a sensational comeback against an in form Paraguay. Ecuador had come from a man down – defender Augusto Poroso was sent off after 19 minutes – and a goal behind – Jose Cardozo put Paraguay ahead in the 27th minute. Delgado equalised on the stroke of half time and scored the winner in the 53rd minute. Even more amazing was that Ecuador finished the game with nine men after midfielder Wellington Sanchez was also shown a red card in the last minute.

There followed another startling last minute victory as Ecuador won their fifth successive qualifier in Lima against Peru. Ecuador had gone behind in the second minute, but Edison Mendez, who did an excellent man-marking job on Brazil's Rivaldo, equalised ten minutes later. Ecuador weathered Peru's storm but seemed to have blown it with less than ten minutes to play when Mendez was sent off. However, in injury time Delgado broke free scoring a dramatic late winner. The result put Ecuador in third place, six points clear of fifth-placed Colombia.

Inevitably beaten by Argentina, the loss was aggravated by the dismissal of Chala, who became the sixth Ecuadorian player to be sent off in the qualifiers. Without Chala, Ecuador secured a 0-0 draw in Colombia and followed it with a sensational 5-1 win against Bolivia at La Paz – Bolivia's first home defeat in 16 years. It left Ecuador needing just a point from their last two games. Qualification, as runners up to Argentina was clinched with a 1-1 draw at home to Uruguay – Ivan Kaviedes scoring the vital goal.

During an 18-match qualifying campaign Ecuador have shown they have more than enough ability to cause an upset at the World Cup, but they remain susceptible to ill discipline.

★ THE LOWDOWN

Population: 13.1 million

Capital: Quito

Leader: Gustavo Nobola

Life Expectancy: Male: 68 yrs Female: 74 yrs

›› In the Ecuadorian Amazon live one third of all the bird species in the entire Amazon region, and 10% of all the tree species on earth.

›› Traditional Ecuadorian cuisine is not for the faint-hearted. Popular dishes include roasted guinea pig and bull penis soup! The less adventurous will be pleased to note that Macdonald's arrived in the country two years ago.

›› 11 different peoples make up the indigenous Ecuadorian population, 50% of whom now live in urban areas.

⋆ **ASSOCIATION:** Asociacion Ecuatoriana de Futbol   ⋆ **CLUBS:** 170
⋆ **JOINED FIFA:** 1926   ⋆ **WEBSITE:** www.ecuafutbolonline.org
⋆ **JOINED CONEMBOL:** 1930   ⋆ **HONOURS:** None
⋆ **PLAYERS:** 15,700

co 'Pancho' Cevallos makes it clear he wants only one sugar in his half-time cuppa.

★ ROAD TO QUALIFICATION

Mar 00 **Venezuela** (h) > (w) **2**-0
Delgado 17, Aguinaga Garzon 50

Apr 00 **Brazil** (a) > (l) 3-**2**
Aguinaga Garzon 12, De La Cruz, U 76

Jun 00 **Paraguay** (a) > (l) 3-**1**
Graziani Lentini 87

Jun 00 **Peru** (h) > (w) **2**-1
Chala 16, Hurtado Roa, E 51

Jul 00 **Argentina** (a) > (l) 2-0

Jul 00 **Colombia** (h) > (d) 0-0

Aug 00 **Bolivia** (h) > (w) **2**-0
Delgado 18, 60

Sep 00 **Uruguay** (a) > (l) 4-**0**

Oct 00 **Chile** (h) > (w) **1**-0 Delgado 76

Nov 00 **Venezuela** (a) > (w) 1-**2**
Kaviedes 4, Sanchez 21

Mar 01 **Brazil** (h) > (w) **1**-0 Delgado 49

Apr 01 **Paraguay** (h) > (w) **2**-1
Delgado 44, 52

Jun 01 **Peru** (a) > (w) 1-**2**
Mendez, E 11, Delgado 90

Aug 01 **Argentina** (h) > (l) **0**-2

Sep 01 **Colombia** (a) > (d) 0-**0**

Oct 01 **Bolivia** (a) > (w) 1-**5**
De La Cruz, U 13, Delgado 23, Kaviedes
56, Fernandez 89, Caceres 90

Nov 01 **Uruguay** (a) > (d) 1-**1** Kaviedes 72

★ FINAL GROUP TABLE

Team	P	W	D	L	F	A	Pts
Argentina	18	13	4	1	42	15	43
Ecuador	18	9	4	5	23	20	31
Brazil	18	9	3	6	31	17	30
Paraguay	18	9	3	6	29	23	30
Uruguay	18	7	6	5	19	13	27
Colombia	18	7	6	5	20	15	27
Bolivia	18	4	6	8	21	33	18
Peru	18	4	4	10	14	25	16
Venezuela	18	5	1	12	18	44	16
Chile	18	3	3	12	15	27	12

★ RECENT RESULTS

Feb 02 **Turkey** (a) > (w) 0-**1** Tenorio 64

Mar 02 **United States** (a) > (l) 1-**0**

Mar 02 **Bulgaria** (h) > (w) **3**-0
Kaviedes 24, 82, Tenorio 51

GROUP G

DID YOU KNOW?

Between July 1965 (v Colombia) and November 2000 (v Venezuela) Ecuador failed to win a single away fixture in World Cup qualifying

In Agustin Delgado and Ivan Kaviedes Ecuador have a useful striking partnership that managed 12 of Ecuador's 23 goals in qualifying. The four-man midfield provides the impetus, driven by Alex Aguinaga, the captain, and supported on the flanks by Cleber Chala and the highly rated Edison Mendez. Both players can swap positions unnerving opponents and breaking through to create chances for Delgado and Kaviedes. Alfonso Obregon provides defensive cover in midfield – largely because of his height, something the back line lacks despite the inclusion of Monterrey's tall central defender Giovani Espinoza. Defensively Ecuador are weak and are especially vulnerable in the air. Remaining defenders Ivan Hurtado, Ulises De La Cruz and Raul Guerron and keeper 'Pancho' Cevallos will be under severe pressure throughout Ecuador's tournament run – after all this is the side that conceded 20 goals in qualifying.

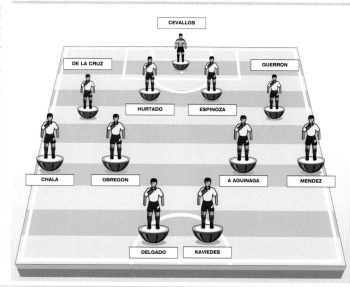

PROBABLE FORMATION 4-4-2

- CEVALLOS
- DE LA CRUZ
- GUERRON
- HURTADO
- ESPINOZA
- CHALA
- OBREGON
- A AGUINAGA
- MENDEZ
- DELGADO
- KAVIEDES

★ MEN THAT MATTER!

AGUSTIN DELGADO

Age 27
Club Soton

'El Tin' scored nine goals in qualifying including the historic winner against Brazil. He is dangerous with both head and feet and the main reason for Ecuador's success.

ULISES DE LA CRUZ

Age 28
Club Hibernian

Attacking right back, De La Cruz was ever present throughout qualifying. His pace and close control causes problems for opposing defences while few forwards can outrun him down the flank.

IVAN KAVIEDES

Age 24
Club Celta Vigo/Porto (loan)

Kaviedes has formed an excellent attacking partnership with Delgado. He is the foil, creator and occasional scorer of many of Ecuador's goals. He is first choice with Ecuador but not his Spanish club.

★ PROBABLE SQUAD ★ QUALIFICATION RECORD

NAME	POSITION	CLUB	APS/GOALS	GAMES	MINS	Y/C	R/C	GOALS
Jose Cevallos	Goalkeeper	Barcelona, Ecuador	58/0	16	1440	5	0	0
Geovani Ibarra	Goalkeeper	El Nacional, Ecuador	20/0	2	180	0	0	0
Jacinto Espinoza	Goalkeeper	LDU Quito, Ecuador	1/0	1	90	0	0	0
Marlon Ayovi	Defender	Deportivo Quito, Ecuador	26/0	7	495	1	0	0
Ulises De La Cruz	Defender	Hibernian, Scotland	48/3	18	1620	1	0	2
Giovany Espinoza	Defender	Monterrey, Mexico	18/0	8	585	0	0	0
Jorge Guagua	Defender	El Nacional, Ecuador	2/0	2	70	0	0	0
Raul Guerron	Defender	Deportivo Quito, Ecuador	16/0	9	787	2	0	0
Ivan Hurtado	Defender	La Piedad, Mexico	86/4	17	1530	0	0	0
Augusto Poroso	Defender	Emelec, Ecuador	21/0	11	927	1	2	0
Carlos Tenorio	Midfielder	LDU Quito, Ecuador	4/1	1	20	0	0	0
Juan Aguinaga	Midfielder	Espoli, Ecuador	6/0	3	74	1	0	0
Juan D Lara Burbano	Midfielder	El Nacional, Ecuador	17/0	8	416	2	0	0
Cleber Chala	Midfielder	Southampton, England	59/6	14	896	0	1	1
Luis Gomez	Midfielder	Barcelona, Ecuador	7/1	1	90	1	0	0
Edison Mendez	Midfielder	Deportivo Quito, Ecuador	20/2	8	658	1	1	1
Alfonso Obregon	Midfielder	Delfin, Ecuador	35/0	14	1154	6	0	0
Edwin Tenorio	Midfielder	Aucas, Ecuador	30/0	14	1114	8	0	0
Alex Aguinaga	Forward	Necaxa, Mexico	88/20	13	950	4	0	2
Nicolas Asencio	Forward	Barcelona, Ecuador	13/0	0	0	0	0	0
Agustin Delgado	Forward	Southampton, England	44/20	16	1305	1	0	9
Angel Fernandez	Forward	El Nacional, Ecuador	66/12	5	198	0	0	1
Ivan Kaviedes	Forward	Celta Vigo, Spain	24/8	13	817	0	0	3

KEY: APPS/GOALS = International Appearances/Goals; GAMES=Qualification Games played; MINS=Minutes played; Y/C= Yellow cards R/C=Red cards

1930 1934 1938 1950 1954 1958 1962 1966 1970 1974 1978 1982 1986 1990 1994 1998

1974 > Ecuador's qualification hopes ended by two draws with Colombia and two defeats by Uruguay.

1978 > Ecuador again fail to win against Chile and Peru in their qualification group.

1970 > Ecuador fail to win any of the World Cup qualifiers.

1986 > Ecuador suffer 6-2 defeat by Chile in qualifying.

1962 > Ecuador's first World Cup qualifier ends in a 6-3 defeat at home to Argentina.

1982 > Ecuador beat Paraguay 1-0 in qualifying but again fail to progress.

1966 > Ecuador lose 2-1 to Chile in a qualification play-off in Peru.

1990 > Ecuador record only a single win over Paraguay in their qualification campaign.

★ WORLD CUP HISTORY

1930 >> Did Not Enter		1970 >> Did Not Qualify	
1934 >> Did Not Enter		1974 >> Did Not Qualify	
1938 >> Did Not Enter		1978 >> Did Not Qualify	
1950 >> Did Not Enter		1982 >> Did Not Qualify	
1954 >> Did Not Enter		1986 >> Did Not Qualify	
1958 >> Did Not Enter		1990 >> Did Not Qualify	
1962 >> Did Not Qualify		1994 >> Did Not Qualify	
1966 >> Did Not Qualify		1998 >> Did Not Qualify	

★ WORLD CUP RECORDS, STORIES AND WEIRDNESS

QUALIFYING GOALS >> Ecuador scored a total of 23 goals in qualifying, making them 29th equal top scorer with Iran, Iraq, Syria, Uzbekistan and Australia (on 73) ahead of them!

GROUP F

OPPONENT	DATE	UK TIME	VENUE
Sweden	**2 June**	10.30	**Saitama, Japan**
Argentina	**7 June**	12.30	**Sapporo, Japan**
Nigeria	**12 June**	07.30	**Osaka, Japan**

"if Becks plays, serious semi-final contenders"

ENGLAND

★ THE LOWDOWN

Population: 52 million

Capital: London

Leader: Tony Blair

Life Expectancy: Male: 75 yrs
Female: 80 yrs

>> Queen Elizabeth II has been the reigning English Monarch for 50 years; she is celebrating her Golden Jubilee in 2002.

>> The World Conker Championships are held every year in Ashton, Northamptonshire during October. Contestants are not allowed to bring their own nuts though – these are both provided and strung by the organisers.

>> In medieval England beer was commonly served for breakfast. Ah, nothing changes!

England are reeling from the news that their captain, midfield supremo and free kick genius is seriously in doubt for the Finals.

A dastardly late lunge by Argentinian Pedro Duscher during Manchester United's quarter-final Champions League clash broke a bone in Beckham's foot and may have ruled him out of the tournament.

It all began in Munich, Germany on September 1st 2001 as England thrash Germany 5-1 in a World Cup qualifier. A hat-trick from Michael Owen, a first goal for Steven Gerrard and an amazing fifth goal from Emile Heskey complete a magical night for England, a night that proves to be a turning point in the group after England had started its qualifying run so disastrously.

Towards the end of 2000 England had hit rock bottom. Marking the closing of Wembley Stadium with a 1-0 home defeat by Germany in their opening World Cup qualifier had followed a disastrous Euro 2000 tournament. Boss Kevin Keegan resigned admitting he was not up to the job leaving the FA's Director of Football Howard Wilkinson to retrieve something from a trip to Finland. A goalless draw, which England fans had to pay to see on television for the first time, led to country-wide pessimism about the state of English football.

The FA took the radical, and controversial, step of appointing foreign coach Swede Sven Goran Eriksson to re-vitalise England's qualification campaign. Eriksson brought to the role a calming and confidence-building influence. Deciding on his favoured 4-4-2 system, he took the common sense step of playing players in their familiar positions and, after watching more English league matches with his assistant Tord Grip than any of his predecessors, unearthed surprising new international talent in left-backs 31-year-old Chris Powell and 19-year-old Ashley Cole.

The return match against Finland at Anfield saw England come back from a goal behind to win 2-1 with goals from Owen and new captain David Beckham. A trip to Tirana saw a resilient Albanian outfit hold out until the 74th minute when Owen, Paul Scholes and Andy Cole scored for a 3-1 win. A successful trip to Athens earned a 2-0 win over Greece with Scholes and Beckham on target.

Then came that magnificent win in Munich followed by a 2-0 win over Albania which put England in the driving seat for the first time. But in their final game against Greece at Old Trafford England, without Owen, made hard work of it. They went a goal down and had goalkeeper Nigel Martyn to thank for not going further behind after he made two superb saves. A vital English substitution brought on Teddy Sheringham, who equalised with his very first touch of the ball, before Greece took the lead again.

At the same time Germany were being held to a goalless draw by Finland and England looked destined for the lottery of the play-offs but, in injury time Sheringham was fouled and Beckham was left with one of the most important free kicks of his career. The England captain did not disappoint – curling a superb kick from 30 yards out and into the back of the net to earn the single point that took England to the World Cup Finals. And now England can only hope…

★ **ASSOCIATION:** The Football Association
★ **JOINED FIFA:** 1946
★ **JOINED UEFA:** 1954
★ **PLAYERS:** 2,250,000

★ **CLUBS:** 42,000
★ **WEBSITE:** www.the-fa.org
★ **HONOURS:** World Cup – 1966; Olympics – 1908, 1912

Beckham, free kick maestro – but will he be fit enough to play?

★ ROAD TO QUALIFICATION

Oct 00 **Germany** (h) > (l) **0-1**

Oct 00 **Finland** (a) > (d) **0-0**

Mar 01 **Finland** (h) > (w) **2-1**
Owen 43, Beckham 49

Mar 01 **Albania** (a) > (w) **1-3**
Owen 73, Scholes 85, Cole, Andy 90

Jun 01 **Greece** (a) > (w) **0-2**
Scholes 63, Beckham 86

Sep 01 **Germany** (a) > (w) **1-5**
Owen 13, 48, 66 Gerrard 45, Heskey 74

Sep 01 **Albania** (h) > (w) **2-0**
Owen 44, Fowler 88

Oct 01 **Greece** (h) > (d) **2-2**
Sheringham 67, Beckham 90

★ FINAL GROUP TABLE

Team	P	W	D	L	F	A	Pts
England	8	5	2	1	16	6	17
Germany	8	5	2	1	14	10	17
Finland	8	3	3	2	12	7	12
Greece	8	2	1	5	7	7	7
Albania	8	1	0	7	5	14	3

★ RECENT RESULTS

Feb 02 **Holland** (a) > (d) **1-1** Vassell 61

Mar 02 **Italy** (h) > (l) **1-2** Fowler 62

DID YOU KNOW?

Bryan Robson scored England's quickest World Cup goal after 2 seconds against Czechoslovakia at Bilbao in Spain on June 16, 1982

Under Sven Goran Eriksson, revitalised England have evolved a settled way of playing in the 4-4-2 formation familiar to Premiership players, and have selected a younger and better balanced squad. David Seaman is England's first choice goalkeeper when fit with Nigel Martyn (probably) as alternative if he's not. Sol Campbell and Rio Ferdinand have established themselves as England's centre backs with Gary Neville and Ashley Cole at full back. In midfield the supremely talented and talismanic Steven Gerrard will be the defensive anchor – if only he can stay fit – while Paul Scholes will play in the hole behind the front two, given free rein to attack from midfield. Owen Hargreaves takes the right of the midfield position if Beckham is ruled out and on England's problematic left side Steve McManaman should get the nod although Emile Heskey could be asked to play the role. Heskey, however, will probably be first choice, among an abundance of other striking talent including Robbie Fowler and Darius Vassell, to play alongside the prolific Michael Owen in attack. Teddy Sheringham's reputation as England's supersub goes before him and he'll be ready to come on to make his mark if Owen or Heskey haven't already made theirs.

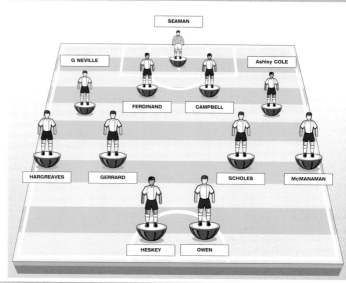

PROBABLE FORMATION 4-4-2

SEAMAN

G NEVILLE · Ashley COLE

FERDINAND · CAMPBELL

HARGREAVES · GERRARD · SCHOLES · McMANAMAN

HESKEY · OWEN

★ MEN THAT MATTER!

DAVID BECKHAM

Age>> 27
Club>> Man. United
Indispensable
Captain, free kick specialist and one of England's most successful players, but fighting to recover from injury in time for the Finals.

MICHAEL OWEN

Age>> 22
Club>> Liverpool
Stormed on to the scene at France 98 scoring a stunning goal against Argentina. Scored a hat-trick against Germany in the qualifiers. Lightening pace and prolific scoring makes him England's main marksman.

STEVEN GERRARD

Age>> 22
Club>> Liverpool
Pivotal player for England in the midfield anchor role that allows Beckham plenty of freedom. This determined and tenacious player has always been excellent for England when free from injury.

★ PROBABLE SQUAD

★ QUALIFICATION RECORD

NAME	POSITION	CLUB	APS/GOALS	GAMES	MINS	Y/C	R/C	GOALS
David James	Goalkeeper	West Ham, England	7/0	0	0	0	0	0
Nigel Martyn	Goalkeeper	Leeds, England	21/0	1	90	0	0	0
David Seaman	Goalkeeper	Arsenal, England	67/0	7	630	0	0	0
Wayne Bridge	Defender	Southampton, England	2/0	0	0	0	0	0
Sol Campbell	Defender	Arsenal, England	44/0	4	299	0	0	0
Jamie Carragher	Defender	Liverpool, England	7/0	2	14	0	0	0
Ashley Cole	Defender	Arsenal, England	7/0	5	438	1	0	0
Rio Ferdinand	Defender	Leeds, England	20/0	6	540	0	0	0
Martin Keown	Defender	Arsenal, England	40/2	4	360	0	0	0
Gary Neville	Defender	Manchester United, England	51/0	6	496	1	0	0
Philip Neville	Defender	Manchester United, England	36/0	2	180	0	0	0
David Beckham	Midfielder	Manchester United, England	49/6	7	623	0	0	3
Nicky Butt	Midfielder	Manchester United, England	17/0	3	93	0	0	0
Kieron Dyer	Midfielder	Newcastle, England	8/0	1	44	0	0	0
Steven Gerrard	Midfielder	Liverpool, England	9/1	5	431	1	0	1
Owen Hargreaves	Midfielder	Bayern Munich, Germany	3/0	1	12	0	0	0
Steve McManaman	Midfielder	Real Madrid, Spain	37/3	7	216	1	0	0
Paul Scholes	Midfielder	Manchester United, England	41/13	8	711	2	0	2
Robbie Fowler	Forward	Leeds, England	23/6	4	190	0	0	1
Emile Heskey	Forward	Liverpool, England	22/3	7	462	1	0	1
Michael Owen	Forward	Liverpool, England	33/14	6	532	0	0	6
Teddy Sheringham	Forward	Tottenham, England	44/11	1	23	0	0	1
Darius Vassell	Forward	Aston Villa, England	2/1	0	0	0	0	0

KEY: APPS/GOALS = International Appearances/Goals; GAMES=Qualification Games played; MINS=Minutes played; Y/C= Yellow cards R/C=Red cards

HISTORY AT THE WORLD CUP

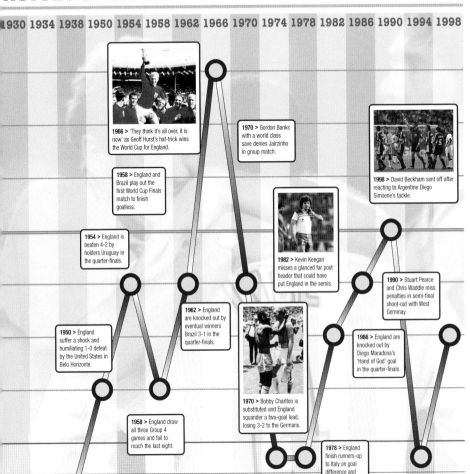

1966 > 'They think it's all over, it is now' as Geoff Hurst's hat-trick wins the World Cup for England.

1970 > Gordon Banks with a world class save denies Jairzinho in group match.

1998 > David Beckham sent off after reacting to Argentine Diego Simoene's tackle.

1958 > England and Brazil play out the first World Cup Finals match to finish goalless.

1954 > England is beaten 4-2 by holders Uruguay in the quarter-finals.

1982 > Kevin Keegan misses a glanced far post header that could have put England in the semis.

1990 > Stuart Pearce and Chris Waddle miss penalties in semi-final shoot-out with West Germnay.

1962 > England are knocked out by eventual winners Brazil 3-1 in the quarter-finals.

1950 > England suffer a shock and humiliating 1-0 defeat by the United States in Belo Horizonte.

1986 > England are knocked out by Diego Maradona's 'Hand of God' goal in the quarter-finals.

1970 > Bobby Charlton is substituted and England squander a two-goal lead, losing 3-2 to the Germans.

1958 > England draw all three Group 4 games and fail to reach the last eight.

1978 > England finish runners-up to Italy on goal difference and miss out on the World Cup Finals.

★ WORLD CUP HISTORY

1930 >> Did Not Enter	1970 >> Quarter-Final
1934 >> Did Not Enter	1974 >> Did Not Qualify
1938 >> Did Not Enter	1978 >> Did Not Qualify
1950 >> First Round	1982 >> Second Round
1954 >> Quarter-Final	1986 >> Quarter-Final
1958 >> First Round	1990 >> Fourth Place
1962 >> Quarter-Final	1994 >> Did Not Qualify
1966 >> Winners	1998 >> Second Round

★ WORLD CUP RECORDS, STORIES AND WEIRDNESS

MOST GOALS >> In 1990 England reached the semi-final of the World Cup, Gary Lineker scoring four goals on the way there. Making him only the 8th player in World Cup history to score 10 goals or more.

CONTROVERSEY >> 1966 and Geoff Hurst's was it over the line goal? Few, if any goals have been as repeatedly discussed. It's 2-2 in extra time in the 1966 Final against West Germany; Hurst receives the ball in the penalty area, turns and shoots – the ball hits the bar and bounces down on or over the line. The referee ultimately awards the goal after conferring with the Russian linesman.

OPPONENT	DATE	UK TIME	VENUE
Senegal	**31 May**	12.30	**Seoul, Korea**
Uruguay	**6 June**	12.30	**Busan, Korea**
Denmark	**11 June**	07.30	**Incheon, Korea**

"defending champions and still the best"

FRANCE

Devastating fluidity in attack, and possessed of an almost impenetrable defence, France are probably the best international side in the world. Frankly, since winning the World Cup on home soil in 1998 and the 2000 European Championship in Rotterdam, no side has come close to matching their flawless organisation, rock-like defence, highly skilled and ferocious midfield and swooping, clinical-finishing attack.

Eighteen players featured in both the 1998 World Cup and Euro 2000 squads with nine players – Lizarazu, Vieira, Djorkaeff, Deschamps, Desailly, Zidane, Thuram, Barthez and Dugarry – playing in both Finals. Laurent Blanc and Didier Deschamps have since retired from the international scene (Blanc's departure has led to some questions about the effectiveness of the new central defence pairing of Manchester United's Mikaël Silvestre and captain Marcel Desailly), but the core of this almost invincible French side remains.

And while coach Roger Lemerre faces certain selection headaches, the seamless blending of new talent has been achieved without any signs of disruption.

An experimental squad of experienced and new players beat Japan 1-0 in the Final of 2001 Confederations Cup held in Japan/Korea with a Vieira goal. What better preparation for the 2002 World Cup Finals? Particularly when you remember that from that point on France would only be playing friendlies (no need to qualify as reigning champions).

Lemerre's side have played teams from the five football-playing continents of varying ability and different styles and almost invariably, beaten them. They've travelled to Africa, Australia, South America and, most importantly, to Asia. Consequently France are the best prepared of any of the finalists. There is a realistic chance that France could become the first team since Brazil in 1958 and 1962 to win successive World Cup Finals.

And France look set to continue to be a major football power for years to come. The production line that led to the current crop of world class players continues to turn out talented youngsters as demonstrated by France lifting the 2000 European Under-18 Championship and 2001 World Under-17 Championship.

★ THE LOWDOWN

Population: 59.5 million

Capital: Paris

Leader: Lionel Jospin

Life Expectancy: Male: 75 yrs
Female: 83 yrs

>> France is the largest Western European nation and is approximately 7 times bigger than England.

>> Most frogs' legs served up in French restaurants come from Asian bullfrogs; mainly from Bangladesh, Malaysia and India.

>> A diet of garlic, frogs' legs and snails, washed down with plenty of vin de table must be good for you; the French football team are the current holders of both the European and the World Cups. Zut alors!!

★ **ASSOCIATION:** Federation Francaise de Football

★ **JOINED FIFA:** 1904

★ **JOINED UEFA:** 1954

★ **PLAYERS:** 1,692,300

★ **CLUBS:** 21,629

★ **WEBSITE:** www.fff.fr

★ **HONOURS:** World Cup – 1998; European Championship – 1984, 2000.

Fabian Barthez launches another French onslaught.

DID YOU KNOW?

France is the first nation to have won both the World Cup (1998) and the European Championship (2000).

The world knows how defending Champions France will play at the 2002 World Cup – Roger Lemerre's team will play how they have always played because, quite frankly, they are so good at it and there is very little the opposition can do to stop them. France is blessed with a depth and quality in their squad that can deal with injuries and suspensions far better than most. And play incisive, tireless attack-minded football. Goalkeeper Fabian Barthez will be protected by a four-man defence of Lilian Thuram and Bixente Lizarazu at full back, with Marcel Desailly and Franck Leboeuf as centre backs. Manchester United's Mikael Silvestre, Roma's Vincent Candela and Bayern Munich's Willy Sagnol provide cover. Robert Pires is still struggling with injury, but Emmanuel Petit and Patrick Vieira can provide both defensive and attacking midfield strategies leaving one of the world's greatest footballers Zinedine Zidane free reign to cause as much damage as possible behind the front men David Trezeguet and Sylvain Wiltord.

PROBABLE FORMATION 4-3-1-2

★ MEN THAT MATTER!

ZINEDINE ZIDANE

Age>> 29

Club>> R. Madrid

Zidane, a former World Player of the Year and Euro 2000 winner, is the world's most expensive player at £47.2 million. He scored twice in the 1998 World Cup Final against Brazil.

DAVID TREZEGUET

Age>> 24

Club>> Juventus

Scored the golden goal against Italy that won France the 2000 European Championship. Played in every match of France 98 except the Final. He is currently France's first choice striker.

PATRICK VIEIRA

Age>> 25

Club>> Arsenal

Widely regarded as one of the best midfielders in the world both in defence and attack. A World Cup Final substitute at France 98 and also a Euro 2000 winner.

★ PROBABLE SQUAD ★ QUALIFICATION RECORD

NAME	POSITION	CLUB	APS/GOALS	GAMES	MINS	Y/C	R/C	GOALS
Fabien Barthez	Goalkeeper	Manchester United, England	44/0	-	-	-	-	-
Gregory Coupet	Goalkeeper	Lyon, France	1/0	-	-	-	-	-
Ulrich Rame	Goalkeeper	Bordeaux, France	8/0	-	-	-	-	-
Vincent Candela	Defender	Roma, Italy	31/2	-	-	-	-	-
Marcel Desailly	Defender	Chelsea, England	88/3	-	-	-	-	-
William Gallas	Defender	Chelsea, England	43/3	-	-	-	-	-
Bixente Lizarazu	Defender	Bayern Munich, Germany	70/2	-	-	-	-	-
Willy Sagnol	Defender	Bayern Munich, Germany	8/0	-	-	-	-	-
Mickael Silvestre	Defender	Manchester United, England	9/1	-	-	-	-	-
Lilian Thuram	Defender	Juventus, Italy	70/2	-	-	-	-	-
Alain Boghossian	Midfielder	Parma, Italy	23/2	-	-	-	-	-
Eric Carriere	Midfielder	Lyon, France	5/2	-	-	-	-	-
Youri Djorkaeff	Midfielder	Bolton Wanderers, England	75/28	-	-	-	-	-
Christian Karembeu	Midfielder	Olympiakos, Greece	51/1	-	-	-	-	-
Claude Makelele	Midfielder	Real Madrid, Spain	12/0	-	-	-	-	-
Emmanuel Petit	Midfielder	Chelsea, England	52/5	-	-	-	-	-
Patrick Vieira	Midfielder	Arsenal, England	47/2	-	-	-	-	-
Zinedine Zidane	Midfielder	Real Madrid, Spain	69/18	-	-	-	-	-
Nicolas Anelka	Forward	Liverpool, England	26/6	-	-	-	-	-
Thierry Henry	Forward	Arsenal, England	31/11	-	-	-	-	-
Laurent Robert	Forward	Newcastle, England	9/1	-	-	-	-	-
David Trezeguet	Forward	Juventus, Italy	32/14	-	-	-	-	-
Sylvain Wiltord	Forward	Arsenal, England	34/12	-	-	-	-	-

KEY: APPS/GOALS = International Appearances/Goals; GAMES=Qualification Games played; MINS=Minutes played; Y/C= Yellow cards R/C=Red cards

HISTORY OF THE WORLD CUP

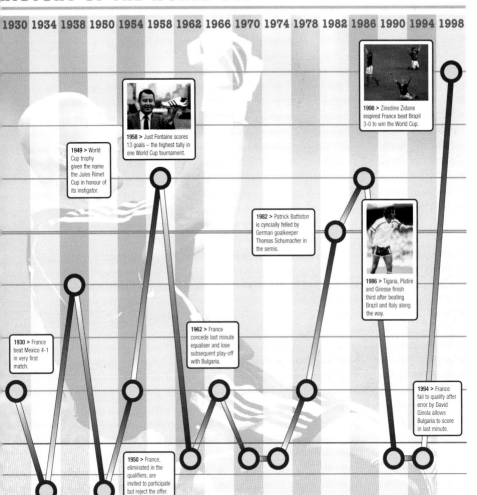

1998 > Zinedine Zidane inspired France beat Brazil 3-0 to win the World Cup.

1958 > Just Fontaine scores 13 goals – the highest tally in one World Cup tournament.

1949 > World Cup trophy given the name the Jules Rimet Cup in honour of its instigator.

1982 > Patrick Battiston is cynically felled by German goalkeeper Thomas Schumacher in the semis.

1986 > Tigana, Platini and Giresse finish third after beating Brazil and Italy along the way.

1930 > France beat Mexico 4-1 in very first match.

1962 > France concede last minute equaliser and lose subsequent play-off with Bulgaria.

1994 > France fail to qualify after error by David Ginola allows Bulgaria to score in last minute.

1950 > France, eliminated in the qualifiers, are invited to participate but reject the offer.

★ WORLD CUP HISTORY

1930 >> First Round	1970 >> Did Not Qualify
1934 >> Did Not Enter	1974 >> Did Not Qualify
1938 >> Quarter-Final	1978 >> First Round
1950 >> Did Not Qualify	1982 >> Fourth Place
1954 >> First Round	1986 >> Third Place
1958 >> Third Place	1990 >> Did Not Qualify
1962 >> Did Not Qualify	1994 >> Did Not Qualify
1966 >> First Round	1998 >> Winners

★ WORLD CUP RECORDS, STORIES AND WEIRDNESS

MOST GOALS IN A TOURNAMENT >> Just Fontaine's record 13 World Cup goals in 1958 included four in the third place play-off against West Germany.

FIRST EVER GOLDEN GOAL >> When France beat Paraguay 1-0 in the second round in 1988, Laurent Blanc scored the first ever Golden Goal in a World Cup match. It is, so far, the only one.

GROUP E

OPPONENT	DATE	UK TIME	VENUE
Saudi Arabia	**1 June**	12.30	**Sapporo, Korea**
Ireland	**5 June**	12.30	**Ibaraki, Japan**
Cameroon	**11 June**	12.30	**Shizuoka, Japan**

"not what they were?"

GERMANY

Germany are no longer the reliable quality side who always do well. After failing to win a single game during Euro 2000, Germany launched a search for a new managerial messiah to deliver them from the decline associated with what was becoming an ageing side. That man was to be Christoph Daum but, dogged by scandal, he was quickly forced to leave the job.

Former German international striker Rudi Voller, appointed caretaker boss, was soon persuaded to take over permanently. Voller started brightly winning his first three games in charge – including World Cup qualifying victories over Greece and, more importantly, over England at Wembley.

After a honeymoon period nothing could disguise the fact that, by previous standards, this was a very ordinary German side. They struggled against Albania in Leverkusen and only secured victory with two minutes to spare through substitute Miroslav Klose. They also surrendered a two-goal lead in Athens against Greece, had Sebastian Deisler sent off on the hour, and had to rely on substitutes Klose and Marco Bode to get the points with two goals in the last nine minutes.

It was a similar story in Helsinki where the Germans gave an awful first half performance that saw them trail 2-0. A Michael Ballack penalty and a Carsten Jancker goal salvaged a point. In Tirana, Marko Rehmer gave Germany the lead but it immediately came under threat when Carsten Ramelow was dismissed. The Germans struggled until Ballack found the net midway through the second half.

But despite the poor quality of these performances, Germany remained unbeaten and the value of the win in England could not be underestimated. Five points clear and with a superior goal difference, Germany looked certain to qualify for the World Cup Finals.

Then, on September 1st in Munich Germany suffered their worst home defeat since 1930, as England thrashed Voller's team 5-1. The *Die Welt* newspaper described it as "the greatest-ever slap in the face for German football". It was a disastrous night for Voller both professionally and personally as his father, Kurt, was rushed to hospital after suffering a heart attack.

A month later Germany faced Finland at home while England entertained Greece. Germany knew they had to better the result of the English and Voller made a point of banning news of events in England from reaching his players. Against the Finns both Oliver Bierhoff and Olivier Neuville missed chances as the Germans failed to score, the game ending 0-0. But automatic qualification still seemed likely with the news that Greece led England 2-1 and just seconds remaining. German midfielder Sebastian Deisler managed to get to a TV set only to witness David Beckham's spectacular equalising free kick.

Paired with a lacklustre Ukraine in the play-offs, Germany put in two of their best performances with a 1-1 draw in Kiev that would make for a tense second leg at home. In the event the tie in Dortmund was over by the 14th minute as Ballack, Neuville and Rehmer found the net on the way to an overall 5-2 aggregate victory.

* **ASSOCIATION:** Deutsche Fussbull-Bund
* **JOINED FIFA:** 1950
* **JOINED UEFA:** 1954
* **PLAYERS:** 5,260,320

* **CLUBS:** 26,800
* **WEBSITE:** www.dfb.de
* **HONOURS:** World Cup - *1954/*74/*90; European Championships: *1972/*80/96; Olympics - **1976. (*as West Germany; **as East Germany)

Sebastien Deisler – a young talented midfielder.

★ ROAD TO QUALIFICATION

Sep 00 Greece (h) > (w) **2-0**
Deisler 17, Ouzounidis 75 og

Oct 00 England (a) > (w) 0-**1** Hamann 13

Mar 01 Albania (h) > (w) **2-1**
Deisler 50, Klose 87

Mar 01 Greece (a) > (w) 2-**4**
Rehmer 6, Ballack 25 pen, Klose 82, Bode 90

Jun 01 Finland (a) > (d) 2-2
Ballack 68 pen, Jancker 72

Jun 01 Albania (a) > (w) **0-2**
Rehmer 28, Ballack 68

Sep 01 England (h) > (l) **1**-5 Jancker 6

Oct 01 Finland (h) > (d) **0-0**

Nov 01 Ukraine (a) > (d) 1-**1** Ballack 31

Nov 01 Ukraine (h) > (w) **4-1** (agg **5**-2)
Ballack 5, 51, Neuville 11, Rehmer 16

★ FINAL GROUP TABLE

Team	P	W	D	L	F	A	Pts
England	8	5	2	1	16	6	17
Germany	8	5	2	1	14	10	17
Finland	8	3	3	2	12	7	12
Greece	8	2	1	5	7	17	7
Albania	8	1	0	7	5	14	3

★ RECENT RESULTS

Feb 02 Israel (h) > (w) **7-1**
Klose 49, 51, 65, Hamann 62, Bierhoff 69, Asamoah 75, Ricken 77

Mar 02 United States (h) > (w) **4-2**
Ziege 44, Neuville 61, Bierhoff 65, Frings 68

DID YOU KNOW?

Lothar Matthaus holds the record for the most World Cup Final appearances, playing a total of 25 games in 1982, 1986, 1990, 1994 and 1998.

Germany have always played 3-5-2 but Rudi Voller's side had to revise this system to achieve adequate results during qualifying. Like France, teams know how Germany will play, but unlike France, Germany currently lacks the quality to be good at it. As something of a last resort, goalkeeper Oliver Kahn has become an increasingly valuable member of the team. Marco Rehmer and Jens Nowotny have been ever present in a shaky back line. No nonsense Thomas Linke completes the defence. In the midfield engine room Michael Ballack, Carsten Ramelow and Sebastian Deisler are regarded as the best, if not the most consistent, combination. Jens Jeremies, if back to form, can play the anchor role and Bernd Schneider on the right and Christian Ziege on the left will play down the flanks. The goals are expected to come from the nippy Oliver Neuville and his towering partner Carsten Jancker.

PROBABLE FORMATION 3-5-2

KAHN

REHMER   LINKE

NOWOTNY

SCHNEIDER   BALLACK   DEISLER   ZIEGE

RAMELOW

NEUVILLE   JANCKER

★ MEN THAT MATTER!

OLIVER KAHN

Age >> 32

Club >> Bayern Munich

Captain of Germany and one of the best goalkeepers in the world. This is his third World Cup but he spent all of USA 94 (third choice) and France 98 (second choice) on the bench.

MICHAEL BALLACK

Age >> 25

Club >> Bayer Leverkusen

Goalscoring midfielder who was Germany's leading marksman in qualifying. He was superb in the play-offs against Ukraine scoring three goals – two far post headers and a tap in.

SEBASTIEN DEISLER

Age >> 22

Club >> Hertha Berlin

Deisler is one of the few creative players in the German side. This will be the first World Cup for this young talented midfielder although he did feature at Euro 2000.

★ PROBABLE SQUAD   ★ QUALIFICATION RECORD

NAME	POSITION	CLUB	APS/GOALS	GAMES	MINS	Y/C	R/C	GOALS
Hans-Jorg Butt	Goalkeeper	Bayer Leverkusen, Germany	1/0	0	0	0	0	0
Oliver Kahn	Goalkeeper	Bayern Munich, Germany	42/0	10	900	0	0	0
Jens Lehmann	Goalkeeper	Borussia Dortmund, Germany	13/0	0	0	0	0	0
Frank Baumann	Defender	Werder Bremen, Germany	7/2	2	9	0	0	0
Jorg Heinrich	Defender	Borussia Dortmund, Germany	34/2	2	136	1	0	0
Thomas Linke	Defender	Bayern Munich, Germany	28/0	6	494	1	0	0
Jens Nowotny	Defender	Bayer Leverkusen, Germany	35/0	10	900	1	0	0
Marko Rehmer	Defender	Hertha Berlin, Germany	27/4	10	852	0	0	3
Christian Worns	Defender	Borussia Dortmund, Germany	38/0	4	316	1	0	0
Michael Ballack	Midfielder	Bayer Leverkusen, Germany	21/6	9	787	3	0	6
Marco Bode	Midfielder	Werder Bremen, Germany	32/6	5	347	1	0	1
Sebastian Deisler	Midfielder	Hertha Berlin, Germany	16/2	7	623	0	1	2
Dietmar Hamann	Midfielder	Liverpool, England	37/3	5	406	3	0	1
Jens Jeremies	Midfielder	Bayern Munich, Germany	28/1	2	182	0	0	0
Carsten Ramelow	Midfielder	Bayer Leverkusen, Germany	22/0	9	718	1	1	0
Lars Ricken	Midfielder	Borussia Dortmund, Germany	14/0	4	141	1	0	0
Mehmet Scholl	Midfielder	Bayern Munich, Germany	35/8	3	270	2	0	0
Christian Ziege	Midfielder	Tottenham, England	63/8	7	475	1	0	0
Gerald Asamoah	Forward	Schalke, Germany	7/1	5	337	0	0	0
Oliver Bierhoff	Forward	Monaco, France	60/32	5	265	0	0	0
Carsten Jancker	Forward	Bayern Munich, Germany	21/6	8	555	0	0	2
Oliver Neuville	Forward	Bayer Leverkusen, Germany	29/2	7	484	2	0	1
Alexander Zickler	Forward	Bayern Munich, Germany	8/2	3	183	0	0	0

KEY: APPS/GOALS = International Appearances/Goals; GAMES=Qualification Games played; MINS=Minutes played; Y/C= Yellow cards R/C=Red cards

HISTORY AT THE WORLD CUP

1930 1934 1938 1950 1954 1958 1962 1966 1970 1974 1978 1982 1986 1990 1994 1998

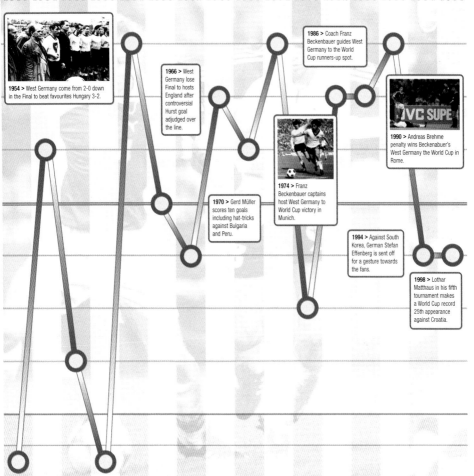

1954 > West Germany come from 2-0 down in the Final to beat favourites Hungary 3-2.

1966 > West Germany lose Final to hosts England after controversial Hurst goal adjudged over the line.

1986 > Coach Franz Beckenbauer guides West Germany to the World Cup runners-up spot.

1990 > Andreas Brehme penalty wins Beckenabuer's West Germany the World Cup in Rome.

1970 > Gerd Müller scores ten goals including hat-tricks against Bulgaria and Peru.

1974 > Franz Beckenbauer captains host West Germany to World Cup victory in Munich.

1994 > Against South Korea, German Stefan Effenberg is sent off for a gesture towards the fans.

1998 > Lothar Matthaus in his fifth tournament makes a World Cup record 25th appearance against Croatia.

★ WORLD CUP HISTORY

1930 >>	Did Not Enter	1970 >>	Third Place
1934 >>	Third Place	1974 >>	Winners
1938 >>	First Round	1978 >>	Second Round
1950 >>	Did Not Enter	1982 >>	Runners-Up
1954 >>	Winners	1986 >>	Runners-Up
1958 >>	Fourth Place	1990 >>	Winners
1962 >>	Quarter-Finals	1994 >>	Quarter-Final
1966 >>	Runners-Up	1998 >>	Quarter-Final

★ WORLD CUP RECORDS, STORIES AND WEIRDNESS

MOST GOALS >> Gerd Müller, "Der Bomber", is the most prolific striker in World Cup history with a record of 14 goals in two tournaments.

SUCCES AS PLAYER AND MANAGER >> Franz Beckenbauer was appointed national coach in 1984 and steered West Germany to the final in both 1986 and 1990. At the latter he became only the second man in World Cup history, Zagalo of Brazil was the other, to achieve success as both a player and manager.

OPPONENT	DATE	UK TIME	VENUE
Cameroon	1 June	07.30	Niigata, Japan
Germany	5 June	12.30	Ibaraki, Japan
Saudi Arabia	11 June	12.30	Yokohama, Japan

"second round candidates, with luck"

IRELAND

The Republic of Ireland must have dreaded the prospect of a play-off after finishing unbeaten but second to Portugal (on goal difference) in European Qualifying Group Two. Three previous competitions – Euro 96, World Cup 98 and Euro 2000 – had seen the Irish denied a place in the Finals after falling at the play-off stage. The draw for the 2002 World Cup play-offs paired them with Iran.

As it happens this time the Irish had nothing to fear. The first leg in Dublin saw the Irish defeat the Iranians 2-0 thanks to a penalty from Ian Harte on the stroke of half time and a 51st minute goal from Robbie Keane. Despite losing to a last minute goal in Tehran, Ireland's qualification was never really threatened.

Mick McCarthy's team deserved to reach Japan/Korea after some stunning performances, which ultimately led to the elimination of Holland. A particularly satisfying outcome, since the Dutch had denied the Irish a place at the last World Cup and Euro 96.

The Irish began their campaign with their two toughest away fixtures against Holland and Portugal – securing a point from each game – but it could have easily been much more. Robbie Keane and Jason McAteer established a two-goal lead against the Dutch with 25 minutes left. Holland fought back to claim a point. In Lisbon, McCarthy's team were under enormous pressure throughout, but Matt Holland managed to find the target cancelling out Sergio Conceicao's effort.

Maximum points were achieved against Estonia, Cyprus and Andorra before Portugal arrived in Dublin. It was an eventful game for captain Roy Keane as the Manchester United midfielder put the Irish in the lead with a deflected shot and was later sent off. Luis Figo's goal secured the draw. Both Keanes, Roy (suspension) and Robbie (injury), missed the trip to Estonia four days later, but the Irish strolled to a comfortable 2-0 win.

Then came the night when all Ireland supped from the cold dish of revenge. A single goal from Jason McAteer proved enough to beat Holland and knock the Dutch out of the World Cup.

The 4-0 win over Cyprus was marked by Niall Quinn's long awaited 21st goal for his country making him the Republic of Ireland's all-time top goalscorer.

This will be Ireland's third time at the World Cup Finals after the glory days of Italia 90 and USA 94. England 1966 World Cup winner Jack Charlton was in charge with a squad in 1990 that reached the last eight and featured Mick McCarthy, Leeds boss David O'Leary and Niall Quinn. Four years later Quinn was joined by current squad members Gary Kelly, Jason McAteer and Steve Staunton, as the Irish reached the second round (beaten by Holland).

Ireland can be expected to do well again. Mick McCarthy's team has shown they can, on their day, match any side in the world and it will require a very good team to stop the boys in green progressing.

★ THE LOWDOWN

Population: 3.8 million

Capital: Dublin

Leader: Bertie Ahern

Life Expectancy: Male: 74 yrs Female: 80 yrs

>> Southern Ireland is divided into 27 counties and 5 county boroughs. Irish-speaking areas are known as "Gaeltacht".

>> The harp is a national Irish symbol. Arthur Guinness deliberately chose it as his logo for this reason. However, the Guinness harp faces left, whilst the official government version faces right. After 7 or 8 pints of the black stuff who cares?!

>> St Patrick's Day is celebrated the world over on March 17th.

★ **ASSOCIATION:** Football Association of Ireland
★ **JOINED FIFA:** 1923
★ **JOINED UEFA:** 1954
★ **PLAYERS:** 124,700

★ **CLUBS:** 3,190
★ **WEBSITE:** www.fai.ie
★ **HONOURS:** None

Roy Keane shows balletic poise under pressure.

★ ROAD TO QUALIFICATION

Sep 00 **Holland** (a) > (d) 2-**2**
Keane, Robbie 21, McAteer 65

Oct 00 **Portugal** (a) > (d) 1-**1** Holland 73

Oct 00 **Estonia** (h) > (w) **2**-0
Kinsella 24, Dunne 50

Mar 01 **Cyprus** (a) > (w) 0-**4**
Keane, Roy 32, 88, Harte 42 pen,
Kelly, G 80

Mar 01 **Andorra** (a) > (w) 0-**3**
Harte 32 pen, Kilbane 75, Holland 80

Apr 01 **Andorra** (h) > (w) **3**-1
Kilbane 33, Kinsella 36, Breen 73

Jun 01 **Portugal** (h) > (d) 1-**1**
Keane, Roy 67

Jun 01 **Estonia** (a) > (w) 0-**2**
Dunne 9, Holland 39

Sep 01 **Holland** (h) > (w) **1**-0 McAteer 67

Oct 01 **Cyprus** (h) > (w) **4**-0
Harte 3, Quinn, N 11, Connolly 63,
Keane, Roy 66

Nov 01 **Iran** (h) > (w) **2**-0
Harte 44 pen, Keane, Robbie 50

Nov 01 **Iran** (a) > (l) 1-**0** (agg **2**-1)

★ FINAL GROUP TABLE

Team	P	W	D	L	F	A	Pts
Portugal	10	7	3	0	33	7	24
Rep of Ireland	10	7	3	0	23	5	24
Netherlands	10	6	2	2	30	9	20
Estonia	10	2	2	6	10	26	8
Cyprus	10	2	2	6	13	31	8
Andorra	10	0	0	10	5	36	0

★ RECENT RESULTS

Feb 02 **Russia** (h) > (w) **2**-0
Reid 3, Keane, Robbie 20

Mar 02 **Denmark** (h) > (w) **3**-0
Harte 19, Keane, Robbie 54, Morrison 90

DID YOU KNOW?

On their World Cup debut in 1990 the Republic of Ireland reached the quarter-finals by virtue of just scoring two goals against England and Holland, and without winning a game.

Nobody really expected Mick McCarthy's Republic of Ireland side to qualify for the Finals out of "the group of death" that included Portugal and Holland, but here they are again, finalists for the third time. Lining up in a strict 4-4-2 formation, we can expect the Irish to be tough act to deal with, especially now that their captain and midfield powerhouse, Roy Keane, is delivering at international level as he has for his club for the last few years. Keane's influence over his Irish teammates can't be underestimated as he lifts their performances to levels they'd rarely achieve on their own. Keane will be keeping good company in Japan/Korea with a young and fast-developing side. The midfield is full of skill and invention featuring Matt Holland, who can also deputise for Keane if necessary, Kevin Kilbane – excellent on the left flank and Jason McAteer, who's back in favour on the right. Ireland's main striker Robbie Keane would hold a place in any European club and will be partnered with the height of either Niall Quinn, if fit, or David Connolly. Shay Given is first choice keeper and at right back either Gary Kelly or Steve Finnan should get the nod. Otherwise the back line, which is always difficult to break down, picks itself.

PROBABLE FORMATION 4-4-2

GIVEN

Gary KELLY   HARTE

BREEN   STAUNTON

McATEER   Roy KEANE   HOLLAND   KILBANE

Robbie KEANE   QUINN

★ MEN THAT MATTER!

ROY KEANE

Age >> 30
Club >> Man. United
Inspirational captain of the Irish side, who played at USA 94, leads by example scoring four goals in qualifying. He is a no-nonsense midfielder who has won a host of honours with his club.

ROBBIE KEANE

Age >> 21
Club >> Leeds United
Ireland's most expensive player after two moves totalling £20 million in transfer fees. A young striker who is always a handful for defences. Scored the first and last goals in Ireland's qualifying campaign.

IAN HARTE

Age >> 24
Club >> Leeds United
Ever present at left back and Ireland's first choice penalty-taker. He converted three penalties — against Cyprus, Andorra and Iran — and is also a real danger at set pieces.

★ PROBABLE SQUAD   ★ QUALIFICATION RECORD

NAME	POSITION	CLUB	APS/GOALS	GAMES	MINS	Y/C	R/C	GOALS
Shay Given	Goalkeeper	Newcastle, England	36/0	9	840	0	0	0
Alan Kelly	Goalkeeper	Blackburn, England	34/0	3	270	0	0	0
Dean Kiely	Goalkeeper	Charlton, England	4/0	0	0	0	0	0
Gary Breen	Defender	Coventry, England	42/5	9	832	0	0	1
Gary Doherty	Defender	Tottenham, England	8/0	5	249	0	0	0
Richard Dunne	Defender	Manchester City, England	12/3	7	630	0	0	2
Steve Finnan	Defender	Fulham, England	12/1	8	359	0	0	0
Ian Harte	Defender	Leeds, England	36/7	12	1110	0	0	4
Gary Kelly	Defender	Leeds, England	43/2	9	599	1	1	1
Steve Staunton	Defender	Aston Villa, England	95/7	8	543	0	0	0
Lee Carsley	Midfielder	Everton, England	19/0	1	26	0	0	0
Matt Holland	Midfielder	Ipswich, England	15/3	10	732	0	0	3
Roy Keane	Midfielder	Manchester United, England	57/9	9	840	2	0	4
Mark Kennedy	Midfielder	Wolves, England	33/3	2	154	0	0	0
Kevin Kilbane	Midfielder	Sunderland, England	30/3	12	1040	0	0	2
Mark Kinsella	Midfielder	Charlton, England	25/2	8	697	1	0	2
Jason McAteer	Midfielder	Sunderland, England	45/3	7	531	2	0	2
David Connolly	Forward	Wimbledon, England	30/8	6	404	0	1	1
Damien Duff	Forward	Blackburn, England	22/1	7	399	0	0	0
Dominic Foley	Forward	QPR, England	6/2	1	3	0	0	0
Robbie Keane	Forward	Leeds, England	29/8	9	754	2	0	2
Clinton Morrison	Forward	Crystal Palace, England	3/1	2	36	0	0	0
Niall Quinn	Forward	Sunderland, England	87/21	8	480	1	0	1

KEY: APPS/GOALS = International Appearances/Goals; GAMES=Qualification Games played; MINS=Minutes played; Y/C= Yellow cards R/C=Red cards

HISTORY AT THE WORLD CUP

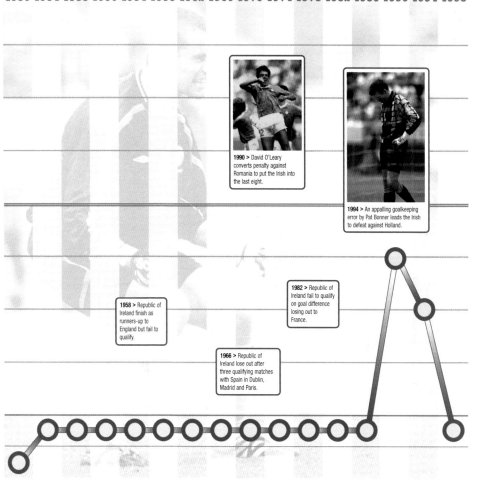

1990 > David O'Leary converts penalty against Romania to put the Irish into the last eight.

1994 > An appalling goalkeeping error by Pat Bonner leads the Irish to defeat against Holland.

1982 > Republic of Ireland fail to qualify on goal difference losing out to France.

1958 > Republic of Ireland finish as runners-up to England but fail to qualify.

1966 > Republic of Ireland lose out after three qualifying matches with Spain in Dublin, Madrid and Paris.

★ WORLD CUP HISTORY

1930 >> Did Not Enter	**1970** >> Did Not Qualify
1934 >> Did Not Qualify	**1974** >> Did Not Qualify
1938 >> Did Not Qualify	**1978** >> Did Not Qualify
1950 >> Did Not Qualify	**1982** >> Did Not Qualify
1954 >> Did Not Qualify	**1986** >> Did not Qualify
1958 >> Did Not Qualify	**1990** >> Quarter-Finals
1962 >> Did Not Qualify	**1994** >> Second Round
1966 >> Did Not Qualify	**1998** >> Did Not Qualify

★ WORLD CUP RECORDS, STORIES AND WEIRDNESS

MOST DRAWS >> Ireland hold the unlikely record of having secured more (4 in 1990) successive draws than any other team.

GROUP G

OPPONENT	DATE	UK TIME	VENUE
Ecuador	**3 June**	**12.30**	**Sapporo, Japan**
Croatia	**8 June**	**10.00**	**Ibaraki, Japan**
Mexico	**13 June**	**12.30**	**Oita, Japan**

"a last-four certainty"

ITALY

★ THE LOWDOWN

Population: 57.6 million

Capital: Rome

Leader: Silvio Berlusconi

Life Expectancy: Male: 76 yrs Female: 82 yrs

>> Bocce is the name given to a popular Italian sport. It is similar to bowls; each player tries to throw his or her four bowls nearest to a target bowl which is about 25 feet away.

>> Eating is an important part of Italian culture. Some shops close for many hours during meal times and about half the primary school children return home for lunch.

>> Ferrari cars are made in Italy, although they are now 51% owned by Fiat. Just think, the Testerossa is owned by the same people that came up with the Fiat Cinquecento - aahh bless!

Coach Giovanni Trapattoni expects Italy to at least reach the semi-finals at the 2002 World Cup. A not unreasonable expectation considering Italy were runners up at Euro 2000 and quarter-finalists at France 98. In both tournaments Italy were knocked out by eventual tournament winners France – in 1998 on a penalty shoot-out and by a golden goal in 2000.

Trapattoni took over Italy after Euro 2000, inheriting a comparatively young side that he has nurtured through qualification. Italy still lack a couple of players that would make them the equal of Italy's 1982 World Cup-winning side, but it should be noted that since Euro 2000 only World Cup favourites Argentina have beaten them.

Alessandro Del Piero netted from one of his trademark free kicks for the winning goal against Hungary in their last group game to confirm qualification, but Italy's place in the Finals would have been booked a game earlier but for a disappointing below par performance in Lithuania, where the hosts earned a well-deserved 0-0 draw.

Throughout qualification, the real goalscoring hero has been Milan's Filippo Inzaghi who scored seven goals in just six appearances. He scored both first half goals in the 2-2 draw with Hungary in Budapest; opened the scoring for the 3-0 home drubbing of Romania and netted both goals in the 2-0 win in Bucharest. Inzaghi also scored two goals, as did Del Piero, in the 4-0 home thrashing of Lithuania.

The national side has been a boon to Italian soccer, where the league game has been rocked by a series of scandals involving drugs, faked passports and match fixing. On top of that Italian clubs – which have been a dominant force in European competition for the past 20 years – have not been performing at anything like the same level. The last Italian club to lift a major European trophy was Lazio which won the European Cup Winners' Cup in 1999.

The national side currently has a plethora of playmakers and lethal attackers. In the former category are Demetrio Albertini, Luigi Di Biagio, Alessio Tacchinardi, Damiano Tommasi and Gianluca Zambrotta. In attack, where often three players are selected, Del Piero and Inzaghi are joined or replaced by Marco Delvecchio and Francesco Totti.

Such an abundance of midfield and attacking talent, when combined with Italy's traditional ability to defend, and defend well, makes a serious challenge for the trophy a real possibility. Italy has always done well at the World Cup; they have won the competition three times in 1934, 1938 and 1982 and have been runners-up twice (both times to Brazil) in 1970 and 1994. Such a history and impressive recent form at major tournaments breeds a high level of expectation from both fans and the Italian media. Anything less than a place in the last four will be considered a disaster for the Italians!

* **ASSOCIATION:** Federazione Italiana Giuoco Calcio
* **JOINED FIFA:** 1905
* **JOINED UEFA:** 1954
* **PLAYERS:** 1,421,000
* **CLUBS:** 20,961
* **WEBSITE:** www.figc.it
* **HONOURS:** World Cup – 1934, 1938, 1982; European Championship – 1968; Olympic Games – 1936.

Alessandro Del Piero models the best shirts in football.

★ ROAD TO QUALIFICATION

Sep 00 **Hungary** (a) > (d) 2-**2**
Inzaghi, F 26, 35

Oct 00 **Romania** (h) > (w) **3**-0
Inzaghi, F 12, Delvecchio 16, Totti 41

Oct 00 **Georgia** (h) > (w) **2**-0
Del Piero 46 pen, 88 pen

Mar 01 **Romania** (a) > (w) 0-**2**
Inzaghi, F 28, 32

Mar 01 **Lithuania** (h) > (w) **4**-0
Inzaghi, F 17, 64, Del Piero 49, 79

Jun 01 **Georgia** (a) > (w) 1-**2**
Delvecchio 45, Totti 66

Sep 01 **Lithuania** (a) > (d) 0-**0**

Oct 01 **Hungary** (h) > (w) **1**-0 Del Piero 44

★ FINAL GROUP TABLE

Team	P	W	D	L	F	A	Pts
Italy	8	6	2	0	16	3	20
Romania	8	5	1	2	10	7	16
Georgia	8	3	1	4	12	12	10
Hungary	8	2	2	4	14	13	8
Lithuania	8	0	2	6	3	20	2

★ RECENT RESULTS

Feb 02 **United States** (h) > (w) **1**-0
Del Piero 61

Mar 02 **England** (a) > (w) 1-**2**
Montella 67, 90

DID YOU KNOW?

Christian Vieri received 264 bottles of wine from Italy's National Wine Cities Association for scoring Italy's first goal at France 98.

Italy's 3-5-2 line-up was introduced at France 98 – a change from their traditional 4-4-2 – but the emphasis remains on strong defence, quality midfield and lethal strikers. A truly world class back three in Fabio Cannavaro, Alessandro Nesta and captain Paolo Maldini can be bolstered, if needed, by right wing-back Gianluca Zambrotta. The right side is perhaps not Italy's strongest but Zambrotta is effective and Francesco Coco offers the same service on the left. Demetrio Albertini is the conductor of the Italian side, dictating pace and strategy – aided by the improving Damiano Tommasi. Francesco Totti plays just behind the front two of Filippo Inzaghi and Alessandro Del Piero. These three players will be a serious handful for any defence and if, for some reason, they don't do the job then there are always Marco Delvecchio and Christian Vieri to call upon. Quality pervades the whole squad.

PROBABLE FORMATION 3-5-2

BUFFON

CANNAVARO — MALDINI

NESTA

ZAMBROTTA — TOMMASI — ALBERTINI — COCO

TOTTI

INZAGHI — DEL PIERO

★ MEN THAT MATTER!

FILIPPO INZAGHI

Age >> 28
Club >> AC Milan
Inzaghi is £26 million worth of

goal poaching excellence who, in six appearances, netted seven goals during qualifying. Substitute at France 98 managing 50 minutes play over two games.

ALESSANDRO DEL PIERO

Age >> 27
Club >> Juventus
Hailed as Italy's golden boy since his goalscoring debut against Wales in 1995. This is his fourth major tournament appearance, including a disappointing France 98.

ALESSANDRO NESTA

Age >> 26
Club >> Lazio

Damaged ligaments ruled him out of the France 98 knock out stage. He is regarded as one of the best central defenders in Italian soccer and on the international scene.

★ PROBABLE SQUAD   ★ QUALIFICATION RECORD

NAME	POSITION	CLUB	APS/GOALS	GAMES	MINS	Y/C	R/C	GOALS
Christian Abbiati	Goalkeeper	Milan, Italy	0/0	0	0	0	0	0
Gianluigi Buffon	Goalkeeper	Juventus, Italy	23/0	5	450	0	0	0
Francessco Toldo	Goalkeeper	Internazionale, Italy	20/0	3	270	0	0	0
Fabio Cannavaro	Defender	Parma, Italy	54/0	8	720	1	0	0
Mark Iuliano	Defender	Juventus, Italy	13/1	1	90	0	0	0
Paolo Maldini	Defender	Milan, Italy	121/7	7	630	0	0	0
Marco Materazzi	Defender	Internazionale, Italy	4/0	2	120	0	0	0
Alessandro Nesta	Defender	Lazio, Italy	40/0	7	600	0	0	0
Giuseppe Pancaro	Defender	Lazio, Italy	12/0	5	320	2	0	0
Demetrio Albertini	Midfielder	Milan, Italy	78/2	5	432	1	0	0
Francesco Coco	Midfielder	Barcelona, Spain	9/0	5	368	0	0	0
Luigi Di Biagio	Midfielder	Internazionale, Italy	23/2	2	38	0	0	0
Stefano Fiore	Midfielder	Lazio, Italy	21/2	6	289	0	0	0
Gennaro Gattuso	Midfielder	Milan, Italy	9/0	3	80	0	0	0
Alessio Tacchinardi	Midfielder	Juventus, Italy	10/0	4	298	2	0	0
Damiano Tommasi	Midfielder	Roma, Italy	10/1	5	450	1	0	0
Gianlucca Zambrotta	Midfielder	Juventus, Italy	20/0	6	522	1	0	0
Alessandro Del Piero	Forward	Juventus, Italy	47/17	8	520	0	5	5
Marco Delvecchio	Forward	Roma, Italy	14/3	4	218	0	0	2
Filippo Inzaghi	Forward	Milan, Italy	36/15	6	445	0	0	7
Francesco Totti	Forward	Roma, Italy	28/5	7	606	2	0	2
Christian Vieri	Forward	Internazionale, Italy	22/10	1	90	0	0	0
Vincenzo Montella	Forward	Roma, Italy	12/3	4	44	0	0	0

KEY: APPS/GOALS = International Appearances/Goals; GAMES=Qualification Games played; MINS=Minutes played; Y/C= Yellow cards R/C=Red cards

HISTORY AT THE WORLD CUP

1930 1934 1938 1950 1954 1958 1962 1966 1970 1974 1978 1982 1986 1990 1994 1998

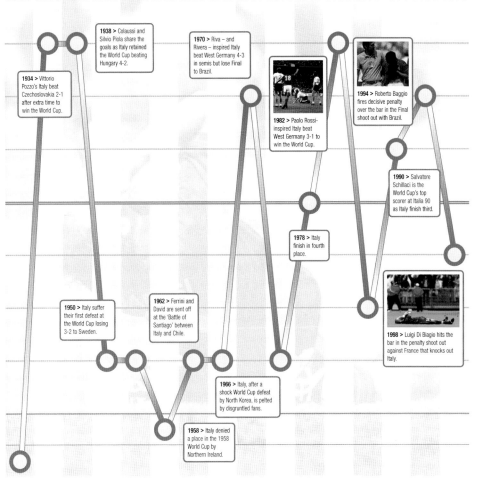

1938 > Colaussi and Silvio Piola share the goals as Italy retained the World Cup beating Hungary 4-2.

1970 > Riva – and Rivera – inspired Italy beat West Germany 4-3 in semis but lose Final to Brazil.

1934 > Vittorio Pozzo's Italy beat Czechoslovakia 2-1 after extra time to win the World Cup.

1994 > Roberto Baggio fires decisive penalty over the bar in the Final shoot out with Brazil.

1982 > Paolo Rossi-inspired Italy beat West Germany 3-1 to win the World Cup.

1990 > Salvatore Schillaci is the World Cup's top scorer at Italia 90 as Italy finish third.

1978 > Italy finish in fourth place.

1950 > Italy suffer their first defeat at the World Cup losing 3-2 to Sweden.

1962 > Ferrini and David are sent off at the 'Battle of Santiago' between Italy and Chile.

1998 > Luigi Di Biagio hits the bar in the penalty shoot out against France that knocks out Italy.

1966 > Italy, after a shock World Cup defeat by North Korea, is pelted by disgruntled fans.

1958 > Italy denied a place in the 1958 World Cup by Northern Ireland.

★ WORLD CUP HISTORY

1930	Did Not Enter	1970	Runners Up
1934	Winners	1974	First Round
1938	Winners	1978	Fourth Place
1950	First Round	1982	Winners
1954	First Round	1986	Second Round
1958	Did Not Qualify	1990	Third Place
1962	First Round	1994	Runners-Up
1966	First Round	1998	Quarter-Finals

★ WORLD CUP RECORDS, STORIES AND WEIRDNESS

MOST GOALS IN A TOURNAMENT >> At the 1982 Final Paolo Rossi made a poor start, but in a memorable game where Brazil only needed a draw to reach the semi-final, Rossi scored a magnificent hat-trick, Italy winning 3-2. He continued to impress in the semi-final against Poland, scoring both goals in the 2-0 win. In the final he scored the first in the 3-1 victory over West Germany and with that goal secured the topscorer title of the tournament.

OPPONENT	DATE	UK TIME	VENUE
Belgium	**4 June**	**10.00**	**Saitama, Japan**
Russia	**9 June**	**12.30**	**Yokohama, Japan**
Tunisia	**14 June**	**07.30**	**Osaka, Japan**

"desperately seeking second round success"

JAPAN

★ THE LOWDOWN

Population: 126.6 million

Capital: Tokyo

Leader: Junichiro Koizumi

Life Expectancy: Male: 77 yrs
Female: 84 yrs

>> Japan has one of the world's largest fishing fleets and accounts for nearly 15% of the world's global catch – eat your heart out John Wilson!

>> It is considered quite rude in Japan to blow your nose in public.

>> Of the world's 720,000 working robots, 410,000 are slaving away in Japan.

>> Japan has 18 active volcanoes and is subject to earthquakes. So you'd better take a helmet!

For World Cup co-hosts Japan, reaching the second-round would make Japanese footballing history. Even so, their fanatical supporters will be expecting much more. The Japanese side is undoubtedly the stronger of the two co-hosts and under coach Philippe Troussier there's been three years of solid preparation – resulting in huge improvement on the side that looked outclassed at France 98.

Japan's long overdue debut at the last World Cup was a big disappointment. The newcomers failed to pick up a single point losing to Argentina (1-0), Croatia (1-0) and Jamaica (2-1), although Masashi Nakayama delighted in the honour of scoring Japan's first ever World Cup goal.

Troussier inherited a relatively young squad and has developed them into a mature outfit. He has positively encouraged Japanese players to move abroad to improve their game. Goalkeeper Yoshikatsu Kawaguchi and midfielder Junichi Inamoto both play in England for Portsmouth and Arsenal respectively. A third player, defender Tsuneyasu Miyamoto, was bound for West Ham but visa problems stalled the move. Japan's most famous player Hidetoshi Nakata plays in Italy with Parma while fellow midfielder Shinji Ono plays in Holland for Feyenoord. Forward Naohiro Takahara, meanwhile, has joined Boca Juniors of Argentina.

Japan's World Cup Squad will be drawn from a pool of 28 tried and tested players all of whom possess good technique and pace, but more recently controlled aggression has been an added feature of their playing style – as was amply demonstrated during their 1-1 draw with Italy, one of the tournament favourites.

Confidence has been built up and this has been reflected in two impressive tournament performances. In 2000, Japan became Asian Champions, winning the title for the second time in eight years. Japan overcame Asia's best beating Saudi Arabia 4-1, Uzbekistan 8-1 (in which both Akinori Nishizawa and Naohiro Takahara got hat-tricks) and drew 1-1 with Qatar. Iraq were defeated 4-1 in the quarter-finals and China 3-2 in the semi-finals.

In the Final, Japan faced Saudi Arabia again for an incident-packed game. Shigeyoshi Mochizuki, playing only because Inamoto was suspended, gave away a penalty in the seventh minute but goalkeeper Kawaguchi survived the spot kick as Talal Al-Meshal put it wide. The relieved Mochizuki went on to score the winning goal in the 29th minute stabbing home Shunsuke Nakamura's free kick. Hiroshi Nanami was voted Player of the Tournament.

Nine months later, Japan co-hosted the Confederations Cup with South Korea and gave a magnificent performance. They went all the way to the Final beating Canada 2-0, Cameroon 2-0 and drawing 0-0 with Brazil before defeating Australia with a Nakata goal. In the Final, Japan suffered defeat by World Cup holders France by a single goal.

Goalkeeper Yawaguchi was once again in superb form while Shonji Ono showed why he was such a danger at free kicks with the goal of the tournament against Canada.

★ **ASSOCIATION:** The Football Association of Japan
★ **JOINED FIFA:** 1950
★ **JOINED AFC:** 1954
★ **PLAYERS:** 359,000

★ **CLUBS:** 13,100
★ **WEBSITE:** www.jfa.or.jp
★ **HONOURS:** Asian Championship – 1992, 2000

On my rising head, son!

DID YOU KNOW?

Japan reached the World Youth Cup Final in Nigeria under national team coach Philippe Troussier.

Japan's 3-5-2 formation is built for a quick passing game that can quickly turn defence into attack. Coach Philippe Troussier has instilled much needed aggression into the side and Japan can now compete to win the ball instead of relying on interceptions and their opposition's wayward passes. However, once the pressure is on, the five-man midfield drifts back to act as a five-man defence and struggles to regain any sort of attacking impetus thereafter. Many of their attacks come from the lightening pace and crossing ability of Yasuhiro Hato and Toshiro Hattori, but if these two are pushed back to defend their attacking ability is nullified. Hidetoshi Nakata will be the main creator in midfield. The Kashima Antlers' striking pair of Takayuki Suzuki and Atsushi Yanagisawa can cause problems around the goal, if they get any sort of service, and it's noticeable that Japan have begun to score more goals of late.

PROBABLE FORMATION 3-5-2

KAWAGUCHI

MORIOKA K NAKATA

MIYAMOTO

HATO INAMOTO ONO HATTORI

H NAKATA

YANAGISAWA SUZUKI

★ MEN THAT MATTER!

JUNICHI INAMOTO

Age>> 22
Club>> Arsenal
Defensive
midfielder Inamoto
is a pivotal player for Japan. He has represented Japan at every level from schoolboy (age 14) upwards. He was an influential member of Japan's 2000 Asian Cup team.

HIDETOSHI NAKATA

Age>> 25
Club>> Parma
Japan's most
famous export has
made an impressive mark in Italy with Roma and Parma. He played at France 98 but chose to miss Japan's 2000 Asian Cup triumph.

SHINJI ONO

Age>> 22
Club>> Feyenoord
Recovered from a
ligament injury
suffered in Olympic qualifying and went onto impress at the 2001 Confederations Cup after being restricted to substitute at France 98 and the 2000 Asian Cup.

★ PROBABLE SQUAD   ★ QUALIFICATION RECORD

NAME	POSITION	CLUB	APS/GOALS	GAMES	MINS	Y/C	R/C	GOALS
Yoshi Kawaguchi	Goalkeeper	Portsmouth, England	51\0	-	-	-	-	-
Seigo Narazaki	Goalkeeper	Nagoya Grampus Eight, Japan	15\0	-	-	-	-	-
Hitoshi Sogahata	Goalkeeper	Kashima Antlers, Japan	1\0	-	-	-	-	-
Yasuhiro Hato	Defender	Yokohama F Marinos, Japan	10/0	-	-	-	-	-
Toshihiro Hattori	Defender	Jubilo Iwata, Japan	35/2	-	-	-	-	-
Naoki Matsuda	Defender	Yokohama F Marinos, Japan	24/0	-	-	-	-	-
Tsuneyasu Miyamoto	Defender	Gamba Osaka, Japan	5/0	-	-	-	-	-
Ryuzo Morioka	Defender	Shimizu S-Pulse, Japan	32/0	-	-	-	-	-
Koji Nakata	Defender	Kashima Antlers, Japan	20/0	-	-	-	-	-
Junichi Inamoto	Midfielder	Arsenal, England	25/1	-	-	-	-	-
Teruyoshi Ito	Midfielder	Shimizu S-Pulse, Japan	27/0	-	-	-	-	-
Hiroaki Morishima	Midfielder	Cerezo Osaka, Japan	57/11	-	-	-	-	-
Tomokazu Myojin	Midfielder	Kashiwa Reysol, Japan	16/2	-	-	-	-	-
Hidetoshi Nakata	Midfielder	Parma, Italy	40/7	-	-	-	-	-
Daisuke Oku	Midfielder	Jubilo Iwata, Japan	22/2	-	-	-	-	-
Shinji Ono	Midfielder	Feyenoord, Holland	24/2	-	-	-	-	-
Kazuyuki Toda	Midfielder	Shimizu S-Pulse, Japan	10/0	-	-	-	-	-
Masashi Nakayama	Forward	Jubilo Iwata, Japan	47/21	-	-	-	-	-
Akinori Nishizawa	Forward	Cerezo Osaka, Japan	24/9	-	-	-	-	-
Takayuki Suzuki	Forward	Kashima Antlers, Japan	10/3	-	-	-	-	-
Naohiro Takahara	Forward	Boca Juniors, Argentina	15/8	-	-	-	-	-
Atsushi Yanagisawa	Forward	Kashima Antlers, Japan	22/9	-	-	-	-	-
Tatsuhiko Kubo	Forward	Sanfrecce Hiroshima, Japan	7/0	-	-	-	-	-

KEY: APPS/GOALS = International Appearances/Goals; GAMES=Qualification Games played; MINS=Minutes played; Y/C= Yellow cards R/C=Red cards

HISTORY AT THE WORLD CUP

1930 1934 1938 1950 1954 1958 1962 1966 1970 1974 1978 1982 1986 1990 1994 1998

1994 > Japan cruelly missed out on their first Finals when Iraqi score an injury time goal.

1990 > North Korea stops Japan's progress in the qualifiers as the Japanese finish runners-up.

1982 > Japan beaten 1-0 by North Korea in the Asian Qualifying semi-finals.

1978 > Japan finish behind South Korea, again, and Israel.

1998 > Masashi Nakayama scores Japan's first World Cup Finals goal, but they suffer a third successive defeat.

1974 > Japan are beaten 1-0 by Israel in the Asia Qualifying semi-finals.

1954 > Japan, despite playing in Tokyo twice, lose 7-3 on aggregate to South Korea in the qualifiers.

1962 > Japan beaten twice by South Korea 2-1 and 2-0 in Group 10.

1970 > Japan finish bottom of the Asia-Oceania group behind Australia and South Korea.

1986 > Once again Japan lose out to South Korea 3-1 on aggregate.

★ WORLD CUP HISTORY

1930 >> Did Not Enter	1970 >> Did Not Qualify
1934 >> Did Not Enter	1974 >> Did Not Qualify
1938 >> Did Not Enter	1978 >> Did Not Qualify
1950 >> Did Not Enter	1982 >> Did Not Qualify
1954 >> Did Not Qualify	1986 >> Did Not Qualify
1958 >> Did Not Enter	1990 >> Did Not Qualify
1962 >> Did Not Qualify	1994 >> Did Not Qualify
1966 >> Did Not Enter	1998 >> First Round

★ WORLD CUP RECORDS, STORIES AND WEIRDNESS

QUALIFYING PAIN >> Captain Tetsuji Hashiratani was taken from the field weeping after Japan had come within 17 seconds of qualifying for 1994 World Cup Finals. They'd conceded an injury time goal to Iraq, and that was that.

CO-HOSTS >> Japan beat South Korea for the first time ever in a World Cup competition during the 1994 qualification tournament.

PRECOCIOUS DEBUTANTE >> On the 1st of March 1994 Shinji Ono left school, he then averaged a goal a game in the J.League and made his debut for the national side in July, aged 18. From schoolboy to international in just 4 months.

GROUP G

OPPONENT	DATE	UK TIME	VENUE
Croatia	**3 June**	07.30	**Niigata, Japan**
Ecuador	**9 June**	07.30	**Miyagi, Japan**
Italy	**13 June**	12.30	**Oita, Japan**

"Central American super-power under pressure"

MEXICO

★ THE LOWDOWN

Population: 101.9 million

Capital: Mexico City

Leader: Vicente Quesada

Life Expectancy: Male: 68 yrs Female: 75 yrs

∙∙ Mexico was under Spanish rule for three centuries before finally achieving independence in 1810.

∙∙ In the year 2000, it was estimated that 3,900 hectares of arable land in Mexico was being used for cannabis cultivation.

∙∙ Mexico is one of the most seismologically active regions on Earth.

Historically, Mexico has always been the best team of the CONCACAF federation and will be appearing at the World Cup Finals for the 12th time in Japan/Korea. Surprisingly for such a regionally dominant team, they've made very little impact on the tournament itself, reaching the last eight on only two occasions – both when they were hosting the Finals. Otherwise, it's been an early bath for the "Tri-Colores".

Mexico's role as the footballing super-power of the region is not what it was. In recent years the USA have developed into serious challengers and Costa Rica, who Mexico finished six points adrift of in qualification, are now finding the talent and discipline to outshine their Central American opponents.

Between January 2000 and the end of January 2002 Mexico played a staggering 53 full internationals competing not only in the World Cup qualifiers but the Gold Cup (twice), Confederations Cup (twice), Copa America, US Cup and a host of friendlies around the world.

Despite the thrashing of Trinidad & Tobago 7-0 (Jared Borguetti scoring a hat-trick), Mexico finished runners-up to Trinidad & Tobago in the semi-final round to qualify for the six team final round, which included Costa Rica, Honduras, Jamaica and USA. In order to qualify they needed to finish in the top three.

Mexico made a poor start, winning just one of their first five games when, following the 3-1 defeat by Honduras, coach Enrique Meza resigned. Meza's record had been poor – 11 defeats and only five wins. His successor, Javier Aguirre, inherited a dispirited team and was given just ten days to turn things round for the must-win game against the USA.

Aguirre made eight changes to the team that had lost to Honduras with striker Borguetti, "El Emperador" Claudio Suarez, the most capped player in the world, and midfielder Gerardo Torrado the only survivors. America played dreadfully and Borgetti's 15th minute goal proved to be enough for a priceless Mexican victory.

Former striker Cuauchtemoc Blanco, who had been ruled out through injury since October 2000, was recalled to the team and scored both goals in a 2-1 win over Jamaica, ending Jamaica's 51-game unbeaten run at home. Blanco's injury had been caused by Trinidad & Tobago's Ansil Elcock's wild tackle and Elcock, perhaps fearing for his own safety, was absent when Mexico beat them 3-0, Blanco scoring the third from the penalty spot.

A 0-0 draw in Costa Rica left Aguirre's team needing to beat Honduras in their last game to qualify. Blanco was in excellent form again scoring twice and setting up another for Juan Francisco Palencia in a deserved 3-0 win. Keeping Blanco fit will be the key to Mexico's progression at the Finals.

★ **ASSOCIATION:** Federacion Mexicana de Futbol Asociacion
★ **JOINED FIFA:** 1929
★ **JOINED FOOTBALL CONFEDERATION:** 1961
★ **PLAYERS:** 1,402,300
★ **CLUBS:** 77
★ **WEBSITE:** none
★ **HONOURS:** CONCACAF/Gold Cup – 1965, 1971, 1977, 1993, 1996, 1998

Recalled veteran Alberto Garcia Aspe still has what it takes at international level.

★ ROAD TO QUALIFICATION

Jul 00 **Panama** (a) > (w) 0-1 Ramirez, R 86

Jul 00 **Trinidad & Tobago** (a) > (l) 1-0

Aug 00 **Canada** (h) > (w) 2-0
Abundis 38, Fenwick 81 og

Sep 00 **Panama** (h) > (w) 7-1
Ruiz, V 8 pen, Abundis 36, Zepeda 44,
Blanco, C 47 pen, 90, Marquez 54,
Ramirez, R 75

Oct 00 **Trinidad & Tobago** (h) > (w) 7-0
Blanco, C 20, 26 pen, Borquetti 24, 29, 78,
Davino 65, Ruiz, V 74 pen

Nov 00 **Canada** (a) > (d) 0-0

Feb 01 **United States** (a) > (l) 2-0

Mar 01 **Jamaica** (h) > (w) 4-0
De Nigris 15, 17, Borquetti 83, 87

Apr 01 **Trinidad & Tobago** (a) > (d) 1-1
Pardo 61

Jun 01 **Costa Rica** (h) > (l) 1-2 Abundis 7

Jun 01 **Honduras** (a) > (l) 3-1 Ruiz, V 86

Jun 01 **United States** (h) > (w) 1-0
Borquetti 15

Sep 01 **Jamaica** (a) > (w) 1-2
Blanco, C 68, 76

Sep 01 **Trinidad & Tobago** (h) > (w) 3-0
Garcia Aspe 25, Arellano 44, Blanco, C 86

Oct 01 **Costa Rica** (a) > (d) 0-0

Nov 01 **Honduras** (h) > (w) 3-0
Blanco, C 65, 78, Palencia 72

★ FINAL GROUP TABLE

Team	P	W	D	L	F	A	Pts
Costa Rica	10	7	2	1	17	7	23
Mexico	10	5	2	3	16	9	17
United States	10	5	2	3	11	8	17
Honduras	10	4	2	4	17	17	14
Jamaica	10	2	2	6	7	14	8
Trinidad & Tob	10	1	2	7	5	18	5

★ SEMI-FINAL GROUP TABLE

Team	P	W	D	L	F	A	Pts
Trinidad & Tob	6	5	0	1	14	7	15
Mexico	6	4	1	1	17	2	13
Canada	6	1	2	3	1	8	5
Panama	6	0	1	5	1	16	1

★ RECENT RESULTS

Feb 02 **Yugoslavia** (h) > (l) 1-2
Mendoza 75

Mar 02 **Albania** (h) > (w) 4-0
Borquetti 23, Morales 29, Bautista 51, 90

Apr 02 **United States** (a) > (l) 1-0

DID YOU KNOW?

Mexican goalkeeper Antonio Carbajal played at five different World Cup Finals in 1950, 1954, 1958, 1962 and 1966.

The arrival of new coach Javier Aguirre has brought about a change in tactics and recall for Alberto Garcia Aspe. Previously, Mexico played a very cautious 4-4-2, but Aguirre has introduced a more attacking game. Veteran Garcia Aspe combines with Johan Rodriguez, supported by Ramon Morales and Gerardo Torrado on the wings, to provide the protection the back three need and add speed to counter-attacks. The return of Cuauhtemoc Blanco after injury also sees his role change from forward to playmaker in an attacking midfielder position playing behind a front two. Young forward Jared Borgetti has gained support up front from the experienced Francisco Palencia. These changes have improved Mexico's results, but have not transformed them into a thrilling side. Mexico lacks strength in depth and the return of the old guard of Garcia Aspe and Blanco has really only added experience to a very ordinary Mexican side.

PROBABLE FORMATION 3-5-2

PEREZ

VIDRIO · BROWN

MARQUEZ

H MORALES · RODRIGUEZ · GARCIA ASPE · TORRADO

BLANCO

PALENCIA · BORGUETTI

★ MEN THAT MATTER!

CUAUHTEMOC BLANCO

Age » 29
Club » Valladolid
Scored nine goals (four penalties) from seven appearances (including three as sub) having been kept out by a severe injury sustained in qualifying. He returned in time to help clinch qualification.

GERARDO TORRADO

Age » 23
Club » Sevilla
An attacking midfielder, more of a creative player than a goalscorer. Last year he earned a move from from Mexico's Pumas UNAM to Sevilla.

FRANCISCO PALENCIA

Age » 29
Club » Espanyol
Palencia is an automatic choice for Mexico because of his thrilling pace and occasional goals. Can play as a striking partner for Blanco or Borguetti or as an attacking midfielder.

★ PROBABLE SQUAD ★ QUALIFICATION RECORD

NAME	POSITION	CLUB	APS/GOALS	GAMES	MINS	Y/C	R/C	GOALS
Jorge Campos	Goalkeeper	Pumas UNAM, Mexico	127/0	8	720	0	0	0
Oscar Perez	Goalkeeper	Cruz Azul, Mexico	26/0	5	450	0	0	0
Oswaldo Sanchez	Goalkeeper	Guadalajara, Mexico	20/0	3	270	0	0	0
Salvador Carmona	Defender	Toluca, Mexico	51/0	5	397	2	0	0
Duilio Davino	Defender	America, Mexico	66/1	7	630	1	0	1
Rafael Marquez	Defender	Monaco, France	31/2	11	969	3	1	1
Heriberto Morales	Defender	Atletico Morelia, Mexico	12/0	3	270	1	0	0
Pavel Pardo	Defender	America, Mexico	85/2	10	900	3	0	1
Alberto Rodriguez	Defender	Pachuca, Mexico	8/0	2	90	0	0	0
Manuel Vidrio	Defender	Pachuca, Mexico	22/1	5	450	1	0	0
Jesus Arellano	Midfielder	Monterrey, Mexico	35/4	7	435	1	1	1
Alberto Garcia Aspe	Midfielder	Puebla, Mexico	102/19	5	355	2	0	1
Ramon Morales	Midfielder	Guadalajara, Mexico	6/0	4	271	1	0	0
Johan Rodriguez	Midfielder	Santos Laguna, Mexico	12/2	4	261	1	1	0
Victor Ruiz	Midfielder	Necaxa, Mexico	16/6	10	696	0	0	3
Gerardo Torrado	Midfielder	Sevilla, Spain	24/1	4	283	4	0	0
German Villa	Midfielder	America, Mexico	61/0	9	702	3	0	0
Miguel Zepeda	Midfielder	Cruz Azul, Mexico	16/2	11	633	0	0	1
Cuauhtemoc Blanco	Forward	Valladolid, Spain	68/29	7	472	1	0	9
Jared Borgetti	Forward	Santos Laguna, Mexico	23/11	8	574	0	0	6
Luis Hernandez	Forward	America, Mexico	79/35	9	582	2	0	0
Francisco Palencia	Forward	Espanyol, Spain	66/8	14	908	0	0	1
Antonio De Nigris	Forward	Monterrey, Mexico	14/4	3	185	0	0	2

KEY: APPS/GOALS = International Appearances/Goals; GAMES=Qualification Games played; MINS=Minutes played; Y/C= Yellow cards R/C=Red cards

1930 1934 1938 1950 1954 1958 1962 1966 1970 1974 1978 1982 1986 1990 1994 1998

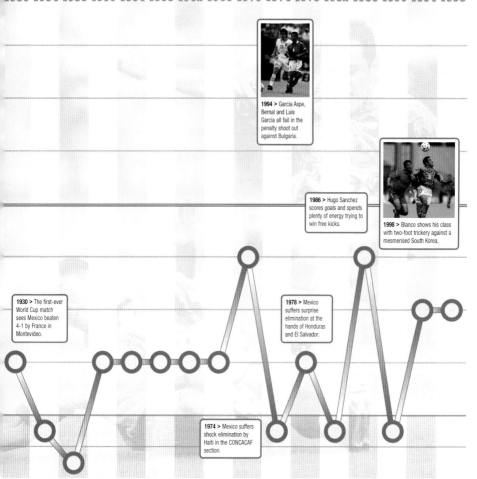

1994 > Garcia Aspe, Bernal and Luis Garcia all fail in the penalty shoot out against Bulgaria.

1986 > Hugo Sanchez scores goals and spends plenty of energy trying to win free kicks.

1998 > Blanco shows his class with two-foot trickery against a mesmerised South Korea,

1930 > The first-ever World Cup match sees Mexico beaten 4-1 by France in Montevideo.

1978 > Mexico suffers surprise elimination at the hands of Honduras and El Salvador.

1974 > Mexico suffers shock elimination by Haiti in the CONCACAF section.

★ WORLD CUP HISTORY

1930	First Round	1970	Quarter-Finals
1934	Did Not Qualify	1974	Did Not Qualify
1938	Did Not Enter	1978	First Round
1950	First Round	1982	Did Not Qualify
1954	First Round	1986	Quarter-Finals
1958	First Round	1990	Banned
1962	First Round	1994	Second Round
1966	First Round	1998	Second Round

★ WORLD CUP RECORDS, STORIES AND WEIRDNESS

FIRST SUBSTITUTE TO SCORE >> Mexico's Juan Basaguren was the first substitute to score in a World Cup Final, netting in Mexico's 1970 4-0 win over El Salvador.

QUICKEST GOAL >> Mexico were on the wrong end of the fastest goal ever scored in the World Cup, put in by Czechoslovakia's Vaclav Masek after just 16 seconds in 1962.

GROUP F

OPPONENT	DATE	UK TIME	VENUE
Argentina	**2 June**	06.30	**Ibaraki, Japan**
Sweden	**7 June**	07.30	**Kobe, Japan**
England	**12 June**	07.30	**Osaka, Japan**

"will the final be Sunday's Sunday?"

NIGERIA

★ THE LOWDOWN

Population: 126.6 million

Capital: Abuja

Leader: Olusegun Obasanjo

Life Expectancy: Male: 51 yrs Female: 51 yrs

>> Nigeria is Africa's most populous country and is made up of over 250 ethnic groups.

>> On 12th December 1991 the capital was officially transferred from Lagos to Abuja.

>> Although English is the official government language, there are 350 to 400 other languages spoken in Nigeria, with many different dialects!

Nigeria is the leading country of West Africa and has the largest population of any state on the continent, which has produced upwards of 200 professional footballers playing around the world. The country has an incredible pool of football talent and is widely regarded as Africa's best hope for World Cup success.

The 'Super Eagles' started embarrassingly on the road to World Cup qualification. In the preliminary round they were drawn against World Cup debutantes Eritrea and for the away first leg only 14 players turned up including two goalkeepers. Adding insult to the injured feelings of the Nigerian stars, who just two months earlier had finished African Nations Cup runners-up, the game had to be played on a school field because the stadium was under repair. Embarrassingly, the Nigerians were held to a 0-0 draw. A fortnight later, pride was restored with an easy 4-0 win and a place in the qualifying draw.

Nigeria began in Lagos against Sierra Leone with a team that only featured three regulars in Jay-Jay Okocha, Sunday Oliseh and Nwankwo Kanu. Such was the makeshift nature of the team that both Oliseh and Kanu found themselves playing alongside their younger brothers Azubike and Christopher. Okocha and Benedict Okwuegbu got the goals in a 2-0 win, but the team was criticised for not scoring more.

Defeats in Liberia and Sierra Leone, and a draw away to Ghana, had Nigeria on the back foot facing the prospect of not qualifying. The draw with Ghana was all the more galling since the Nigerians had put out their best team, many of their players called up from Europe leagues, while Ghana opted for local players. It was a game everyone had expected Nigeria to win.

Worse was to follow when Sierra Leone scored their first goal of the qualifiers inflicting a shock defeat on Nigeria. A bout of sustained criticism followed leading five days later to the dismissal of coach Jo Bonfrere, who had in any case, been under pressure since Nigeria had failed to defend their Olympic title in September 2000. Nigeria, five points adrift of leaders Liberia, needed not only to win their last three games but also hoped Liberia would slip up.

The new coach Shaibi Amodu's first match in charge was against Liberia in Port Harcourt and the players responded with an excellent performance producing a 2-0 win with goals from Nwankwo Kanu and Victor Agali, closing the gap to two points. Then Liberia suffered a surprise 2-1 home defeat by Ghana and although they finished with a 1-0 win over Sierra Leone, Nigeria's 4-0 drubbing of Sudan meant the Super Eagles knew they could fly to the top of the group by beating Ghana in their final game.

All 16,000 tickets at the Liberty Stadium in Port Harcourt were sold out and victory for Nigeria looked even more likely when Ghana were forced to field a makeshift team after several of their foreign-based stars failed to turn up. A minute after kick off and qualification looked certain when 2000 African Player of the Year, Victor Agali, opened the scoring. Tijani Babangida scored twice before the break to set up an untroubled second half and an easy 3-0 win. The result meant Nigeria became the fifth and last of the African nations to qualify for the World Cup Finals – their third appearance at the Finals in succession.

★ **ASSOCIATION:** Nigeria Football Association
★ **JOINED FIFA:** 1959
★ **JOINED CAF:** 1959
★ **PLAYERS:** 80,190

★ **CLUBS:** 326
★ **WEBSITE:** www.nfaonline.com
★ **HONOURS:** African Nations Cup – 1980, 1994.

Taribo West can't wait to head East.

★ ROAD TO QUALIFICATION

Apr 00 **Eritrea** (a) > (d) 0-**0**

Apr 00 **Eritrea** (h) > (w) **4**-0 (agg **4**-0)
Akwuegbu 13, Lawal 20, Akpoborie 65,
Kanu, N 89

Jun 00 **Sierra Leone** (h) > (w) **2**-0
Okocha 12, Akwuegbu 79

Jul 00 **Liberia** (a) > (l) 2-**1** Kanu, N 35

Jan 01 **Sudan** (h) > (w) **3**-0
Agali 56, 68, Kanu, N 79

Mar 01 **Ghana** (a) > (d) 0-**0**

Apr 01 **Sierra Leone** (a) > (l) 1-**0**

May 01 **Liberia** (h) > (w) **2**-0
Kanu, N 11, Agali 59

Jul 01 **Sudan** (a) > (w) 0-**4**
Okocha 40, Ayegbeni 47, 87, Aghahowa 78

Jul 01 **Ghana** (h) > (w) **3**-0
Agali 1, Babangida 18, 32

★ FINAL GROUP TABLE

Team	P	W	D	L	F	A	Pts
Nigeria	8	5	1	2	15	3	16
Liberia	8	5	0	3	10	8	15
Sudan	8	4	0	4	8	10	12
Ghana	8	3	2	3	10	9	11
Sierra Leone	8	1	1	6	2	15	4

★ RECENT RESULTS

Mar 02 **Paraguay** (a) > (d) 1-**1**
Okocha 82 pen

DID YOU KNOW?

In 1994 Augustine Efuavoen avoided being sent off against Argentina after the referee mistakenly booked Sunday Oliseh for a foul on Claudio Caniggia.

Nigeria's 4-4-2 formation is all about providing ample goal chances for strikers Victor Agali and Nwankwo Kanu (or Julius Aghahowa). The midfield is one of Africa's most experienced with right-sided Finidi George, Nigeria's longest serving international, playing in his third World Cup. The hugely exciting Sunday Oliseh supports the attack with help on the left from Garbo Lawal. Defensive midfield duties fall to Austin Okocha, whose presence in front of the back four will be important since the back line, with the exception of Taribo West, is relatively inexperienced at this level. The full backs are Joseph Yobo and Ifeanyi Udeze, who can play on both sides of the field. Partnering West in the centre is Ukrainian-based Isaac Okoronkwo. Ike Shorunmu is Nigeria's first choice goalkeeper.

PROBABLE FORMATION 4-4-2

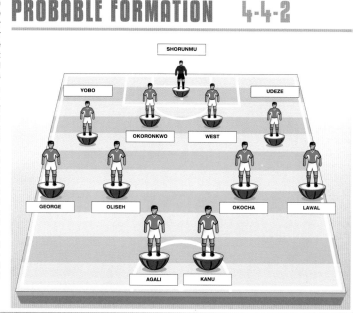

SHORUNMU

YOBO — UDEZE

OKORONKWO — WEST

GEORGE — OLISEH — OKOCHA — LAWAL

AGALI — KANU

★ MEN THAT MATTER!

NWANKWO KANU

Age>> 25

Club>> Arsenal

Diagnosed with a serious heart condition in 1996 and written off. Since then Kanu has been showered with numerous club, international and individual honours including African and Olympic titles.

VICTOR AGALI

Age>> 23

Club>> Schalke

Nigerian Player of the Year in 2000 who made a goal scoring debut against Zambia in an African Nations Cup qualifier in January 2001. Now established as first choice attacker.

SUNDAY OLISEH

Age>> 27

Club>> Borussia Dortmund

Experienced midfielder who has won the African Nations Cup (1994) and Olympics (1996) and played in Belgium, Germany, Holland and Italy. Scored a stunning World Cup goal against Spain at France 98.

★ PROBABLE SQUAD ★ QUALIFICATION RECORD

NAME	POSITION	CLUB	APS/GOALS	GAMES	MINS	Y/C	R/C	GOALS
Ademole Bankole	Goalkeeper	Crewe Alexandra, England	0/0	0	0	0	0	0
Ndubuisi Egbo	Goalkeeper	SK Tirana, Albania	8/0	1	90	0	0	0
Ike Shorunmu	Goalkeeper	unattached	28/0	7	630	0	0	0
Celestine Babayaro	Defender	Chelsea, England	23/0	1	16	0	0	0
Eric Ejiofor	Defender	Maccabi Haifa, Israel	8/0	2	170	2	0	0
Emeka Ifejiagwa	Defender	Wolfsburg, Germany	10/0	4	260	0	0	0
Isaac Okoronkwo	Defender	Shakhtar Donetsk, Ukraine	5/0	1	90	0	0	0
Godwin Okpara	Defender	Standard Liege, Belgium	19/0	4	360	2	0	0
Ifeanyi Udeze	Defender	PAOK Salonika, Greece	9/0	6	524	2	0	0
Taribo West	Defender	Kaiserslautern, Germany	33/0	7	630	1	0	0
Joseph Yobo	Defender	Marseille, France	7/0	4	360	0	0	0
Tijani Babangida	Midfielder	Vitesse Arnhem, Holland	33/5	5	177	0	0	2
Justice Christopher	Midfielder	Royal Antwerp, Belgium	4/0	2	180	0	0	0
Finidi George	Midfielder	Ipswich, England	57/7	7	560	2	0	0
Garba Lawal	Midfielder	Roda JC, Holland	26/3	7	534	0	0	0
Pascal Ojigwe	Midfielder	Bayer Leverkusen, Germany	14/1	3	144	0	0	0
Austin Okocha	Midfielder	Paris Saint-Germain, France	49/7	8	720	1	0	2
Sunday Oliseh	Midfielder	Borussia Dortmund, Germany	50/2	8	673	0	0	0
Victor Agali	Forward	Schalke, Germany	8/5	6	498	1	0	4
Julius Aghahowa	Forward	Shakhtar Donetsk, Ukraine	9/5	4	186	3	0	1
Yakubu Aiyegbeni	Forward	Maccabi Haifa, Israel	7/3	3	202	0	0	2
Benedict Akwuegbu	Forward	Grazer AK, Austria	13/5	3	247	1	0	1
Nwankwo Kanu	Forward	Arsenal, England	27/6	9	594	0	0	3

KEY: APPS/GOALS = International Appearances/Goals; **GAMES**=Qualification Games played; **MINS**=Minutes played; **Y/C**= Yellow cards **R/C**=Red cards

HISTORY AT THE WORLD CUP

1998 > Sunday Oliseh's half volley proves the winner as Nigeria shock Spain 3-2.

1994 > Emmanuel Amunike's goal puts Nigeria within two minutes of beating Italy in the second round.

1974 > Nigeria trail Ghana 3-2 in an abandoned game, but Ghana given 2-0 win and out go Nigeria.

1978 > Nigeria finish bottom of the final round behind Tunisia and Egypt.

★ WORLD CUP HISTORY

1930 >> Did Not Enter	1970 >> Did Not Qualify
1934 >> Did Not Enter	1974 >> Did Not Qualify
1938 >> Did Not Enter	1978 >> Did Not Qualify
1950 >> Did Not Enter	1982 >> Did Not Qualify
1954 >> Did Not Enter	1986 >> Did Not Qualify
1958 >> Did Not Enter	1990 >> Did Not Qualify
1962 >> Did Not Qualify	1994 >> Second Round
1966 >> Did Not Enter	1998 >> Second Round

★ WORLD CUP RECORDS, STORIES AND WEIRDNESS

TOP SCORER>> Nigeria's best all-time international scorer is Rashidi Yekini.

TOP SCORER IN QUALIFYING>> Victor Agali with 4.

WORLD CUP WEIRDNESS>> Nigeria alleges that an unknown group is attempting to force the cancellation of its World Cup warm-up matches. A spokesman said that in an attempt to sabotage Nigeria's World Cup build up, a nameless group has "written to those involved in our pre-World Cup matches to inform them we are not interested in the matches anymore"

OPPONENT	DATE	UK TIME	VENUE
South Africa	**2 June**	08.30	**Busan, Korea**
Spain	**7 June**	10.00	**Jeonju, Korea**
Slovenia	**12 June**	12.30	**Seogwipo, Korea**

"what will Maldini make of his new charges?"

PARAGUAY

araguay is the team with the goalscoring goalkeeper and had a magnificent coach who was sacked!

José Luis Chilavert, Paraguay's number one goalkeeper and team captain, loves to take free kicks, penalties and corners and is often found roaming the pitch. Remarkably, he scored four times during the qualifiers, including Paraguay's second goal in the 90th minute of a 2-0 win in Colombia. In the next game he converted an 84th minute penalty to complete a 5-1 home thrashing of Peru, contributed a goal in the 5-1 demolition of Bolivia and then converted a penalty in the big clash with Argentina. And how often can it be said of an international goalkeeper that he has had a penalty saved?! On this occasion by Chile's Sergio Vargas, but Chilavert's blushes were also saved by Carlos Paredas's winner in the third minute of injury time. At the start of the 2001-02 season he chose to remain with relegated French club Strasbourg when he could have played easily in the higher league. Sadly he will miss the opening World Cup match against South Africa through suspension.

Now to that magnificent coach: Sergio Markarian, Uruguayan by birth, managed a tough qualification programme by beating Brazil, holding favourites Argentina home and away and earning qualification with two games to spare after Uruguay drew their penultimate match. It was the first time Paraguay had qualified for

successive World Cup Finals – an impressive result from a countr whose population only amounts to million.

Paraguay had come through the toughest World Cup qualifying group playing superb football and Markarian who had coached Paraguay at the 1992 Olympics, was a popular boss Nevertheless, halfway through qualification, Markarian had quit following criticism of a 2-1 defeat by Ecuador, but there was such a clamour from fans and players alike that he retracted his resignation a week later. Markarian's popularity did not extend, however, to the Paraguayan FA and media and after Paraguay had qualified, the team perhaps understandably, took their collective feet off the pedal, suffering defeats by Venezuela (1-3) and Colombia (0-4) in their last two games And that was considered sufficien cause to dismiss Markarian.

Ex-Italy boss Cesare Maldini has been appointed his successor. It wil be interesting to see how they get on with the new man who has little time to impose his ideas on a squad with whom he does not share a common language. Under Markarian, Paraguay played to a 4-4-2 system, the formation Maldini favours and which he used to such great effect with Italy at France 98. Retaining it may well be the key to Paraguay's impact on this year's Finals. Four years ago Paraguay reached the second round where they were knocked out by the World Cup's first-ever golden goal.

★ THE LOWDOWN

Population: 5.7 million

Capital: Asuncion

Leader: Luis Macchi

Life Expectancy: Male: 71 yrs Female: 76 yrs

>> 200 years ago sightseers were not welcome at the Palacio de Gobierno, the royal residence in Paraguay; during the reign of the military dictator Rodriguez de Francia anyone found staring at the building was shot on sight. Things are friendlier now; even a souvenir shop has been opened!

>> Paraguay is a land-locked country surrounded by Argentina, Bolivia and Brazil.

★ **ASSOCIATION:** Asociacion Paraguaya de Futbol
★ **JOINED FIFA:** 1921
★ **JOINED CONEMBOL:** 1921
★ **PLAYERS:** 140,000

★ **CLUBS:** 1,500
★ **WEBSITE:** none.
★ **HONOURS:** Copa America – 1953, 1979.

José Luis Chilavert, penalty taker, free kick specialist and part-time goalkeeper.

★ ROAD TO QUALIFICATION

Mar 00 **Peru** (a) > (l) 2-**0**

Apr 00 **Uruguay** (h) > (w) **1**-0 Ayala 17

Jun 00 **Ecuador** (h) > (w) 3-1
Toledo 11, Brizuela 43, 64

Jun 00 **Chile** (a) > (l) 3-**1** Cardozo 71

Jul 00 **Brazil** (h) > (w) 2-1
Paredes 6, Campos 83

Jul 00 **Bolivia** (a) > (d) 0-0

Aug 00 **Argentina** (a) > (d) 1-1 Acuna 61

Sep 00 **Venezuela** (h) > (w) 3-0
Gonzalez, G 30, Cardozo 35, Paredes 44

Oct 00 **Colombia** (a) > (w) 0-**2**
Santa Cruz 4, Chilavert 90

Nov 00 **Peru** (h) > (w) 5-1
Santa Cruz 15, Del Solar 25 og,
Cardozo 44, Paredes 65, Chilavert 84 pen

Mar 01 **Uruguay** (a) > (w) 0-**1**
Alvarenga 64

Apr 01 **Ecuador** (a) > (l) 2-**1** Cardozo 26

Jun 01 **Chile** (h) > (w) **1**-0 Paredes 90

Aug 01 **Brazil** (a) > (l) 2-**0**

Sep 01 **Bolivia** (h) > (w) 5-1
Paredes 33, Cardozo 45, 89, Chilavert 50,
Santa Cruz 69

Oct 01 **Argentina** (h) > (d) 2-2
Chilavert 51 pen, Morinigo 70

Nov 01 **Venezuela** (a) > (l) 3-**1** Arce 28 pen

Nov 01 **Colombia** (h) > (l) **0**-4

★ FINAL GROUP TABLE

Team	P	W	D	L	F	A	Pts
Argentina	18	13	4	1	42	15	43
Ecuador	18	9	4	5	23	20	31
Brazil	18	9	3	6	31	17	30
Paraguay	18	9	3	6	29	23	30
Uruguay	18	7	6	5	19	13	27
Colombia	18	7	6	5	20	15	27
Bolivia	18	4	6	8	21	33	18
Peru	18	4	4	10	14	25	16
Venezuela	18	5	1	12	18	44	16
Chile	18	3	3	12	15	27	12

★ RECENT RESULTS

Feb 02 **Bolivia** (h) > (d) 2-2
Cardozo 3, Struway 90

Mar 02 **Nigeria** (h) > (d) **1**-1 Gamarra 24

DID YOU KNOW?

Cesare Maldini is not the first Italian to take charge of Paraguay Vessilio Bartoli was given the job almost 50 years ago.

The Paraguay line-up could undergo radical change if new boss Cesare Maldini decides to switch from Paraguay's regular 4-4-2 to a 3-5-2; the formation he used with Italy during France 98. Assuming Maldini opts for no change at this late stage, the back four will consist of full backs Francisco Arce and Denis Canizaand Carlos Gamarra and Celso Ayala in the centre. If Maldini goes for 3-5-2 then Pedro Sarabia will join them. Roberto Acuna is the key player out on the right of midfield – Maldini might want to switch him inside with the tenacious Carlos Paredes in the middle alongside Victor Quintana. Guido Alvarenga provides the speed down the left (or probable wing-back role along with Arce, if the formation is changed). Hugo Brizuela and Roque Santa Cruz provide the little and large in attack. Free roaming goalkeeper José Luis Chilavert (and aspirant goalscorer) misses the first game with Ricardo Tavarelli his probable replacement.

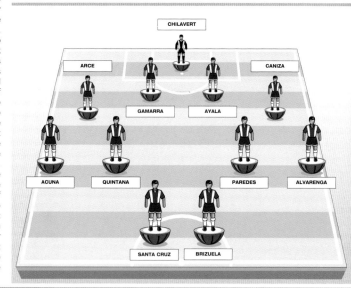

PROBABLE FORMATION 4-4-2

CHILAVERT

ARCE
CANIZA

GAMARRA
AYALA

ACUNA
QUINTANA
PAREDES
ALVARENGA

SANTA CRUZ
BRIZUELA

★ MEN THAT MATTER!

JOSÉ LUIS CHILAVERT

Age>> 36
Club>> Strasbourg
Suspended from the first match following a spitting incident in the qualifiers. Takes and saves penalties and free kicks and intends to become the first goalkeeper to score at a World Cup.

CARLOS PAREDES

Age>> 25
Club>> FC Porto
This versatile midfielder can be used as a man-marker or as a creative player. He has been an automatic choice for Paraguay ever since the last World Cup.

ROBERTO ACUNA

Age>> 30
Club>> Real Zaragoza
Paraguay's most capped international is a major creative influence and presence on the right side of midfield. Played at the last World Cup and missed just two games during qualifying.

★ PROBABLE SQUAD   ★ QUALIFICATION RECORD

NAME	POSITION	CLUB	APS/GOALS	GAMES	MINS	Y/C	R/C	GOALS
Aldo Bobadilla	Goalkeeper	Cerro Porteno, Paraguay	3/0	2	180	0	0	0
Jose Luis Chilavert	Goalkeeper	Strasbourg, France	67/8	14	1260	5	0	4
Ricardo Tavarelli	Goalkeeper	Olimpia, Paraguay	17/0	1	90	0	0	0
Francisco Arce	Defender	Palmeiras, Brazil	48/5	10	880	0	0	1
Celso Ayala	Defender	River Plate, Argentina	73/6	16	1431	2	1	1
Denis Caniza	Defender	Santos Laguna, Mexico	46/1	12	1080	2	0	0
Paula Da Siva	Defender	Venezia, Italy	3/0	3	252	0	0	0
Carlos Gamarra	Defender	AEK Athens, Greece	73/4	13	1100	0	0	0
Claudio Rodriguez	Defender	San Lorenzo, Argentina	4/0	4	288	1	0	0
Pedro Sarabia	Defender	River Plate, Argentina	39/0	8	720	0	0	0
Roberto Acuna	Midfielder	Real Zaragoza, Spain	76/5	15	1266	4	0	1
Guido Alvarenga	Midfielder	Leon, Mexico	15/2	7	441	1	0	1
Jorge Campos	Midfielder	Universidad Catilica, Chile	29/3	6	187	0	0	1
Julio Cesar Enciso	Midfielder	Olimpia, Paraguay	59/2	8	546	1	0	0
Diego Gavilan	Midfielder	Newcastle, England	17/0	5	254	2	0	0
Gustavo Morinigo	Midfielder	Libertad, Paraguay	8/1	3	146	2	0	1
Carlos Paredes	Midfielder	Porto, Portugal	38/6	14	1182	3	0	3
Victor Quintana	Midfielder	Olimpia, Paraguay	18/0	13	706	2	1	0
Estanislao Struway	Midfielder	Libertad, Paraguay	67/3	13	847	3	0	0
Miguel Benitez	Forward	Olimpia, Paraguay	29/11	5	73	1	0	0
Hugo Brizuela	Forward	Pachuca, Mexico	21/3	7	364	1	1	2
Jose Cardozo	Forward	Toluca, Mexico	55/15	15	1218	2	0	6
Roque Santa Cruz	Forward	Bayern Munich, Germany	21/7	12	904	1	0	3

KEY: APPS/GOALS = International Appearances/Goals; GAMES=Qualification Games played; MINS=Minutes played; Y/C= Yellow cards R/C=Red cards

HISTORY AT THE WORLD CUP

1930 1934 1938 1950 1954 1958 1962 1966 1970 1974 1978 1982 1986 1990 1994 1998

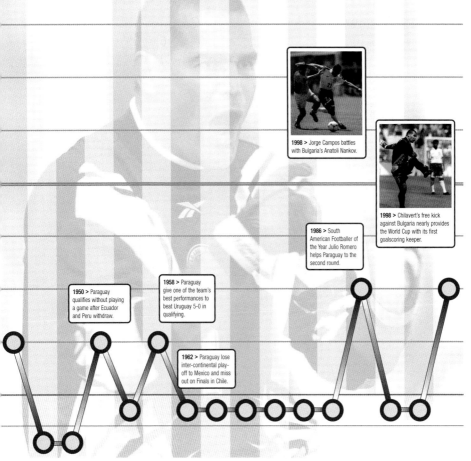

1998 > Jorge Campos battles with Bulgaria's Anatoli Nankov.

1998 > Chilavert's free kick against Bulgaria nearly provides the World Cup with its first goalscoring keeper.

1986 > South American Footballer of the Year Julio Romero helps Paraguay to the second round.

1950 > Paraguay qualifies without playing a game after Ecuador and Peru withdraw.

1958 > Paraguay give one of the team's best performances to beat Uruguay 5-0 in qualifying.

1962 > Paraguay lose inter-continental play-off to Mexico and miss out on Finals in Chile.

★ WORLD CUP HISTORY

1930 >> First Round	1970 >> Did Not Qualify
1934 >> Did Not Enter	1974 >> Did Not Qualify
1938 >> Did Not Enter	1978 >> Did Not Qualify
1950 >> First Round	1982 >> Did Not Qualify
1954 >> Did Not Qualify	1986 >> Second Round
1958 >> First Round	1990 >> Did Not Qualify
1962 >> Did Not Qualify	1994 >> Did Not Qualify
1966 >> Did Not Qualify	1998 >> Second Round

★ WORLD CUP RECORDS, STORIES AND WEIRDNESS

FIRST OWN GOAL >> Ramon Gonzales of Paraguay holds the honour of scoring the World Cup's first ever own goal – against the United States in 1930. The USA won 3-0.

GROUP D

OPPONENT	DATE	UK TIME	VENUE
South Korea	**4 June**	**12.30**	**Busan, Korea**
Portugal	**10 June**	**12.30**	**Jeonju, Korea**
USA	**14 June**	**12.30**	**Daejeon, Korea**

"back to form and a tournament dark horse"

POLAND

★ THE LOWDOWN

Population: 38.6 million

Capital: Warsaw

Leader: Leszek Miller

Life Expectancy: Male: 69 yrs
Female: 78 yrs

>> Poland is one of the world's largest producers of silver.

>> Despite a reputation as a country with pollution problems, Poland does have many unspoilt regions of natural beauty. It is home to the last surviving virgin forest of the European mainland, which is inhabited by the largest herd of European bison.

>> In 1989, after over 40 years of communist rule, the Trade Union leader Lech Walesa formed the first post-communist democratic government.

It's easy to forget that Poland were once one of the best sides in world football. By the end of the 1999-2000 season Poland had not won a single match of their eight internationals and had once again failed to qualify for a major tournament. Their new boss Jerzy Engel saw his team score just once in his first five games in charge and few, if any, gave the Poles a hope of reaching the 2002 World Cup Finals.

Then Nigerian-born striker Emmanuel Olisadebe took Polish Citizenship and set about transforming the national team – with a staggering 10 goals in his first 13 internationals. He scored on his debut in a friendly against Romania in Bucharest to earn a 1-1 draw, starting a run of 13 matches without a defeat; the longest unbeaten run by a Polish national side.

Engel's re-vitalised Poland has been built around a well-organised defence and a devastatingly effective counter-attacking game that exploits the pace and power of Olisadebe. The new Poland unveiled itself in Kiev against the Ukraine in front of a 55,000 crowd. Olisadebe gave Poland the lead twice in the 3rd and 33rd minute and midfielder Radoslaw Kaluzny put the result beyond doubt in the 57th. That 3-1 victory ended a 10-match run without a win.

Not that the Polish public thought much of it. Only 7,000 fans turned up for qualifier against the Belarus in which Kaluzny was outstanding, netting a hat-trick in another 3-1 win. A 0-0 draw at home to Wales saw Poland revert to type, but events in Oslo in March 2001 proved once and for all that Poland with Olisadebe was now an attacking, goal scoring side to compare with their illustrious forebears.

Olisadebe found the net twice in si minutes to give Poland a 2-0 lead b the 29th minute. Norway battled bac to level terms by the 66th minute an with just nine minutes to go substitut midfielder Bartosz Karwan scored th winner. Four days later Poland thrashe Armenia 4-0, sparking a rush for ticket (the game in Bydgoszcz was sold out i a day) for the friendly with Scotland month later.

Back on the qualification trail a Cardiff's Millennium Stadium, an Poland trail Wales after just 13 minutes In the past the Poles would have capitulated but now they come from behind – thanks to goals from Pawe Kryszalowicz and, inevitably, Olisadeb for a 2-1 win. A bad-tempered 1-draw in Armenia, which ends in a braw and the sending off of defender Jacek Bak, earns another point, which mean a win at home to Norway would b enough for qualification.

Poland were in the in form team having now gone 12 matches withou defeat – a performance that'd not bee seen since the mid-seventies during the golden age of Polish soccer whe they were semi-finalists at successive World Cups. Poland earned a deserve 3-0 win with goals from Kryszalowicz Olisadebe and Marcin Zewlakow an magnificent goalkeeping performance by Jerzy Dudek.

Poland are back and will be one o the World Cup's dark horses. Coach Jerzy Engel has a settled pool of 25 players of roughly equal ability including goalkeeper Dudek, who at £4.9 millior became Poland's most expensive player ever when he joined Liverpool.

★ **ASSOCIATION:** Polski Zwiazek Pilki Noznej
★ **JOINED FIFA:** 1923
★ **JOINED UEFA:** 1954
★ **PLAYERS:** 317,500

★ **CLUBS:** 5,881
★ **WEBSITE:** www.pzpn.pl
★ **HONOURS:** Olympics – 1972.

Bartosz Karwan and France's Emmanuel Petit.

★ ROAD TO QUALIFICATION

Sep 00 **Ukraine** (a) > (w) **1-3**
Olizadebe 3, Nowak 33, Kaluzny 55

Oct 00 **Belarus** (h) > (w) **3-1**
Kaluzny 25, 62, 73

Oct 00 **Wales** (h) > (d) **0-0**

Mar 01 **Norway** (a) > (w) **2-3**
Olizadebe 23, 30, Karwan 81

Mar 01 **Armenia** (h) > (w) **4-0**
Zewlakow, Mi 15 pen, 81, Olizadebe 41, Karwan 88

Jun 01 **Wales** (a) > (w) **1-2**
Olizadebe 32, Kryszalowicz 72

Jun 01 **Armenia** (a) > (d) **1-1** Kaluzny 5

Sep 01 **Norway** (h) > (w) **3-0**
Kryszalowicz 45, Olizadebe 77, Zewlakow, Ma 87

Sep 01 **Belarus** (a) > (l) **4-1**
Zewlakow, Ma 78

Oct 01 **Ukraine** (h) > (d) **1-1** Olizadebe 40

★ FINAL GROUP TABLE

Team	P	W	D	L	F	A	Pts
Poland	10	6	3	1	21	11	21
Ukraine	10	4	5	1	13	8	17
Belarus	10	4	3	3	12	11	15
Norway	10	2	4	4	12	14	10
Wales	10	1	6	3	10	12	9
Armenia	10	0	5	5	7	19	5

★ RECENT RESULTS

Feb 02 **Northern Ireland** (h) > (w) **4-1**
Kryszalowicz 6, 64, Kaluzny 12, Zewlakow, Mi 69

Mar 02 **Japan** (h) > (l) **0-2**

GROUP D

DID YOU KNOW?

Wladyslaw Zmuda made 22 appearances over four World Cups ⊁ 1974, 1978, 1982 and 1986.

Poland play an attack-minded 4-4-2 system that always looks to release the pace-blessed goalscoring machine Emmanuel Olisadebe. Poland know that given just half a chance, this super-quick and skilful striker will score. Add Olisadebe's partner, the equally quick Pawel Kryszalowicz, and opponents find that they're often hit before they know it. Piotr Swierczewski is the team's experienced midfield playmaker who looks to exploit the pace in attack and on the wings through Bartosz Karwan on the right and Marek Kozminski on the left. Radoslaw Kaluzny anchors the midfield but will show his goalscoring abilities from free kicks and corners. The two Tomaszs, Hajto and Waldoch, are the uncompromising centre backs with Tomasz Klos and the excellent Michal Zewlakow at full back. And once past them, there's Liverpool's Jerzy Dudek in goal.

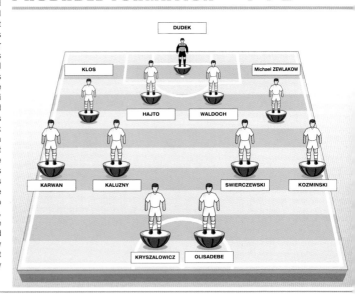

PROBABLE FORMATION 4-4-2

DUDEK
KLOS
Michael ZEWLAKOW
HAJTO
WALDOCH
KARWAN
KALUZNY
SWIERCZEWSKI
KOZMINSKI
KRYSZALOWICZ
OLISADEBE

★ MEN THAT MATTER!

EMMANUAL OLISADEBE

Age>> 23

Club>> Panathiniakos

Nigerian-born striker regarded as one of the most talented players in the world. Boasts an enviable international strike rate — his first 13 games reaped 10 goals including eight in the qualifiers.

JERZY DUDEK

Age>> 29

Club>> Liverpool

Poland's most expensive player, and goalkeeper, after Liverpool signed him from Feyenoord for £4.9 million. Magnificent during qualifying particularly against Norway where Poland clinched their place in the Finals.

MICHAEL ZEWLAKOW

Age>> 26

Club>> Mouscron

A gifted attack-minded left back who was the only Polish player ever-present during qualifiers. He is also a formidable free-kick specialist adding to Poland's thriving array of attacking options.

★ PROBABLE SQUAD   ★ QUALIFICATION RECORD

NAME	POSITION	CLUB	APS/GOALS	GAMES	MINS	Y/C	R/C	GOALS
Jerzy Dudek	Goalkeeper	Liverpool, England	19/0	10	835	0	0	0
Radoslaw Majdan	Goalkeeper	Goztepe, Turkey	2/0	0	0	0	0	0
Adam Matysek	Goalkeeper	Zaglebie, Poland	33/0	1	65	0	0	0
Jacek Bak	Defender	Lens, France	33/1	4	194	0	0	0
Tomasz Hajto	Defender	Schalke, Germany	41/5	7	546	2	0	0
Tomasz Klos	Defender	Kaiserslautern, Germany	34/1	9	804	1	0	0
Mariusz Kukielka	Defender	Amica Wronki, Poland	8/0	1	90	0	0	0
Tomasz Waldoch	Defender	Schalke, Germany	68/2	6	540	0	0	0
Michal Zewlakow	Defender	Mouscron, Belgium	21/1	10	888	0	0	2
Jacek Zielinski	Defender	Legia Warsaw, Poland	48/1	5	450	0	0	0
Arkadiusz Bak	Midfielder	Birmingham, England	8/0	4	360	1	0	0
Tomasz Iwan	Midfielder	Austria Wien, Austria	37/4	5	327	1	0	0
Jacek Krynowek	Midfielder	Nurnberg, Germany	15/2	5	182	1	0	0
Radoslaw Kaluzny	Midfielder	Energie Cottbus, Germany	26/9	7	578	3	0	5
Bartosz Karwan	Midfielder	Legia Warsaw, Poland	15/3	7	467	0	0	2
Marek Kozminski	Midfielder	Brescia, Italy	38/1	8	632	1	0	0
Jacek Krzynowek	Midfielder	Nurnberg, Germany	19/1	4	150	0	0	0
Piotr Swierczewski	Midfielder	Marseille, France	62/1	9	795	2	0	0
Tomasz Zdebel	Midfielder	Genclerbirligi, Turkey	9/0	3	71	1	0	0
Pawel Kryszalowicz	Forward	Eintracht Frankfurt, Germany	19/3	8	507	1	0	2
Emmanuel Olisadebe	Forward	Panathiaikos, Greece	13/10	9	707	0	0	7
Radoslav Gilewicz	Forward	Tirol Innsbruck, Austria	9/0	3	106	0	0	0
Maciej Zurawski	Forward	Wisla Krakow, Poland	7/0	0	0	0	0	0

KEY: APPS/GOALS = International Appearances/Goals; GAMES=Qualification Games played; MINS=Minutes played; Y/C= Yellow cards R/C=Red cards

HISTORY AT THE WORLD CUP

1930 1934 1938 1950 1954 1958 1962 1966 1970 1974 1978 1982 1986 1990 1994 1998

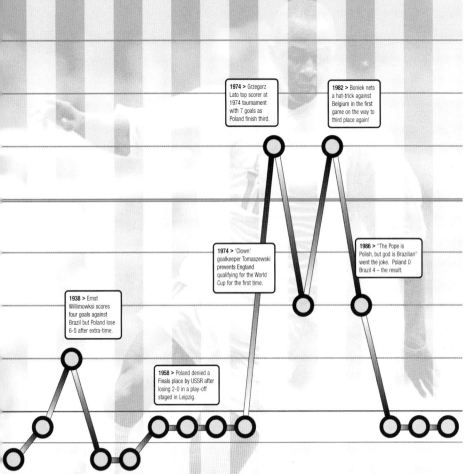

1974 > Grzegorz Lato top scorer at 1974 tournament with 7 goals as Poland finish third.

1982 > Boniek nets a hat-trick against Belgium in the first game on the way to third place again!

1974 > 'Clown' goalkeeper Tomaszewski prevents England qualifying for the World Cup for the first time.

1986 > "The Pope is Polish, but god is Brazilian" went the joke. Poland 0 Brazil 4 – the result.

1938 > Ernst Willimowksi scores four goals against Brazil but Poland lose 6-5 after extra-time.

1958 > Poland denied a Finals place by USSR after losing 2-0 in a play-off staged in Leipzig.

★ WORLD CUP HISTORY

1930 >> Did Not Enter	1970 >> Did Not Qualify
1934 >> Did Not Qualify	1974 >> Third Place
1938 >> First Round	1978 >> Second Round
1950 >> Did Not Enter	1982 >> Third Place
1954 >> Did Not Enter	1986 >> Second Round
1958 >> Did Not Qualify	1990 >> Did Not Qualify
1962 >> Did Not Qualify	1994 >> Did Not Qualify
1966 >> Did Not Qualify	1998 >> Did Not Qualify

★ WORLD CUP RECORDS, STORIES AND WEIRDNESS

MOST APPEARANCES IN FINALS >> Grzegorz Lato with 20 appearances is 4th on the all-time list.

MOST GOALS >> Along with Deyna and Szarmach, Grzegorz Lato was one of the stars of the Polish side which took third place in the 1974 World Cup. Lato scored 7 times in the 1974 finals and totalled 10 in all his World Cup appearances.

MOST GOALS IN A MATCH >> Ernst Willimowski with 4 against Brazil in 1938.

OPPONENT	DATE	UK TIME	VENUE
USA	**5 June**	**10.00**	**Suwon, Korea**
Poland	**10 June**	**12.30**	**Jeonju, Korea**
South Korea	**14 June**	**12.30**	**Incheon, Korea**

"flair wrapped in an enigma"

PORTUGAL

Portugal are an enigmatic side blessed with one of the world's most talented and expensive midfield partnerships. European Footballer of the Year and highly influential Luis Figo, Portugal's most capped player with 80 appearances, is worth a staggering £37.5 million to Real Madrid and his partner Rui Costa is a £28 million Serie A midfielder with AC Milan. Both players performed gloriously at Euro 2000 as the creative engine of Portugal's free flowing, exciting side.

At Euro 2000 Portugal reached the semi-finals playing some fantastic football, most notably against Kevin Keegan's England. The Portuguese came from 2-0 down to win 3-2 in their opening game, beat Romania with an injury-time winner from Francisco Da Costa and outclassed Germany with a Sergio Conceicao hat-trick before defeating Turkey 2-0 in the quarter-finals.

Their thrilling run came to an end at the semi-final stage when they were knocked out by a golden goal, France's Zinedane Zidane converting from the penalty spot after Abel Xavier was adjudged, by the linesman, to have handled Sylvain Wiltord 's shot. While France celebrated, Portugal's too vigorous protests led to the dismissal of Nuno Gomes and later suspensions for Abel Xavier.

More controversy was to follow when Portuguese defender Fernando Couto tested positive for banned substance nandrolone while playing with Lazio. He received a worldwide 10-month ban (later reduced to four months).

Back on the field Portugal continued to play their entertaining brand of football, winning their World Cup qualifying group and seeing to the elimination of Holland in the process. The Portuguese took four points off the Dutch, winning in Eindhoven with two goals from Sergio Conceicao and Pauleta. In the return fixture, the Dutch looked to have taken their revenge establishing a two-goal lead. But a late goal from Pauleta and a last minute penalty from Figo forced the draw.

Against the Republic of Ireland Portugal drew 1-1 both home and away. Their main rivals dealt with, Portugal were left with an easy last few qualification furlongs and in flew the goals; against Cyprus 6-0, Moldova 3-0 (a Figo hat trick), Andorra 7-1 (Nuno Gomes 4 goals), Cyprus again 3-1 and Estonia 5-0. They deservedly topped the group.

Portugal have only ever been occasional World Cup participants. In 1966, the Eusebio-inspired team reached the semi-finals, losing to England at Wembley. In the heat of Mexico in 1986, defeats by Poland and Morocco, after they'd beaten England led to a first round exit. The Portuguese have certainly got better since then and have added strength and resilience (in players like Nuno Frechaut, Jorge Costa and Petit) to their undoubtedly skilful game. Now they are much less likely to be pushed aside.

On their day, as they have shown frequently over the past two years, Portugal can be flair personified and just about impossible to deal with. An unpredictable World Cup dark horse that could surprise us all.

★ THE LOWDOWN

Population: 10 million

Capital: Lisbon

Leader: Antonio Gutteres

Life Expectancy: Male: 72 yrs Female: 79 yrs

>> Portugal is one of the oldest European nations and Portuguese is the most commonly spoken language in South America.

>> At over 1000 metres, Guarda in central Portugal is claimed by its inhabitants to be the highest city in Europe.

>> Bobby Robson, the former England and current Newcastle United Manager, has managed Portugal's two biggest football clubs – F C Porto and Sporting Lisbon.

* **ASSOCIATION:** Federacao Portuguese de Futebol
* **JOINED FIFA:** 1928
* **JOINED UEFA:** 1954
* **PLAYERS:** 79,300

* **CLUBS:** 204
* **WEBSITE:** www.fpf.pt
* **HONOURS:** None

Luis Figo – the world's best player.

★ ROAD TO QUALIFICATION

Sep 00 **Estonia** (a) > (w) **1-3**
Rui Costa 15, Figo 49, Sa Pinto 56

Oct 00 **Rep of Ireland** (h) > (d) **1-1**
Conceicao 57

Oct 00 **Holland** (a) > (w) **0-2**
Conceicao 10, Pauleta 44

Feb 01 **Andorra** (h) > (w) **3-0**
Figo 1, 49, Pauleta 35

Mar 01 **Holland** (h) > (d) **2-2**
Pauleta 85, Figo 90 pen

Jun 01 **Rep of Ireland** (a) > (d) **1-1** Figo 79

Jun 01 **Cyprus** (h) > (w) **6-0**
Pauleta 36, 71, Barbosa 55, 59,
Pinto 76, 81

Sep 01 **Andorra** (a) > (w) **1-7**
Nuno Gomes 36, 40, 45, 90, Pauleta 39,
Rui Jorge 45, Conceicao 58

Sep 01 **Cyprus** (a) > (w) **1-3**
Nuno Gomes 47, Pauleta 64, Conceicao 71

Oct 01 **Estonia** (h) > (w) **5-0**
Pinto 29, Nuno Gomes 49, 65, Pauleta 59,
Figo 79

★ FINAL GROUP TABLE

Team	P	W	D	L	F	A	Pts
Portugal	10	7	3	0	33	7	24
Rep of Ireland	10	7	3	0	23	5	24
Netherlands	10	6	2	2	30	9	20
Estonia	10	2	2	6	10	26	8
Cyprus	10	2	2	6	13	31	8
Andorra	10	0	0	10	5	36	0

★ RECENT RESULTS

Feb 02 **Spain** (a) > (d) **1-1** Costa 28

Mar 02 **Finland** (h) > (l) **1-4** Conceicao 40

DID YOU KNOW?

In Portugal's first World Cup they reached the semi-finals. They were due to play England at Goodison Park, where the Portuguese had been based, but the tie was switched to Wembley.

Impressively, Portugal scored 33 goals in ten qualifying games – amazing when you consider that the Portuguese play with only one recognised striker, Pauleta. But what Pauleta had in support would make any lone forward green with envy. A quality five-man midfield that can quickly get forward in numbers led by central play-maker Rui Costa of Milan. To Rui Costa's right is FIFA World Player of the Year Luis Figo. To his left is the pacy Nuno Capucho. Just hanging slightly back from that trio is the defensive midfield pairing of Beto and Petit, with the latter encouraged to join the attack whenever possible. The experienced defenders, Fernando Couto, Jorge Costa and Rui Jorge, are joined by new boy Frechaut to complete a back four. While Vitor Baia has been out injured, Ricardo has been first choice goalkeeper and could well retain his place.

PROBABLE FORMATION 4-4-2

RICARDO
FERNANDO COUTO — JORGE COSTA
FRECHAUT — RUI JORGE
FIGO — BETO — RUI COSTA — PETIT
NUNO CAPUCHO
PAULETA

★ MEN THAT MATTER!

LUIS FIGO
Age>> 29
Club>> R. Madrid
The FIFA World Player of the Year signed by Real Madrid for £37.5 million. He was outstanding for Portugal at Euro 2000 and throughout Portugal's qualifying group.

RUI COSTA
Age>> 29
Club>> AC Milan
Rui Costa is an attacking midfielder worth £28 million of Milan's money. His influence alongside Figo cannot be underestimated often producing an exciting and unexpected piece of play. An exquisite penalty taker too!

PAULETA
Age>> 29
Club>> Bordeaux
Pauleta was Portugal's top scorer during qualifying with eight goals. His agility, speed and accuracy finally earned his place in the starting line-up.

★ PROBABLE SQUAD | ★ QUALIFICATION RECORD

NAME	POSITION	CLUB	APS/GOALS	GAMES	MINS	Y/C	R/C	GOALS
Quim	Goalkeeper	Sp Braga, Portugal	12/0	5	450	1	0	0
Ricardo	Goalkeeper	Boavista, Portugal	7/0	5	450	0	0	0
Pereira	Goalkeeper	Boavista, Portugal	7/0	0	0	0	0	0
Beto	Defender	Sp Lisbon, Portugal	16/1	6	540	0	0	0
Fernando Couto	Defender	Lazio, Italy	80/6	6	496	1	0	0
Fernando Meira	Defender	Stuttgart, Germany	7/0	4	145	0	0	0
Nuno Frechaut	Defender	Boavista, Portugal	7/0	5	400	0	0	0
Manuel Dimas	Defender	Sp Lisbon, Portugal	44/0	2	178	1	0	0
Jorge Costa	Defender	Charlton, England	44/2	7	566	1	0	0
Rui Jorge	Defender	Sp Lisbon, Portugal	18/1	8	646	1	0	1
Nuno Capucho	Midfielder	Porto, Portugal	28/2	8	379	0	0	0
Luis Figo	Midfielder	Real Madrid, Spain	80/27	9	810	2	0	6
Paulo Bento	Midfielder	Porto, Portugal	30/0	3	100	0	0	0
Paulo Sousa	Midfielder	Panathinaikos, Greece	50/0	2	114	0	0	0
Petit	Midfielder	Boavista, Portugal	7/0	5	417	1	0	0
Rui Costa	Midfielder	Milan, Italy	67/20	8	717	0	0	1
Sergio Conceicao	Midfielder	Internazionale, Italy	39/9	6	508	0	0	4
Pedro Barbosa	Midfielder	Sp Lisbon, Portugal	20/5	2	143	0	0	2
Joao Pinto	Forward	Sp Lisbon, Portugal	74/23	8	455	0	0	3
Nuno Gomes	Forward	Fiorentina, Italy	27/13	6	280	0	0	7
Pauleta	Forward	Bordeaux, France	30/12	10	740	0	0	8
Ricardo Sa Pinto	Forward	Sp Lisbon, Portugal	45/10	4	188	0	0	1
Sabrosa Simao	Forward	Benfica, Portugal	11/1	6	182	0	0	0

KEY: APPS/GOALS = International Appearances/Goals; GAMES=Qualification Games played; MINS=Minutes played; Y/C= Yellow cards R/C=Red cards

HISTORY AT THE WORLD CUP

1930 1934 1938 1950 1954 1958 1962 1966 1970 1974 1978 1982 1986 1990 1994 1998

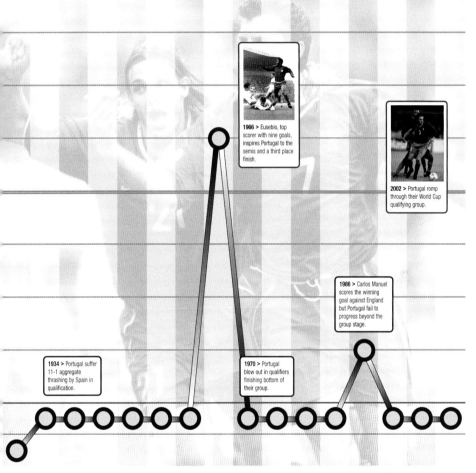

1966 > Eusebio, top scorer with nine goals, inspires Portugal to the semis and a third place finish.

2002 > Portugal romp through their World Cup qualifying group.

1986 > Carlos Manuel scores the winning goal against England but Portugal fail to progress beyond the group stage.

1934 > Portugal suffer 11-1 aggregate thrashing by Spain in qualification.

1970 > Portugal blow out in qualifiers finishing bottom of their group.

★ WORLD CUP HISTORY

1930 >> Did Not Enter		**1970** >> Did Not Qualify	
1934 >> Did Not Qualify		**1974** >> Did Not Qualify	
1938 >> Did Not Qualify		**1978** >> Did Not Qualify	
1950 >> Did Not Qualify		**1982** >> Did Not Qualify	
1954 >> Did Not Qualify		**1986** >> First Round	
1958 >> Did Not Qualify		**1990** >> Did Not Qualify	
1962 >> Did Not Qualify		**1994** >> Did Not Qualify	
1966 >> Third Place		**1998** >> Did Not Qualify	

★ WORLD CUP RECORDS, STORIES AND WEIRDNESS

MOST GOALS >> Eusebio won the first of his 64 caps in 1961, but will be best remembered for his contribution to the 1966 World Cup. "The Black Pearl" was quite brilliant, scoring some outstanding goals. Nine goals made him the tournament's top scorer and he managed to net four in Portugal's remarkable fight-back against North Korea

"old bears hope for a quarter-final place"

RUSSIA

The Russian national side is an ageing team. The fragmentation of the Soviet Union in the early 90s meant Russia having to create a new side without a host of players from the former Soviet Republics and since that time Russia's national side has largely remained the same. Players such as Valeri Karpin, Alexander Mostovoi, Victor Onopko, Dmitri Khlestov, Vladimir Beschastnykh and Omari Tetradze were wearing the Russian shirt in 1992 and are still.

As younger players they qualified for both World Cup 94 and Euro 96, although failing to progress beyond the group stage of either tournament. But it must be said that as the squad has got older their threat has lessened and Russia failed to qualify for either France 98 or Euro 2000.

Euro 96 coach Oleg Romantsev was recalled to manage the Russian side (he retains his day job as coach of the country's dominant club, Spartak Moscow) and immediately expressed a wish to return to the old Soviet-style system of a national side based around one club – Spartak Moscow. But things aren't what they were and even the Russian League has seen an influx of foreign players – as has Spartak themselves. So, as it is all over Europe, young home-grown talent has been hard to find.

Romantsev has been forced to abandon the 'Spartak as Russia' plan, but continues a policy of selecting predominantly Russian-based players, which has led to a Russian squad mainly selected from the Russian League with many players such as Beschastnykh, Sergei Ovchinnikov, Alexander Panov and Tetradze returning home. About a quarter of the potential squad still play abroad, mostly in Spain, but all are playing regularly for their clubs.

Much needed new blood has managed to squeeze its way into the side, notably midfielders Rolan Gusev (aged 24) and Marat Izmailov (aged 19) resulting in a switch from a short passing game to a set up that encourages wing play and long passing, although this has not been an overwhelmingly successful ploy – yet.

Russia won their qualifying group grinding out results against modest and downright weak opposition. At home they scored but a single goal against the mighty Faroe Islands and it needed a first international goal from Sergei Semak late in the game to beat Luxembourg 2-1.To Russia's credit they did take four points off a very disappointing Yugoslavia side and did the double over Switzerland. They had needed just a point to qualify in their final game at home to the Swiss with their best performance of the competition ran out 4-0 winners – Beschastnykh scoring a hat trick with Yegor Titov netting the fourth.

Russia has set the target of reaching at least the quarter-finals in Japan/Korea, but with a defence lacking pace and over reliance on goalkeeper Ruslan Nigmatullin – who does not yet bear comparison with the most successful Russian footballer of all time, Lev Yashin – that may be over ambitious. They're a team that tries to make the best of what it has got but lacks the all round strengths that tougher, more skilful teams will bring to the tournament.

★ **ASSOCIATION:** Football Union of Russia
★ **JOINED FIFA:** 1992
★ **JOINED UEFA:** 1992
★ **PLAYERS:** 785,000

★ **CLUBS:** 43,700
★ **WEBSITE:** www.rfs.ru
★ **HONOURS:** Olympics* – 1956,1988.
European Championships* – 1960
*As USSR

Rising midfield star Marat Izmailov in full flight.

★ ROAD TO QUALIFICATION

Sep 00 **Switzerland** (a) > (w) 0-**1**
Beschastnykh 74

Oct 00 **Luxembourg** (h) > (w) **3**-0
Buznikin 20, Khokhlov 58, Titov 90

Mar 01 **Slovenia** (h) > (d) **1**-1 Khlestov 8

Mar 01 **Faroe Islands** (h) > (w) **1**-0
Mostovoi 20

Apr 01 **Yugoslavia** (a) > (w) 0-**1**
Beschastnykh 72

Jun 01 **Yugoslavia** (h) > (d) **1**-1 Kovtun 25

Jun 01 **Luxembourg** (a) > (w) 1-**2**
Alenitchev 16, Semak 76

Sep 01 **Slovenia** (a) > (l) 2-**1** Titov 72

Sep 01 **Faroe Islands** (a) > (w) 0-**3**
Beschastnykh 19, 30, Shirko 88

Oct 01 **Switzerland** (h) > (w) **4**-0
Beschastnykh 14 pen, 19, 39, Titov 82

★ FINAL GROUP TABLE

Team	P	W	D	L	F	A	Pts
Russia	**10**	**7**	**2**	**1**	**18**	**5**	**23**
Slovenia	10	5	5	0	17	9	20
Yugoslavia	10	5	4	1	22	8	19
Switzerland	10	4	2	4	18	12	14
Faroe Islands	10	2	1	7	6	23	7
Luxembourg	10	0	0	10	4	28	0

★ RECENT RESULTS

Feb 02 **Rep of Ireland** (a) > (l) 2-0

Mar 02 **Estonia** (a) > (l) 2-**1**
Beschastnykh 18

DID YOU KNOW?

World Cup squads have featured brothers on more than one occasion, but Victor and Vyacheslav Chanov share a unique place in football history. Both were selected for the 1982 Soviet Union squad — as goalkeepers!

Russia's 4-4-2 formation boasts an excellent last line of defence in goalkeeper Ruslan Nigmatullin and an outstanding front line led by striker Vladimir Beschastnykh, who will be partnered by the experienced Alexander Mostovoi. In midfield Russia have two brilliant playmakers in Yegor Titov and rising star Marat Izmailov. It's questionable whether they can or will play together, in which case Dmitri Khoklov is the likely choice. Khoklov can also play in the striker role where he would take Mostovoi's place. While Valeri Karpin is an automatic choice on the right of midfield, the left is problematic. CSKA's Rolan Gusev or Porto's Dmitri Alenichev are the likely candidates. Behind them is Yuri Kovtun at left back. Yuri Drozdov man-marks with more subtlety than Kovtun on the right. In the centre of defence Victor Onopko, Russia's old war-horse, is joined by Igor Chugainov. Yuri Nikiforov, a former forward, is an alternative in the middle of the back four.

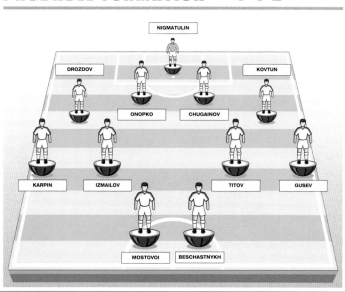

PROBABLE FORMATION   4-4-2

NIGMATULIN

DROZDOV • KOVTUN

ONOPKO • CHUGAINOV

KARPIN • IZMAILOV • TITOV • GUSEV

MOSTOVOI • BESCHASTNYKH

★ MEN THAT MATTER!

RUSLAN NIGMATULLIN

Age>> 27
Club>> Verona
The 2001 Russian Player of the Year who has the reputation as one of the best goalkeepers around after his outstanding performances during qualifying conceding only five goals in ten games.

VLADIMIR BESCHASTNYKH

Age>> 28
Club>> Moscow Spartak
Beschastnykh is Russia's main striker with seven goals in qualifying. At 18 years, four months and 16 days he was the youngest Russian player ever to make his debut in August 1992 against Mexico.

MARAT IZMAILOV

Age>> 19
Club>> Lokomotiv Moscow
Izmailov is Russia's teenage sensation who blazed on to the scene at the back end of last year. He can play in attack or as a playmaker. Wanted by both Under-21 and Senior Russian sides.

★ PROBABLE SQUAD   ★ QUALIFICATION RECORD

NAME	POSITION	CLUB	APS/GOALS	GAMES	MINS	Y/C	R/C	GOALS
Alexander Filimonov	Goalkeeper	Kyiv Dynamo, Ukraine	15\0	0	0	0	0	0
Ruslan Nigmatullin	Goalkeeper	Verona, Italy	15\0	10	900	0	0	0
Sergei Goncharov	Goalkeeper	Moscow Spartak, Russia	0\0	0	0	0	0	0
Alexei Smertin	Defender	Bordeaux, France	23\0	6	454	0	0	0
Igor Chugainov	Defender	Uralan Elista, Russia	24\0	1	90	0	0	0
Omari Tetradze	Defender	Alaniya Vladikavkaz, Russia	36\1	4	270	0	0	0
Victor Onopko	Defender	Oviedo, Spain	90\6	10	900	1	0	0
Vyacheslav Dayev	Defender	CSKA Moscow, Russia	3\0	2	155	1	0	0
Yuri Drozdov	Defender	Lokomotiv Moscow, Russia	10\0	5	295	3	0	0
Yuri Kovtun	Defender	Moscow Spartak, Russia	42\2	8	720	1	0	0
Yuri Nikiforov	Defender	PSV Eindhoven, Holland	48\6	4	360	1	0	0
Alexander Mostovoi	Midfielder	Celta Vigo, Spain	41\9	7	630	4	0	1
Dmitri Alenichev	Midfielder	Porto, Portugal	41\6	8	561	1	0	1
Dmitri Khokhlov	Midfielder	Real Sociedad, Spain	35\3	10	718	0	0	0
Marat Izmailov	Midfielder	Lokomotiv Moscow, Russia	4\0	3	224	1	0	0
Andrei Karyaka	Midfielder	Kryliya Sovetov, Russia	3\0	1	7	0	0	0
Rolan Gusev	Midfielder	CSKA Moscow, Russia	10\0	5	324	0	0	0
Sergei Semak	Midfielder	CSKA Moscow, Russia	29\1	7	153	1	0	1
Valeri Karpin	Midfielder	Celta Vigo, Spain	65\16	8	720	2	0	0
Yegor Titov	Midfielder	Moscow Spartak, Russia	30\4	10	856	0	0	3
Maxim Buznikin	Forward	Lokomotiv Moscow, Russia	8\5	4	268	0	0	1
Vladimir Beschastnykh	Forward	Moscow Spartak, Russia	61\23	10	640	0	0	7
Alexander Panov	Forward	Dinamo Moscow, Russia	16\4	1	42	0	0	0

KEY: APPS/GOALS = International Appearances/Goals; GAMES=Qualification Games played; MINS=Minutes played; Y/C= Yellow cards R/C=Red cards

HISTORY AT THE WORLD CUP

1930 1934 1938 1950 1954 1958 1962 1966 1970 1974 1978 1982 1986 1990 1994 1998

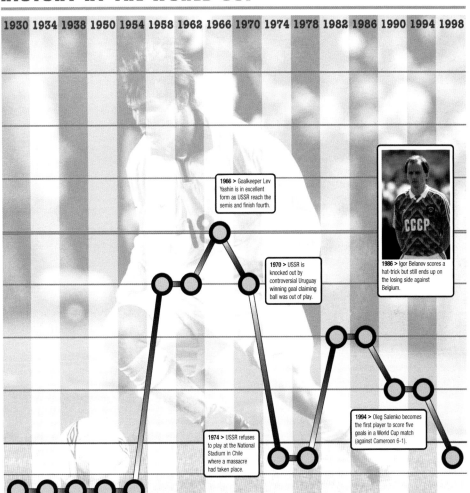

1966 > Goalkeeper Lev Yashin is in excellent form as USSR reach the semis and finish fourth.

1970 > USSR is knocked out by controversial Uruguay winning goal claiming ball was out of play.

1986 > Igor Belanov scores a hat-trick but still ends up on the losing side against Belgium.

1974 > USSR refuses to play at the National Stadium in Chile where a massacre had taken place.

1994 > Oleg Salenko becomes the first player to score five goals in a World Cup match (against Cameroon 6-1).

★ WORLD CUP HISTORY

1930 >> Did Not Enter	1970 >> Quarter-Finals
1934 >> Did Not Enter	1974 >> Did Not Qualify
1938 >> Did Not Enter	1978 >> Did Not Qualify
1950 >> Did Not Enter	1982 >> Second Round
1954 >> Did Not Enter	1986 >> Second Round
1958 >> Quarter-Finals	1990 >> First Round
1962 >> Quarter-Finals	1994 >> First Round
1966 >> Fourth Place	1998 >> Did Not Qualify *1930-1990 as Soviet Union

★ WORLD CUP RECORDS, STORIES AND WEIRDNESS

MOST GOALS IN A TOURNAMENT >> Centre-forward Oleg Salenko took his tally to 6 at USA '94, scoring 5 against the hapless Cameroons. Salenk would not have been playing in the Cameroon game at all if his compatriot Yuran had not squabbled with Russian manager, Sadyrin.

OPPONENT	DATE	UK TIME	VENUE
Germany	**1 June**	**12.30**	**Sapporo, Korea**
Cameroon	**6 June**	**10.00**	**Saitama, Japan**
Ireland	**11 June**	**12.30**	**Yokohama, Japan**

"Pride of the Gulf"

SAUDI ARABIA

★ THE LOWDOWN

Population: 22.7 million

Capital: Riyadh

Leader: King Fahd bin Abd al-Aziz Al Saud

Life Expectancy: Male: 66 yrs Female: 69 yrs

>> Money from petrol sales makes up 75% of the Saudi budget revenue. It has the world's largest oil reserves — a quarter of all known deposits.

>> The Monarch, which is hereditary, is both the Chief of State and Head of Government and there are no elections.

>> Saudi Arabia is the world's largest producer and user of desalinated water – seawater minus the salt – mmm nice!

Saudi Arabia deservedly qualified from Asian Group A for their third successive World Cup appearance. With five appearances in a row in the final of the Asian Cup since 1984, winning the title a record-equalling three times, Saudi Arabia have been the continent's best international side for the last 20 years. Best side in the Gulf they may be, but it was not until their last qualification game that the Saudis booked their place in the Finals – ahead of rivals Iran.

They started poorly with a home draw against Bahrain and a 2-0 defeat by the Iranians, results which led to the dismissal of head coach, Slobodan Santrac, and Nasser Al-Johar's re-appointment to the job. Al-Johar has been assured that after an unbeaten run in World Cup qualifying and winning the 2002 Gulf Cup he will be in charge at the World Cup Finals. Not a promise to be taken lightly. Since Eduardo Vingada guided the Saudis to the Asian Cup title in 1996, there have been no fewer than eight changes of head coach, with Otto Pfister and Nasser Al Johar both holding the position twice

From now on the Saudis would always be playing catch-up. With a play-off looking likely, the Saudis faced Thailand while Iran travelled to Bahrain. Luck was finally with the Saudis as they romped to a 4-1 win with goals from Abdullah Bin Shehan, Abdullah Al-Dosary, Sami Al-Jaber and Ibrahim Al-Haib. Meanwhile the Iranians experienced their first defeat – going down 3-1 to Bahrain. The Saudis leapfrogged over the Iranians in the table to qualify.

In an earlier group Saudi Arabia had demonstrated their unarguable superiority, scoring, in six games, 30 goals without reply. Talal Al-Meshal scored nine of those goals including hat-tricks against Bangladesh and Vietnam. Sami Al-Jaber, who will become the first Arab player to appear in three World Cups, also scored a hat-trick against Vietnam.

In their two previous World Cup appearances the Saudis were under foreign coaches. In 1994 it was Argentine Jorge Solari and in 1998, Brazilian Carlos Alberto Parreira. At USA 94 Saudi Arabia made an impressive debut beating Morocco 2-1, in the World Cup's first ever all-Arab clash, and Belgium 1-0, to progress to the second round, where they lost to in form Sweden. A Saudi fan was so impressed with his team's showing that he gave each squad member a Volvo. A generous but ultimately redundant gesture as the Saudi FA had already handed the entire squad a Mercedes each as a reward for qualifying.

At France 98, the Saudis managed just a point thanks to a 2-2 draw with South Africa in a group that included France and Denmark. "We was robbed" might be the timeless refrain of losing teams, but in the case of the Saudis it turned out to be the literal and annoying truth – as they discovered on return to their hotel which had been broken in to while they were busy playing their opening game against Denmark.

The Saudis find themselves in a tough group once again, featuring an improving Germany, a difficult Republic of Ireland side and the African Champions Cameroon. But if experience has its rewards then, with goalkeeper Mohammed Al-Deayea, defenders Mohammed Al Khlawi and Abdullah Zubromawi and forward Sami Al-Jaber all set to appear in their third World Cup Finals, we can expect to see the Pride of the Gulf competing with the best.

- ★ **ASSOCIATION:** Saudi Arabian Football Federation
- ★ **JOINED FIFA:** 1959
- ★ **JOINED AFC:** 1972
- ★ **PLAYERS:** 9,600
- ★ **CLUBS:** 120
- ★ **WEBSITE:** None.
- ★ **HONOURS:** Asian Championship – 1984, 1988, 1996.

Sami Al-Jaber gallops to his third World Cup Finals appearance.

★ ROAD TO QUALIFICATION

Feb 01 **Mongolia** (h) > (w) **6-0**
Al Shelhoub 10, 26, Al Dossary 22,
Sulimani 30, 59, Al Otabi 70

Feb 01 **Bangladesh** (a) > (w) 0-**3**
Al Meshal 30, 88, Al-Jaber 63

Feb 01 **Vietnam SR** (h) > (w) **5-0**
Al Meshal 18, 89, Al-Jaber 30, 60, 90

Feb 01 **Mongolia** (a) > (a) 0-**6**
Al-Jaber 20, Al Shelhoub 24, Al Meshal 24,
Al Dossary 40, 86, Al-Khilaiwi 76

Feb 01 **Bangladesh** (h) > (w) **6-0**
Harthi 5, Al Meshal 28, 29, 43, Al Dossary
32, 38

Feb 01 **Vietnam SR** (a) > (w) 0-**4**
Al Meshal 31, 71, 80, Al Dossary 89

Aug 01 **Bahrain** (h) > (d) **1-1** Al Dossary 83

Aug 01 **Iran** (h) > (l) 2-0

Aug 01 **Iraq** (h) > (w) **1-0** Al Dossary 45

Sep 01 **Thailand** (a) > (w) 1-**3**
Al-Jaber 47, Bin Shehan 63, Al Dossary 70

Sep 01 **Bahrain** (a) > (w) 0-**4**
Al Dossary 26, Bin Shehan 28,
Al Shahrani, A 39, Al-Jaber 88

Sep 01 **Iran** (h) > (d) **2-2**
Al-Shahrani, I 20, Al Yami 59

Oct 01 **Iraq** (a) > (w) 1-**2** Bin Shehan 1, 80

Oct 01 **Thailand** (h) > (w) **4-1**
Bin Shehan 41, Al Dosary, A 50,
Al-Jaber 67, Al Harbi 73

★ 2ND RND GROUP TABLE

Team	P	W	D	L	F	A	Pts
Saudi Arabia	8	5	2	1	17	8	17
Iran	8	4	3	1	10	7	15
Bahrain	8	2	4	2	8	9	10
Iraq	8	2	1	5	9	10	7
Thailand	8	0	4	4	5	15	4

★ 1ST RND GROUP TABLE

Team	P	W	D	L	F	A	Pts
Saudi Arabia	6	6	0	0	30	0	18
Vietnam SR	6	3	1	2	9	9	10
Bangladesh	6	1	2	3	5	15	5
Mongolia	6	0	1	5	2	22	1

★ RECENT RESULTS

Feb 02 **Brazil** (h) > (l) **0-1**

Feb 02 **Denmark** (h) > (l) **0-1**

Mar 02 **Uruguay** (h) > (w) **3-2**
Al Dossary 8, 18, Al Shahrani 17

DID YOU KNOW?

Saudi Arabia was the first team to sack their coach at France 98. Brazilian Carlos Alberto Parreira was fired following defeats by Denmark and France.

Saudi Arabia played to a 4-4-2 formation during France 98 and, while failing to win a single game, showed that with their pace they could, at times, outwit their opponents. In the interim, the Saudis have experimented with 3-5-2 line up – with some success – but coach Nasser Al-Johar is likely to stick with 4-4-2, opting for a more conservative strategy. Goalkeeper Mohammed Al-Deayea retains his place and has an experienced back four in front of him. However, it is a defence that is susceptible to set pieces. The return from injury of Nawaf Al-Temyat is a boost to a midfield that can be overrun, although it did hold its own against Romania and Brazil earlier this year. Sami Al-Jaber and Mohammed Al-Shlhoob will be looking to find the net when they can and not rely on penalties as the team did four years ago.

PROBABLE FORMATION 4-4-2

AL-DEAYEA

SULIMANI · AL-HARBI

AL-KHILAIWI · ZUBROMAWI

AL-GHAMDI · S AL-DOSARI · AL-TEMYAT · AL-MESHAL

AL-JABER · AL-SHLHOOB

★ MEN THAT MATTER!

SAMI AL-JABER

Age>> 29
Club>> Al Hilal

Sami Al-Jaber, who made his international debut in 1990, will be one of the first Arab Players to play in three World Cups. He scored a penalty against South Africa in 1998.

NAWAF AL-TEMYAT

Age>> 27
Club>> Al-Hilal

One of Saudi Arabia's most successful players who has won almost every domestic trophy. In 2000 he was voted Asia's Player of the Year. One of the national side's most influential players.

MOHAMMED AL-DEAYEA

Age>> 29
Club>> Al-Hilal

Al-Deayea is regarded as Asia's best goalkeeper who will be playing in his third World Cup Finals and looks set to establish the Saudi Arabian all-time appearance record.

★ PROBABLE SQUAD / ★ QUALIFICATION RECORD

NAME	POSITION	CLUB	APS/GOALS	GAMES	MINS	Y/C	R/C	GOALS
Tisir Al-Antaif	Goalkeeper	Al Ahli, Saudi Arabia	-	1	44	0	0	0
Mohammed Al-Deayea	Goalkeeper	Al Hilal, Saudi Arabia	-	8	592	0	0	0
Mohammed Babkr	Goalkeeper	Al Nassr, Saudi Arabia	-	7	624	2	0	0
Ahmed Dukhi Al-Dosari	Defender	Al Hilal, Saudi Arabia	-	12	1034	0	0	0
Ahmed Khalil Al-Dosari	Defender	Al Hilal, Saudi Arabia	-	7	546	0	0	0
Mohammed Al-Jahani	Defender	Al Ahli, Saudi Arabia	-	3	224	0	0	0
Mohammed Al-Khilaiwi	Defender	Al Ittihad, Saudi Arabia	-	12	659	1	0	1
Saleh Al-Saqri	Defender	Al Ittihad, Saudi Arabia	-	5	233	2	1	0
Hussain Sulimani	Defender	Al Ahli, Saudi Arabia	-	13	1133	1	0	2
Abdullah Zubromawi	Defender	Al Hilal, Saudi Arabia	-	11	896	0	0	0
Saad Al-Dosari	Midfielder	Al Ahli, Saudi Arabia	-	6	532	1	0	0
Omar Al-Ghamdi	Midfielder	Al Hilal, Saudi Arabia	-	9	551	1	0	0
Ibrahim Al-Harbi	Midfielder	Al Nassr, Saudi Arabia	-	11	679	0	0	1
Abdullah Al-Shahrani	Midfielder	Al Shabab, Saudi Arabia	-	4	320	0	0	0
Ibrahim Al-Shahrani	Midfielder	Al Ahli, Saudi Arabia	-	9	540	2	0	1
Mohammed Al-Shlhoob	Midfielder	Al Hilal, Saudi Arabia	-	6	471	0	0	3
Nawaf Al-Temyat	Midfielder	Al Hilal, Saudi Arabia	-	5	375	0	1	0
Mohammed Hawsawi	Midfielder	Al Ittihad, Saudi Arabia	-	9	646	3	0	0
Obaid Al-Dosari	Forward	Al Ahli, Saudi Arabia	-	12	950	0	0	10
Sami Al-Jaber	Forward	Al Hilal, Saudi Arabia	-	12	954	1	0	8
Talal Al-Meshal	Forward	Al Ahli, Saudi Arabia	-	6	457	0	0	11
Marzouk Al-Otaibi	Forward	Al Ittihad, Saudi Arabia	-	8	314	0	1	1
Al Hassan Al-Yami	Forward	Al Ittihad, Saudi Arabia	-	4	146	1	0	1

KEY: APPS/GOALS = International Appearances/Goals; GAMES=Qualification Games played; MINS=Minutes played; Y/C= Yellow cards R/C=Red cards

HISTORY AT THE WORLD CUP

1930 1934 1938 1950 1954 1958 1962 1966 1970 1974 1978 1982 1986 1990 1994 1998

1998 > Captain Youssef Al-Thyniyan accuses boss Carlos Alberto Parreira of 'cowardly tactics' as Saudis go out.

1994 > Saeed Owairan scores the goal of the tournament with the winner against Belgium.

★ WORLD CUP RECORDS, STORIES AND WEIRDNESS

COACHING RECORD >> Saudi Arabia have shared the services of Brazilian coach Carlos Alberto Parreira (1998) with three other countries – a World Cup coaching record Parreira shares with Yugoslavian Bora Milutinovic.

GROUP A

OPPONENT	DATE	UK TIME	VENUE
France	**31 May**	12.30	Seoul, Korea
Denmark	**6 June**	07.30	Daegu, Korea
Uruguay	**11 June**	07.30	Suwon, Korea

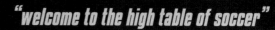

"welcome to the high table of soccer"

SENEGAL

★ THE LOWDOWN

Population: 10.2 million

Capital: Dakar

Leader: Madior Boye

Life Expectancy: Male: 61 yrs Female: 64 yrs

>> Senegal is the western most country on the African Continent.

>> Dances are not allowed during the farming season.

>> Yela is the name given to the music of women. Apparently it mimics the sound they make when pounding grain. It's said that this sound was the primary influence on the development of reggae in the Caribbean – thank goodness they weren't using a multi-chef!

Senegal's President Abdoulaye Wade cut short a state visit to Europe in order to bestow the prestigious National Order of the Lion upon the "Lions of Teranga" in recognition of the national side's qualification for their first ever World Cup Finals. Senegal's veteran German coach, Peter Schnittger, had laughed out loud when the qualifying draw was made as his side had been grouped with past African World Cup representatives Algeria, Egypt and Morocco along with Namibia. Arguably the toughest group in the continental qualifiers, it looked beyond Senegal's abilities. In fact after two drawn games, Schnittger stepped down to make way for French coach Bruno Metsu.

A third draw in Morocco, thanks to goalkeeper Tony Sylva, was followed by two impressive home wins. Lone striker El Hadji Ousseynou Diouf scored successive hat-tricks against Namibia (4-0) and Algeria (3-0). However, defeat by Egypt allowed Morocco to take a six-point lead. Senegal then faced Morocco, who needed just a single point to qualify from their final fixture, but sensationally, Senegal's Diouf scored the only goal of the game.

This result meant Morocco topped the table with 15 points. Senegal and Egypt were locked on 12 points, but the Egyptians had the superior goal difference. Egypt were to visit Algeria and Senegal travelled to Namibia. The task looked daunting; Senegal would have to win by a three-goal greater margin than Egypt to qualify.

By half-time Senegal led 3-0 thanks to goals from Pape Thiaw (2) and, inevitably, Diouf, his eighth of the qualifiers. It was goalless at the break between Algeria and Egypt. Then on the hour the Egyptians were awarded a controversial penalty, which they converted. In response the Algerian crowd began throwing missiles, forcing the Egyptians to quit the field, and delaying the game by 15 minutes. Meanwhile, back in Namibia, Senegal had increased their lead to 5-0. Then Algeria equalised, making the whole of Senegal desperate for the final whistle to blow in Annaba, hoping against hope that Egypt wouldn't find the net again. They didn't and Senegal were on their way to Japan/Korea.

Senegal's success owes as much to Peter Schnittger as it does to Bruno Metsu. Schnittger had been involved with African soccer since 1968 and in 1995 he began working on a development programme for Senegalese soccer and the national team. FA President Oumar Seck toured Europe searching for players to strengthen the squad – players like Khalilou Fadiga who was on the point of becoming a Belgian citizen when Seck stepped in.

The strategy which has so lifted Senegalese football involves picking a squad with players who turn out, almost exclusively, for European clubs, mostly French, and who are playing regular first team football. Metsu has also stuck with a consistent selection. He knows his best side and tinkers very rarely with the starting line-up. The results speak for themselves – earlier this year Senegal reached the African Nations Cup Final for the first time losing to Cameroon in a penalty shoot-out. It was Metsu's 19th match in charge and only his third defeat.

However, Senegal's experience is almost exclusively African, so we should welcome them to a place at soccer's high table, where they'll no doubt bring much charm and laughter, while it lasts.

★ **ASSOCIATION:** Federation Senegalaise de Football
★ **JOINED FIFA:** 1962
★ **JOINED CAF:** 1963
★ **PLAYERS:** 4,000

★ **CLUBS:** 75
★ **WEBSITE:** None.
★ **HONOURS:** None.

Henri Camara chasing World Cup glory.

★ ROAD TO QUALIFICATION

Apr 00 **Benin** (a) > (d) 1-**1** N'Diaye 15

Apr 00 **Benin** (h) > (w) **1**-0 Ba 63 (agg **2**-1)

Jun 00 **Algeria** (a) > (d) 1-**1** Diop 16

Jul 00 **Egypt** (h) > (d) **0-0**

Feb 01 **Morocco** (a) > (d) 0-**0**

Mar 01 **Namibia** (h) > (w) **4**-0
Diouf 24, 44, 52, Camara, H 64

Apr 01 **Algeria** (h) > (w) **3**-0
Diouf 2, 47, 75

May 01 **Egypt** (a) > (l) 1-**0**

Jul 01 **Morocco** (h) > (w) **1**-0 Diouf 17

Jul 01 **Namibia** (a) > (w) 0-**5**
Thiaw 15, 30, Diouf 23, Fadiga 79,
N'Diaye 81

★ FINAL GROUP TABLE

Team	P	W	D	L	F	A	Pts
Senegal	8	4	3	1	14	2	15
Morocco	8	4	3	1	8	3	15
Egypt	8	3	4	1	16	7	13
Algeria	8	2	2	4	11	14	8
Namibia	8	0	2	6	3	26	2

★ RECENT RESULTS

Mar 02 **Bolivia** (h) > (w) **2**-1
Diop 44, Niang 64

DID YOU KNOW?

Senegal's French coach Bruno Metsu has taken his commitment to his adopted home to a new level by marrying a Senegalese woman.

Senegal play a French style 4-4-2 formation, which is appropriate since nearly all the squad play in the French League. Senegal are a skilful passing side, capable of producing a tournament upset. In Monaco's Tony Sylva they've unearthed a decent goalkeeper. Captain Aliou Cisse of Montpellier plays as centre back alongside Rennes' Lamine Diatta with Sochaux's Omar Daf as right back – he can also play on the left – a position that should be occupied by Lens' Pape Sarr or Ferdinand Coly. In midfield Salif Alassane Diao and Pape Bouba Diop play in the centre with Makhtar N'Diaye of Rennes (or Moussa N'Diaye of Sedan) and Khalilou Fadiga, a strong source of creativity, providing the width. In attack is another Lens player El Hadji Diouf who has a real knack for getting goals with Henri Camara, who can also play in midfield, or Pape Thiaw as his partner up front.

PROBABLE FORMATION 4-4-2

SYLVA

DAF · COLY

DIATTA · A CISSE

Makhtar N'DIAYE · DIAO · PB DIOP · FADIGA

DIOUF · H CAMARA

★ MEN THAT MATTER!

EL HADJI DIOUF

Age>> 21
Club>> Lens
Averages a goal a game at international level, Diouf has shone on the international scene since his debut against Benin in April 2000. Scored successive hat-tricks against Algeria and Namibia.

KHALILOU FADIGA

Age>> 25
Club>> Auxerre
Born in Senegal, raised in France, a success in Belgium and almost became a Belgian international until snapped by the Senegalese FA. He can play as an attacking midfielder or a forward.

FERDINAND COLY

Age>> 28
Club>> Lens
Defender Coly has impressed over the past two years. He can play on either flank of defence or midfield and won plaudits for his performances in the 2002 African Nations Cup.

★ PROBABLE SQUAD ★ QUALIFICATION RECORD

NAME	POSITION	CLUB	APS/GOALS	GAMES	MINS	Y/C	R/C	GOALS
Oumar Diallo	Goalkeeper	Olympique Khourigba, Senegal	42/0	3	270	0	0	0
Samuel Monin	Goalkeeper	Raith, Scotland	1/0	0	0	0	0	0
Tony Sylva	Goalkeeper	Monaco, France	13/0	4	360	1	0	0
Habib Beye	Defender	Strasbourg, France	5/0	2	92	0	0	0
Aliou Cisse	Defender	Montpellier, France	18/0	6	484	3	0	0
Ferdinand Coly	Defender	Lens, France	14/0	5	450	2	0	0
Omar Daf	Defender	Sochaux, France	30/0	7	630	2	0	0
Lamine Diatta	Defender	Rennes, France	17/1	5	450	0	0	0
Pape Sarr	Defender	Lens, France	21/1	5	450	2	1	0
Salif Diao	Midfielder	Sedan, France	18/2	4	347	0	0	0
Pape Bouba Diop	Midfielder	Lens, France	10/2	1	13	0	0	0
Pape Malick Diop	Midfielder	Lorient, France	25/2	1	90	0	0	0
Khalilou Fadiga	Midfielder	Auxerre, France	23/2	6	520	0	0	1
Makhtar N'Diaye	Midfielder	Rennes, France	10/0	0	0	0	0	0
Sylvain N'Diaye	Midfielder	Lille, France	4/0	0	0	0	0	0
Alassane Ndour	Midfielder	Saint-Etienne, France	6/0	1	6	0	0	0
Henri Camara	Forward	Sedan, France	34/7	6	478	0	0	1
El Hadji Diouf	Forward	Lens, France	19/12	7	630	1	0	8
Moussa N'Diaye	Forward	Sedan, France	37/4	5	323	0	0	1
Pape Thiaw	Forward	Strasbourg, France	12/5	3	143	0	0	2
Amara Traore	Forward	Gueugnon, France	11/2	1	12	0	0	0
Ousmane Diop Papa	Forward	Xanthi, Greece	3/0	3	189	1	0	0
Souleymane Camara	Forward	Monaco, France	7/1	0	0	0	0	0

KEY: APPS/GOALS = International Appearances/Goals; GAMES=Qualification Games played; MINS=Minutes played; Y/C = Yellow cards R/C=Red cards

HISTORY AT THE WORLD CUP

1930 1934 1938 1950 1954 1958 1962 1966 1970 1974 1978 1982 1986 1990 1994 1998

1970 > Senegal lose an African first round play-off to Morocco staged in Las Palmas, Spain.

1974 > Senegal bow out to Morocco in the first round of African qualifying.

★ WORLD CUP HISTORY

1930 >> Did Not Enter	**1970** >> Did Not Qualify
1934 >> Did Not Enter	**1974** >> Did Not Qualify
1938 >> Did Not Enter	**1978** >> Did Not Qualify
1950 >> Did Not Enter	**1982** >> Did Not Qualify
1954 >> Did Not Enter	**1986** >> Did Not Qualify
1958 >> Did Not Enter	**1990** >> Did Not Enter
1962 >> Did Not Enter	**1994** >> Did Not Qualify
1966 >> Did Not Enter	**1998** >> Did Not Qualify

★ WORLD CUP RECORDS, STORIES AND WEIRDNESS

APPEARANCES IN THE COMPETITION >> Senegal currently occupy 100th position in the ranking of all countries that have played in the World Cup – qualifiers and finals. They've appeared in a total of 21 matches (including qualifiers), winning 5, drawing 5 and losing 11 with a –7 goal difference.

GROUP B

OPPONENT	DATE	UK TIME	VENUE
Spain	**2 June**	**12.30**	**Gwangju, Korea**
South Africa	**8 June**	**07.30**	**Daegu, Korea**
Paraguay	**12 June**	**12.30**	**Seogwipo, Korea**

"surprise qualifiers, worth watching on their day"

SLOVENIA

★ THE LOWDOWN

Population: 1.9 million

Capital: Ljubljana

Leader: Janez Drnovsek

Life Expectancy: Male: 71 yrs Female: 79 yrs

>> Slovenia succeeded in establishing its independence from Yugoslavia in 1991.

>> There are over 300 waterfalls in Slovenia, the highest is 130 metres! There are over 7000 caves in the country and the longest is 19 miles!

>> During the eighteenth century, Slovenes would paint pictures of Saints on their beehives; these are so rare now they've become collector's items.

P art of Yugoslavia until 1991, this small nation of two million souls has defied all the odds to reach their first World Cup Finals; but how exactly does a team that are held by the Faroe Islands to a 2-2 draw in their opening qualifying match and go on to win only one of their first five games manage to qualify at all?

Slovenia, the surprise qualifiers of Euro 2000, shocked the football world again by booking a place in Japan/Korea at the expense of Yugoslavia, Switzerland and Romania. From the start they were never expected to get through one of Europe's tightest groups and it certainly looked as if they were playing to the script when they threw away a two-goal lead with just two minutes to play against the part-time fishermen of the Faroe Islands.

Their first five games delivered just one win – a narrow 2-1 victory over Luxembourg – and four draws against Switzerland (coming from behind twice), Russia (an Aleksandr Knavs goal), Yugoslavia (injury time equaliser from Zlatko Zahovic) and the aforementioned opener against the Faroe Islands. Slovenia might have been undefeated up until now, but not even a second, predictable win over Luxembourg was going to make them contenders – was it?

A turning point of sorts came on the trip to Basle in early June 2001 with a 1-0 win over Switzerland. 26-year-old first-half substitute Sebastjan Cimerotic scored the winner, netting his first international goal.

Three months later in the Slovenian capital Ljubljana, coach Srecko Katanec's team defeated Russia with a dramatic and controversial injury time penalty – awarded by English ref Graham Poll. Midfielder Milenko Acimovic coolly scored from the spot for a 2-1 win that gave Slovenia a realistic chance of a play-off place. An impressive 1-1 draw in Yugoslavia followed, which left Slovenia needing only a win over the Faroe Islands to clinch the play-off spot behind Russia.

Two first-half goals from Nastja Ceh were never considered enough, remembering what had happened 13 months earlier, but when substitute Senad Tiganj, on his debut, netted the third goal in the 82nd minute, Slovenia knew the play-off spot was theirs.

They had been in a play-off situation before – successfully booking their place for Euro 2000 – but this time they were considered the underdogs going up against an experienced Romanian team. In the event they proved to be the better team, winning 3-2 on aggregate with goals from Acimovic, Osterc (first leg) and Rudonja (second leg).

While they may have actually remained unbeaten throughout qualifying, Slovenia are regarded as the weakest of the European teams destined for Japan/Korea. Although they scored in every one of the qualifying games, keeping a clean sheet is something of a Slovenian rarity. They're an erratic, often unpredictable team as much within a game as between matches. During their Euro 2000 clash with Yugoslavia they played thrilling football, storming to a 3-0 lead and then threw it away allowing Yugoslavia to score three goals in the last quarter of the game. That breathless performance was in stark contrast to their goalless drudge of a game with Norway.

The chances are that the world will see all shades of Slovenian football at the World Cup Finals, with a side battling against its own inconsistencies as much as their opponents. But they'll be well worth watching – just in case it's one of their good days.

★ **ASSOCIATION:** Nogometna Zveza Slovenije
★ **JOINED FIFA:** 1993
★ **JOINED UEFA:** 1992
★ **PLAYERS:** 20,200

★ **CLUBS:** 375
★ **WEBSITE:** www.nzs.si
★ **HONOURS:** None

ate to add glamour to their squad, Slovenia recruit a rather bemused Hugh Grant.

★ ROAD TO QUALIFICATION

Sep 00 **Faroe Islands** (a) > (d) 2-**2**
Udovic 25, Osterc 87

Oct 00 **Luxembourg** (a) > (w) 1-**2**
Zahovic 39, Milinovic 40

Oct 00 **Switzerland** (h) > (d) 2-2
Siljak 44, Acimovic 77

Mar 01 **Russia** (a) > (d) 1-**1** Knavs 22

Mar 01 **Yugoslavia** (h) > (d) **1**-1
Zahovic 90

Jun 01 **Luxembourg** (h) > (w) **2**-0
Zahovic 35, 66 pen

Jun 01 **Switzerland** (a) > (w) 0-**1**
Cimirotic 83

Sep 01 **Russia** (h) > (w) **2**-1
Osterc 62, Acimovic 90 pen

Sep 01 **Yugoslavia** (a) > (d) 1-**1**
Milinovic 10

Oct 01 **Faroe Islands** (h) > (w) **3**-0
Ceh 13, 31, Tiganj 82

Nov 01 **Romania** (h) > (w) **2**-1
Acimovic 41, Osterc 73

Nov 01 **Romania** (a) > (d) 1-**1** (agg **3**-2)
Rudonja 57

★ FINAL GROUP TABLE

Team	P	W	D	L	F	A	Pts
Russia	10	7	2	1	18	5	23
Slovenia	10	5	5	0	17	9	20
Yugoslavia	10	5	4	1	22	8	19
Switzerland	10	4	2	4	18	12	14
Faroe Islands	10	2	1	7	6	23	7
Luxembourg	10	0	0	10	4	28	0

★ RECENT RESULTS

Feb 02 **Honduras** (n) > (l) **1**-5
Zahovic 52 pen

Feb 02 **China PR** (n) > (d) 0-0
(Slovenia won 4-3 on pens)

Mar 02 **Croatia** (a) > (d) 0-0

DID YOU KNOW?

Coach Srecko Katanec was a Slovenian international making five appearances after previously playing 31 times for Yugoslavia including the 1990 World Cup.

Slovenia has stuck with the same strategy and largely the same personnel that entertained fans at Euro 2000 but only produced two draws and a defeat. In the interim Marko Simeunovic has displaced Malden Dabanovic as Slovenia's number one goalkeeper. The three-man defence has Marinko Galic as sweeper with Zelijko Milinovic and Aleksandr Knavs either side of him. Ales Ceh and Miran Pavlin are the defensive midfielders while Amir Karic on the left and Saso Gajser on the right will provide the width. Zlatko Zahovic almost acts as a third striker, playing just behind the front two. This shadowing position has brought Zahovic and Slovenia many goals, but it's a ploy that most opponents now anticipate. The front two consist of main striker Milan Osterc and partner Mladen Rudonja. While Slovenia has a settled side, it is growing long in the tooth and lacks the pace of former years.

PROBABLE FORMATION 3-4-2-1

SIMEUNOVIC

MILINOVIC · KNAVS

GALIC

GAJSER · A CEH · PAVLIN · KARIC

ZAHOVIC · RUDONJA

OSTERC

★ MEN THAT MATTER!

MILAN OSTERC

Age>> 26
Club>> Hapoel Tel Aviv
Previously used as a supersub to good effect, Osterc has established himself as a first choice forward with Slovenia after scoring vitals goals against Russia and, in the play-offs, Romania.

MLADEN RUDONJA

Age>> 30
Club>> Primorje Ajdovscina
Rudonja has become the strike partner to Milan Osterc. A decent forward he faces pressure from Milenko Acimovic. Rudonja has good control and can play on left side of midfield.

ZLATKO ZAHOVIC

Age>> 31
Club>> Benfica
At Euro 2000 Slovenia were seen as a one-man team — with Zahovic being that man. He still continues to score but now plays just behind the front two.

★ PROBABLE SQUAD ★ QUALIFICATION RECORD

NAME	POSITION	CLUB	APS/GOALS	GAMES	MINS	Y/C	R/C	GOALS
Mladen Dabanovic	Goalkeeper	Lokeren, Belgium	19/0	3	186	0	0	0
Dejan Nemec	Goalkeeper	Brugge, Belgium	0/0	0	0	0	0	0
Marko Simeunovic	Goalkeeper	Maribor, Slovenia	41/0	10	894	0	0	0
Spasoje Bulajic	Defender	Koln, Germany	15/1	4	270	0	0	0
Marinko Galic	Defender	No Club, Slovenia	62/0	7	630	0	0	0
Aleksander Knavs	Defender	Kaiserslautern, Germany	35/2	9	810	1	0	1
Zeljko Milinovic	Defender	JEF United, Japan	33/3	11	990	2	0	2
Goran Sankovic	Defender	Slavia Prague, Czech Republic	1/0	1	27	0	0	0
Muamer Vugdalic	Defender	Maribor, Slovenia	11/0	6	540	2	0	0
Milenko Acimovic	Midfielder	Red Star Belgrade, Yugoslavia	36/9	9	522	2	0	3
Ales Ceh	Midfielder	Grazer AK, Austria	69/1	12	1080	3	0	2
Nastja Ceh	Midfielder	Brugge, Belgium	2/2	1	50	0	0	0
Sasa Gajser	Midfielder	Gent, Belgium	17/1	5	398	4	0	0
Amir Karic	Midfielder	Maribor, Slovenia	40/1	8	567	4	0	0
Dzoni Novak	Midfielder	Unterhaching, Germany	66/2	11	990	3	0	0
Miran Pavlin	Midfielder	Porto, Portugal	42/4	11	916	3	0	0
Zoran Pavlovic	Midfielder	No Club, Slovenia	18/0	8	294	0	0	0
Rajko Tavcar	Midfielder	Nurnberg, Germany	5/0	1	35	0	0	0
Zlatko Zahovic	Midfielder	Benfica, Portugal	61/31	8	687	2	0	4
Sebastjan Cimirotic	Forward	Lecce, Italy	11/1	6	288	1	0	1
Milan Osterc	Forward	Hapoel Tel Aviv, Israel	38/8	11	601	1	0	3
Mladen Rudonja	Forward	Portsmouth, England	55/1	10	721	0	0	1
Senad Tiganj	Forward	Olimpija Ljubljana, Slovenia	1/1	1	20	0	0	1

KEY: APPS/GOALS = International Appearances/Goals; GAMES=Qualification Games played; MINS=Minutes played; Y/C= Yellow cards R/C=Red cards

HISTORY AT THE WORLD CUP

1930 1934 1938 1950 1954 1958 1962 1966 1970 1974 1978 1982 1986 1990 1994 1998

1998 > Slovenia fail to win a single game of their first World Cup qualifying campaign.

★ WORLD CUP HISTORY

1930 >> Did Not Enter	1970 >> Did Not Enter
1934 >> Did Not Enter	1974 >> Did Not Enter
1938 >> Did Not Enter	1978 >> Did Not Enter
1950 >> Did Not Enter	1982 >> Did Not Enter
1954 >> Did Not Enter	1986 >> Did Not Enter
1958 >> Did Not Enter	1990 >> Did Not Enter
1962 >> Did Not Enter	1994 >> Did Not Enter
1966 >> Did Not Enter	1998 >> Did Not Qualify

★ WORLD CUP RECORDS, STORIES AND WEIRDNESS

MOST GOALS >> Slovenia's best all-time World Cup scorer is Zlatko Zahovic with 6.

FIFA RANKING >> Their current position is 27 and their best has been 26th.

OPPONENT	DATE	UK TIME	VENUE
Paraguay	**2 June**	08.30	**Busan, Korea**
Slovenia	**8 June**	07.30	**Daegu, Korea**
Spain	**12 June**	12.30	**Daejeon, Korea**

"the Bafana Bafana seek second round glory"

SOUTH AFRICA

★ THE LOWDOWN

Population: 43.5 million

Capital: Pretoria

Leader: Thabo Mbeki

Life Expectancy: Male: 47 yrs Female: 48 yrs

>> There are eleven official languages used in South Africa, including Afrikaans, English, Zulu, Venda and Swazi.

>> The National Flag includes six different colours: red, blue, green, black, yellow and white.

>> South Africa is the world's largest producer of platinum and gold.

It's been a decade since South Africa re-entered the international sporting fold – after years of isolation in response to her apartheid policies – and South Africa coach Carlos Queiroz has made it clear how he wants his team to celebrate the anniversary at this summer's World Cup. He wants the Bafana Bafana to reach the second round. At France 98, in their first World Cup appearance, defeat by France and draws with Denmark and Saudi Arabia saw them make a first round exit.

Queiroz's team has been in a period of transition for the last couple of years; younger players like Delron Buckley, Siyabonga Nomvete and captain Shaun Bartlett are proving their international mettle and the large number of players previously used by the national side has been cut in a bid to become more consistent.

Queiroz took over the reins of the national team in the shadow of one of the World Cup's worst ever human disasters. After defeating Lesotho 3-0 on aggregate with two pretty drab performances in the preliminary round, South Africa opened their qualifying programme proper away to Zimbabwe at the National Sports Stadium in Harare. Delron Buckley gave the visitors a sixth minute lead and thereafter South Africa controlled the game. In the 82nd minute Buckley struck again to secure the points.

However, South Africa's goal celebrations provoked a hail of missiles from the crowd. The crowd's venom was directed both towards the South African players and the Zimbabwean bench. In a bid to quell the disturbances the Zimbabwean Police fired teargas into the crowd causing a stampede that led to the deaths of 13 fans. On the pitch players and officials were forced to lie face down to avoid the clouds of teargas engulfing them. A decision was taken to abandon the game and later FIFA ruled that the result – 2-0 – would stand.

It was six months before South Africa would return to World Cup action when they produced wins over Burkina Faso and Malawi – albeit in a less than convincing fashion. South African World Cup hopes were boosted, as were the hopes of Zimbabwe, when one of the main rivals, Guinea, were expelled from the competition. Zimbabwe's hopes were short lived as South Africa beat them 2-1 thanks to first-half goals from Shaun Bartlett and Benni McCarthy. This big, decisive clash attracted just 15,000 fans at the Soccer City Stadium in Johannesburg. Just a month earlier South Africa had been struck by its own stadium disaster in which 43 people had died.

A 1-1 draw away to Burkina Faso earned South Africa the point they needed to qualify for their second successive Finals.

Since South Africa returned to the international football family it's been a colourful decade for "The Boys". Crowned African Champions in 1996 and successful qualification for two World Cups Finals, such was the confidence in the South African game that they applied to host, and were hot favourites to get, the 2006 World Cup Finals. However, they ultimately lost out to Germany because the Oceania representative refused to follow his Confederation's instructions to vote for South Africa and went home.

★ **ASSOCIATION:** South African Football Association

★ **JOINED FIFA:** 1992

★ **JOINED CAF:** 1992

★ **PLAYERS:** 1,039,900

★ **CLUBS:** 51,944

★ **WEBSITE:** www.safa.org.za

★ **HONOURS:** African Nations Cup – 1996.

His country hopes for exactly what it says on the shirt.

★ ROAD TO QUALIFICATION

Apr 00 **Lesotho** (a) > (w) 0-**2**
Bartlett 40, Pule 71

Apr 00 **Lesotho** (h) > (w) **1**-0 (agg 3-0)
Bartlett 48

Jul 00 **Zimbabwe** (a) > (w) 0-**2**
Buckley 6, 82

Jan 01 **Burkina Faso** (h) > (w) **1**-0
Bartlett 17

Feb 01 **Malawi** (a) > (w) 1-**2**
Masinga 25, Nomvethe 81

May 01 **Zimbabwe** (h) > (w) **2**-1
Bartlett 18, McCarthy 40

Jul 01 **Burkina Faso** (a) > (d) 1-**1**
Zuma 24

Jul 01 **Malawi** (h) > (w) **2**-0
Booth 5, August 54

★ FINAL GROUP TABLE

Team	P	W	D	L	F	A	Pts
South Africa	6	5	1	0	10	3	16
Zimbabwe	7	4	0	3	7	8	12
Guinea	3	2	1	0	7	3	7
Burkina Faso	7	1	2	4	9	11	5
Malawi	7	0	2	5	5	13	2

★ RECENT RESULTS

Jan 02 **Burkina Faso** (n) > (d) **0**-0

Jan 02 **Ghana** (n) > (d) **0**-0

Jan 02 **Morocco** (n) > (w) **3**-1
Zuma 41, Mngomeni 48, Nomvethe 50

Feb 02 **Mali** (n) > (l) 2-**0**

Mar 02 **Georgia** (a) > (l) 4-**1** Buckley 69

DID YOU KNOW?

South Africa will celebrate a decade back in the international fold when they participate in the World Cup Finals after the end of their period of isolation because of their apartheid policies

South Africa's 3-5-2 line up has brought them much success on the African continent in the last few years, but they certainly lost their way at the 2002 African Nations Cup – suggesting that without the right personnel they may well struggle at the World Cup. Hans Vonk has displaced Andre Arendse as first choice goalkeeper. The back three are likely to be Aaraon Mokoena, Pierre Issa and Frank Schoeman, although Mbulelo Mabizela and Bradley Carnell make strong cases for inclusion. Playmaker John Moshoeu, absent from the African Nations Cup, is seen as a vital player who will be supported by Thano Mngomeni and Delron Buckley. South Africa has an abundance of decent wide men at the moment with Manchester United's Quinton Fortune and FC Copenhagen's Sibusiso Zuma providing plenty of creativity if brought into the game. In attack, Benni McCarthy and Shaun Bartlett look the likely pairing, but Siyabonga Nomvete could break them up.

PROBABLE FORMATION 3-5-2

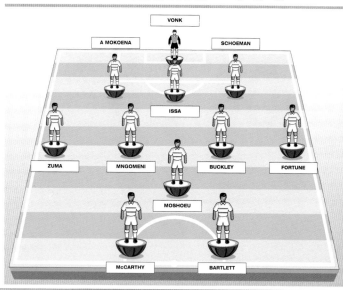

VONK

A MOKOENA   SCHOEMAN

ISSA

ZUMA   MNGOMENI   BUCKLEY   FORTUNE

MOSHOEU

McCARTHY   BARTLETT

★ MEN THAT MATTER!

SUBUSISO ZUMA

Age>> 26
Club>> FC Copenhagen

Right-winger and excellent crosser of the ball who has finally established himself in the side after making his debut in October 1998 against Angola. Voted Denmark's 2000-01 Player of the Year.

BENNI MCCARTHY

Age>> 24
Club>> Celta Vigo/ FC Porto (loan)

Benni McCarthy has had a tough time at club level but has been consistently selected for his country. He scored the vital winning goal in the 2-1 win over Zimbabwe in the qualifiers.

SHAUN BARTLETT

Age>> 29
Club>> Charlton Athletic

Shaun Bartlett has played football in Africa, Europe, America and Britain. He made his international debut in 1995 and he was South Africa's main goalscorer during the qualifiers.

★ PROBABLE SQUAD   ★ QUALIFICATION RECORD

NAME	POSITION	CLUB	APS/GOALS	GAMES	MINS	Y/C	R/C	GOALS
Andre Arendse	Goalkeeper	Santos , South Africa	49/0	2	180	0	0	0
Bryan Baloyi	Goalkeeper	Kaizer Chiefs, South Africa	17/0	1	90	0	0	0
Hans Vonk	Goalkeeper	Heerenveen, Holland	27/0	1	90	1	0	0
Aaron Mokoena	Defender	Germinal Beerschot, Belgium	20/0	3	270	1	0	0
Bradley Carnell	Defender	Stuttgart, Germany	19/0	2	180	0	0	0
David Kannemeyer	Defender	Kaizer Chiefs, South Africa	9/0	2	180	0	0	0
Frank Schoeman	Defender	Farum, Denmark	14/0	3	270	1	0	0
Pierre Issa	Defender	Watford, England	40/0	4	360	2	0	0
Cyril Nzama	Defender	Kaizer Chiefs, South Africa	17/1	2	180	1	0	0
Alfred Phiri	Midfielder	Samsunspor, Turkey	10/2	2	94	2	0	0
Delron Buckley	Midfielder	Bochum, Germany	29/4	3	226	0	0	2
John Moshoeu	Midfielder	Bursaspor, Turkey	63/6	1	90	0	0	0
Helman Mkhalele	Midfielder	Goztepe, Turkey	63/7	3	169	0	0	0
Quinton Fortune	Midfielder	Manchester United, England	38/0	2	146	1	0	0
Eric Tinkler	Midfielder	Barnsley, England	46/1	1	90	0	0	0
Teboho Mokoena	Midfielder	St Gallen, Switzerland	9/0	2	107	0	0	0
Jacob Lekcetho	Midfielder	Lokomotiv Moscow, Russia	13/0	1	90	0	0	0
Matthew Booth	Midfielder	Mamelodi Sundowns, South Africa	13/2	1	90	0	0	1
Benedict McCarthy	Forward	Porto, Portugal	40/17	4	240	0	0	1
Bradley August	Forward	Santos, South Africa	14/3	2	98	0	0	1
Shaun Bartlett	Forward	Charlton, England	60/23	4	352	0	0	2
Siyabongo Nomvete	Forward	Udinese, Italy	29/5	4	152	0	0	1
Sibusiso Zuma	Forward	Copenhagen, Denmark	22/3	4	316	0	0	0

KEY: APPS/GOALS = International Appearances/Goals; GAMES=Qualification Games played; MINS=Minutes played; Y/C= Yellow cards R/C=Red cards

HISTORY AT THE WORLD CUP

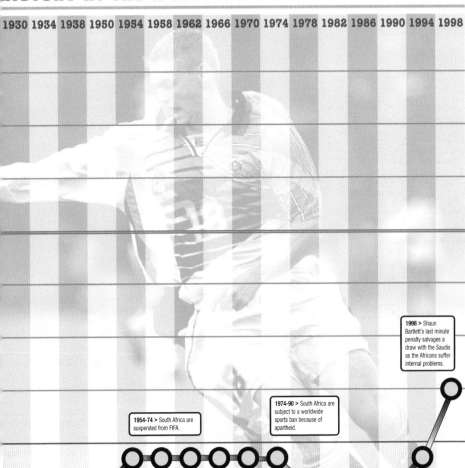

1998 > Shaun Bartlett's last minute penalty salvages a draw with the Saudis as the Africans suffer internal problems.

1954-74 > South Africa are suspended from FIFA.

1974-90 > South Africa are subject to a worldwide sports ban because of apartheid.

★ WORLD CUP HISTORY

1930 >> Did Not Enter		**1970** >> Suspended	
1934 >> Did Not Enter		**1974** >> Suspended	
1938 >> Did Not Enter		**1978** >> Did Not Enter	
1950 >> Did Not Enter		**1982** >> Did Not Enter	
1954 >> Suspended		**1986** >> Did Not Enter	
1958 >> Suspended		**1990** >> Did Not Enter	
1962 >> Suspended		**1994** >> Did Not Qualify	
1966 >> Suspended		**1998** >> First Round	

★ WORLD CUP RECORDS, STORIES AND WEIRDNESS

MOST SENDINGS OFF IN A MATCH >> Denmark against South Africa in 1998 saw three players sent off.

OPPONENT	DATE	UK TIME	VENUE
Poland	**4 June**	12.30	**Busan, Korea**
USA	**10 June**	07.30	**Daegu, Korea**
Portugal	**14 June**	12.30	**Incheon, Korea**

"looking for their first win"

SOUTH KOREA

★ THE LOWDOWN

Population: 46.1 million

Capital: Seoul

Leader: Yi Han-tong

Life Expectancy: Male: 71 yrs
Female: 79 yrs

>> The Korean alphabet was created during the 15th century and is called Hangeul. It consists of 10 vowels and 14 consonants; although considered an easy language to learn, it is one of the most scientific writing systems in the world.

>> Kite flying is a popular traditional sport in Korea. It can be quite competitive and attaching pieces of glass to the string of a kite to cut an opponent's line is considered quite acceptable.

World Cup co-hosts South Korea are undeniably one of Asia's strongest teams. They've qualified for the last four World Cup Finals and were the first Asian side to play in the Finals – back in 1954. However, in all of their 14 World Cup matches, the South Koreans have yet to record a win. And they carry the added burden of knowing that in no previous World Cups have the hosts failed to reach the second round. Oh, how they would love to emulate the heroic achievement of their northern counterparts who, in 1966, reached the quarter-finals.

No need to qualify as co-hosts of course, they were placed in the top group of seeds for the draw (normally they'd be in the bottom group), but the draw itself was far from kind. Two improving European teams, Poland and Portugal, stand in the way of a second round place, as do the United States.

South Korean fans are not entirely optimistic about their team's chances and recognising that they'd come as far as they were likely to without outside help, appointed former Holland national team coach Guus Hiddink in January 2001. He was put in charge of a squad with several talented players, most of whom play their club football at home or in Japan. The Dutchman is the first non-Korean to coach the national side and was given 17 months to sort them out. Lined up were a series of tournaments including the Carlsberg Cup in Hong Kong, the Emirates Cup in Dubai, a tournament in Egypt and the co-hosting of the Confederations Cup and, earlier this year, the Gold Cup in the USA along with a host of friendly internationals.

Hiddink's first step was to adopt the playing system used by Korea's leading clubs, such as the highly successful Suwon Bluewings, which roughly equates to a 4-5-1 formation. This would mean that the national squad would have to switch from a three-man to a four-man defence. The change in organisation led to problems and the defence stuttered especially against strong European opposition. Both France and the Czech Republic thrashed the Koreans 5-0.

The midfield, however, showed improvement thanks to the arrival of youngster Song Chong-gug alongside wide-man Lee Young-pyo and free-kick specialist Park Ji-sung. This five-man midfield supports a single striker such as Choi Yong-soo or the new wonder boy of South Korean football Lee Dong-gook, who led his country to the Asian Under-19 title 1999 and was top scorer at the 2000 Asian Championships – where South Korea finished fourth.

At the Confederations Cup, Korea had a bad case of the *deja vus*, showing the sort of form we can expect to see in the Finals. Despite beating both Mexico and Australia, they unluckily bowed out at the group stage. At the Gold Cup, however, they were semi-finalists beating Mexico in a penalty shoot-out, with two saves from goalkeeper Lee Woon-jae along the way.

Even when you add up the value of Hiddink's experience, home advantage and massive support of a football-mad nation, the Koreans are going to find it difficult. At the last World Cup Hiddink, wearing his Dutch hat, handed out a 5-0 thrashing to the Koreans and they would be wise to limit their ambitions to securing their first World Cup Finals win. Asian soccer also has vested interest in a breakthrough Korean performance as the continent seeks to increase its numbers in future World Cup Finals.

★ **ASSOCIATION:** Korea Football Association
★ **JOINED FIFA:** 1948
★ **JOINED AFC:** 1954
★ **PLAYERS:** 20,050

★ **CLUBS:** 476
★ **WEBSITE:** www.kfa.or.kr
★ **HONOURS:** Asian Championship – 1956, 1960

Kim Do-hoon chasing a World Cup dream.

DID YOU KNOW?

Boss Bora Militinovic is 'Mister World Cup'. This will be his fifth World Cup Finals with a different team each time — Mexico (1986), Costa Rica (1990), USA (1994) and Nigeria (1998)

South Korea's prospects of making an impact at the World Cup are not particularly good. Although their players are technically adept, shortcomings in other aspects of their game, particularly their relative lack of physical presence, make them vulnerable. Dutch coach Guus Hiddink has opted for a 4-4-2 formation that is hugely dependent on keeper Lee Woon-jae and South Korea's best known player, Hong Myung-bo, providing last ditch protection of the goalmouth. In midfield, despite the presence of the popular Song Chong-gug and sweeper captain Hong Myung-bo, the Koreans will find it hard to cope. A bold attacking partnership of Lee Dong-gook, the Michael Owen of Korean football, and the highly paid Kim Do-hoon offers some hope for goals. Getting the ball to these two will be a major problem.

PROBABLE FORMATION   4-4-2

LEE WOON-JAE

KIM TAE-YOUNG

LEE MIN-SUNG

HONG MYUNG-BO   LEE LIM-SAENG

CHOI SUNG-YONG   SONG CHONG-GUG   LEE YONG-PYU   CHOI TAE-UK

KIM DO-HOON   LEE DONG-GOOK

★ MEN THAT MATTER!

HONG MYUNG-BO

Age>> 33

Club>> Kashiwa Reysol

South Korea's most capped player is regarded as the best sweeper in Asia. This will be Hong's fourth successive World Cup.

LEE YOUNG-PYO

Age>> 25

Club>> Anyang Cheetahs

After impressing in the Korean's Olympic Under-23 team he was promoted to the senior team. Lee Young-pyo can play on the left of midfield and equally carve out chances through the middle.

SONG CHONG-GUG

Age>> 23

Club>> Pusan Icons

Song Chong-gug, who impressed at the 2001 Confederations Cup, is the new boy wonder of South Korean football. He plays in midfield and is quick off the mark allowing him to create chances.

★ PROBABLE SQUAD   ★ QUALIFICATION RECORD

NAME	POSITION	CLUB	APS/GOALS	GAMES	MINS	Y/C	R/C	GOALS
Lee Woon-jae	Goalkeeper	Sangmoo, South Korea	25/0	-	-	-	-	-
Kim Byung-ji	Goalkeeper	Pohang Steelers, South Korea	54/0	-	-	-	-	-
Kim Yong-dae	Goalkeeper	Yonsei University, South Korea	12/0	-	-	-	-	-
Hong Myung-bo	Defender	Pohang Steelers, South Korea	122/9	-	-	-	-	-
Kang Chul	Defender	Chunnam Dragons, South Korea	53/1	-	-	-	-	-
Kim Tae-young	Defender	Chunnam Dragons, South Korea	68/3	-	-	-	-	-
Lee Lim-saeng	Defender	Puchon SK, South Korea	24/0	-	-	-	-	-
Lee Min-sung	Defender	Sangmoo, South Korea	54/2	-	-	-	-	-
Sim Jae-won	Defender	Eintracht Frankfurt, Germany	18/2	-	-	-	-	-
Song Chong-gug	Defender	Pusan Icons, South Korea	18/1	-	-	-	-	-
Choi Sung-yong	Midfielder	Suwon Bluewings, South Korea	54/1	-	-	-	-	-
Choi Tai-uk	Midfielder	Anyang Cheetahs, South Korea	11/3	-	-	-	-	-
Ha Seok-ju	Midfielder	Pohang Steelers, South Korea	91/23	-	-	-	-	-
Kim Nam-il	Midfielder	Chunnam Dragons, South Korea	12/1	-	-	-	-	-
Lee Young-pyo	Midfielder	Anyang Cheetahs, South Korea	39/3	-	-	-	-	-
Song Chong-gug	Midfielder	Pusan Icons, South Korea	19/1	-	-	-	-	-
Yoo Sang-chul	Midfielder	Kashiwa Reysol, Japan	90/16	-	-	-	-	-
Yoon Jong-hwan	Midfielder	Cerezo Osaka, Japan	33/2	-	-	-	-	-
Ahn Jung-hwan	Forward	Perugia, Italy	14/2	-	-	-	-	-
Choi Yong-soo	Forward	JEF United Ichihara, Japan	54/27	-	-	-	-	-
Hwang Sun-hong	Forward	Kashiwa Reysol, Japan	92/47	-	-	-	-	-
Kim Do-hoon	Forward	Chonbuk, South Korea	57/20	-	-	-	-	-
Lee Dong-gook	Forward	Pohang Steelers, South Korea	25/9	-	-	-	-	-

KEY: APPS/GOALS = International Appearances/Goals; GAMES=Qualification Games played; MINS=Minutes played; Y/C=Yellow cards R/C=Red cards

HISTORY AT THE WORLD CUP

1930 1934 1938 1950 1954 1958 1962 1966 1970 1974 1978 1982 1986 1990 1994 1998

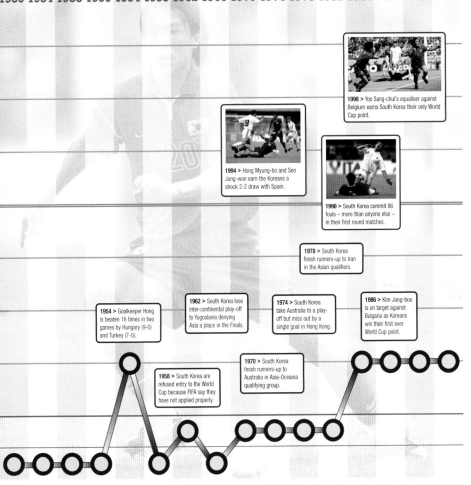

1998 > Yoo Sang-chul's equaliser against Belgium earns South Korea their only World Cup point.

1994 > Hong Myung-bo and Seo Jung-won earn the Koreans a shock 2-2 draw with Spain.

1990 > South Korea commit 86 fouls – more than anyone else – in their first round matches.

1978 > South Korea finish runners-up to Iran in the Asian qualifiers.

1954 > Goalkeeper Hong is beaten 16 times in two games by Hungary (9-0) and Turkey (7-0).

1962 > South Korea lose inter-continental play-off to Yugoslavia denying Asia a place in the Finals.

1974 > South Korea take Australia to a play-off but miss out by a single goal in Hong Kong.

1986 > Kim Jong-boo is on target against Bulgaria as Koreans win their first ever World Cup point.

1958 > South Korea are refused entry to the World Cup because FIFA say they have not applied properly.

1970 > South Korea finish runners-up to Australia in Asia-Oceania qualifying group.

★ WORLD CUP HISTORY

1930 >> Did Not Enter		1970 >> Did Not Qualify	
1934 >> Did Not Enter		1974 >> Did Not Qualify	
1938 >> Did Not Enter		1978 >> Did Not Qualify	
1950 >> Did Not Enter		1982 >> Did Not Qualify	
1954 >> First Round		1986 >> First Round	
1958 >> Did Not Enter		1990 >> First Round	
1962 >> Did Not Qualify		1994 >> First Round	
1966 >> Did Not Enter		1998 >> First Round	

★ WORLD CUP RECORDS, STORIES AND WEIRDNESS

BIGGEST DEFEAT >> South Korea were thrashed 9-0 by Hungary in Zurich in 1954. Between them Kocis and Hungarian great Puskas scored 5.

OPPONENT	DATE	UK TIME	VENUE
Slovenia	**2 June**	12.30	**Gwangju, Korea**
Paraguay	**7 June**	10.00	**Jeonju, Korea**
South Africa	**12 June**	12.30	**Daejeon, Korea**

"perennial under-achievers?"

SPAIN

★ THE LOWDOWN

Population: 40 million

Capital: Madrid

Leader: Jose Maria Aznar

Life Expectancy: Male: 75 yrs **Female:** 82 yrs

>> Take a trip to Pamplona on 7th July if you want to see the Festival of San Fermin. Basically, this involves hundreds of men running for their lives, chased by dozens of bulls through the streets of the town. Now that's entertainment!

>> Whilst Spain managed to avoid active participation in either of the World Wars, it did suffer a devastating civil war between 1936-39 and only became truly democratic 27 years ago.

Spain qualified with ease for the World Cup Finals – as they always do. Unbeaten, scoring 21 goals, shared between 11 different players, in eight games. There was never any doubt that Spain would be in the Finals. The remaining doubt is whether this time they will do anything about their poor record in major tournaments. It takes a Spaniard with a long memory to recall the heady days when his country achieved their best finish in a World Cup Finals, a fourth place all the way back in the 1950 World Cup Brazil.

At France '98 Spain bowed out at the group stage after suffering an opening 3-2 defeat by Nigeria and then held to a 0-0 draw by Paraguay. At Euro 2000 Spain reached the quarter-finals where they were defeated 2-1 by France, but it could have been different but for Raul's last minute penalty miss.

Spain's relative lack of international success is all the more surprising when you look at their domestic game. They boast one of the strongest and richest leagues in the world, attracting many top stars from abroad and, significantly, most of the national squad play for Spanish clubs.

Some sort of breakthrough was thought to have been achieved when Spain, as hosts, lifted the 1992 Olympic Soccer Gold Medal. However, few of the Olympic winning team really established themselves in the national side and ten years on Spain have still to truly thrive at major tournaments.

Undoubtedly, this is a country brimming with football talent. Their star player is Raul who, since making his debut in October 1996 at the age of 19, carries the weight of expectation of fans and media alike for both club and country. He's been ever present in the side since Euro 2000 and is rarely missing from the Real Madrid line up.

Calculations show that over the past two seasons Raul has played more football than any other Spanish player.

Other established figures include goalkeeper Jose Canizares, Luis Enrique (both featured in the Olympic team) and midfielder Fernando Hierro. New coach Jose Antonio Camacho, a former Real Madrid defender, has also been keen to introduce young players into the side, notably, Diego Tristan, who scored on each occasion he started a qualifying game, and midfielder Vicente who had an outstanding debut in the 4-0 home thrashing of Austria.

The Spanish have always blended youth and experience exceedingly well. And whatever system they adopt, the more flamboyant attacking style promoted by Camacho or the cautious defence-packed midfield system of his predecessor, they have always won competitive games. Friendlies are a different matter, usually accorded a lower priority, and it's no surprise that Spain's only defeats since Euro 2000 have been in friendlies by Germany, Holland and England. On the other hand, they've beaten World Cup holders France and World Cup co-hosts Japan, also in friendlies.

Spanish clubs thrive in European competition with Real Madrid European Champions League winners in 2000, and Valencia Champions League runners-up in 2000 and 2001. Alaves too were UEFA Cup finalists last season. Inexplicably, tournament soccer remains a problem for the Spanish national side. Their form, seeding and FIFA Ranking suggest that Spain ought to be serious contenders for a World Cup final, but past experience tips them as an also ran. An indefinable something prevents them making a serious impact on the world stage, despite the multi-million Euros of talent on show.

★ **ASSOCIATION:** Real Federacion Espanola De Futbol
★ **JOINED FIFA:** 1904
★ **JOINED UEFA:** 1954
★ **PLAYERS:** 408,200

★ **CLUBS:** 10,240
★ **WEBSITE:** www.futvol.com
★ **HONOURS:** European Championship – 1964;
Olympics – 1992.

Gaizka Mendieta – style, skill and steel personified. Dodgy barnet though.

★ ROAD TO QUALIFICATION

Sep 00 **Bosnia** (a) > (w) **1-2**
Gerard 39, Etxeberria 72

Oct 00 **Israel** (h) > (w) **2-0**
Gerard 22, Hierro 54

Oct 00 **Austria** (a) > (d) 1-1 Baraja 27

Mar 01 **Liechtenstein** (h) > (w) **5-0**
Helguera 21, Mendieta 37, 82,
Hierro 55 pen, Raul 68

Jun 01 **Bosnia** (h) > (w) **4-1**
Hierro 27, Javi Moreno 76, Raul 89,
Diego Tristan 90

Jun 01 **Israel** (a) > (d) 1-1 Raul 63

Sep 01 **Austria** (h) > (w) **4-0**
Diego Tristan 45, Morientes 79, 84,
Mendieta 90

Sep 01 **Liechtenstein** (a) > (w) **0-2**
Raul 19, Nadal 82

★ FINAL GROUP TABLE

Team	P	W	D	L	F	A	Pts
Spain	8	6	2	0	21	4	20
Austria	8	4	3	1	10	8	15
Israel	8	3	3	2	11	7	12
Bosnia	8	2	2	4	12	12	8
Liechtenstein	8	0	0	8	0	23	0

★ RECENT RESULTS

Feb 02 **Portugal** (h) > (d) **1-1** Morientes 41

Mar 02 **Holland** (a) > (l) **1-0**

DID YOU KNOW?

Spain's biggest international win was 12-1 over Malta in an European Championshi qualifier in December 1983. Santillana and Rincon both scored four times in the gam◄

Oh, how they flatter to deceive, Spain – the perennial under-achievers of international football. Will it be different this time? Well coach Jose Antonio Camacho has yet again a world beating squad at his disposal. A team that starts with goalkeeper Jose Santiago Canizares, runs through centre back Fernando Hierro and midfielder Josep Guardiola and finishes with world class striker Raul Gonzalez Blanco. Four experienced players on whom Spain relies to make things happen – and during qualifying they did just that. Hierro is partnered with Nadal in the centre of defence with Sergi left back and new boy Manuel Pablo, who has made the right back position his own since making his debut in August 2000. Guardiola is still supported by the familiar Luis Enrique on the left while Ivan Helguera and Gaizka Mendieta complete a midfield quartet of style, steel and skill. Raul, still carrying the expectations of the Spanish supporters, has had the pressure taken off him up front with the arrival of the revelation that is Diego Tristan.

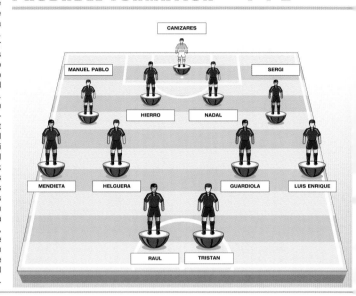

PROBABLE FORMATION 4-4-2

CANIZARES

MANUEL PABLO SERGI

HIERRO NADAL

MENDIETA HELGUERA GUARDIOLA LUIS ENRIQUE

RAUL TRISTAN

★ PROBABLE SQUAD   ★ QUALIFICATION RECORD

NAME	POSITION	CLUB	APS/GOALS	GAMES	MINS	Y/C	R/C	GOALS
Santiago Canizares	Goalkeeper	Valencia, Spain	33/0	3	270	0	0	0
Iker Casillas	Goalkeeper	Real Madrid, Spain	12/0	5	450	0	0	0
Jose F'cisco Molina	Goalkeeper	Deportivo La Coruna, Spain	8/0	0	0	0	0	0
Fernandez Abelardo	Defender	Barcelona, Spain	54/3	3	270	0	0	0
Agustin Aranzabal	Defender	Real Sociedad, Spain	24/0	2	180	0	0	0
Fernando Hierro	Defender	Real Madrid, Spain	83/27	13	1047	0	0	3
Miguel Angel Nadal	Defender	Mallorca, Spain	56/3	5	404	0	0	1
Manuel Pablo	Defender	Deportivo La Coruna, Spain	12/0	7	630	1	0	0
Carles Puyol	Defender	Barcelona, Spain	6/0	2	97	0	0	0
Barjuan Sergi	Defender	Barcelona, Spain	56/1	4	360	1	0	0
Ruben Baraja	Midfielder	Valencia, Spain	9/2	4	263	2	0	1
Luis Enrique	Midfielder	Barcelona, Spain	57/12	4	235	1	0	0
Josep Guardiola	Midfielder	Brescia, Italy	47/5	3	233	0	0	0
Ivan Helguera	Midfielder	Real Madrid, Spain	20/2	6	397	2	0	1
Gaizka Mendieta	Midfielder	Lazio, Italy	31/7	7	517	0	0	3
Juan Carlos Valeron	Midfielder	Deportivo La Coruna, Spain	18/0	3	210	0	0	0
Rodriguez Vicente	Midfielder	Valencia, Spain	4/0	1	84	0	0	0
Javi Moreno	Forward	AC Milan, Italy	5/1	3	195	0	0	1
Fernando Morientes	Forward	Real Madrid, Spain	17/13	2	109	0	0	2
Pedro Munitis	Forward	Real Madrid, Spain	21/2	4	219	2	0	0
Gonzalez Raul	Forward	Real Madrid, Spain	49/23	8	671	0	0	4
Diego Tristan	Forward	Deportivo La Coruna, Spain	6/2	4	210	0	0	2
Ismael Urzaiz	Forward	Athl Bilbao, Spain	25/8	3	200	0	0	0

KEY: APPS/GOALS = International Appearances/Goals; **GAMES**=Qualification Games played; **MINS**=Minutes played; **Y/C**= Yellow cards **R/C**=Red cards

1930 1934 1938 1950 1954 1958 1962 1966 1970 1974 1978 1982 1986 1990 1994 1998

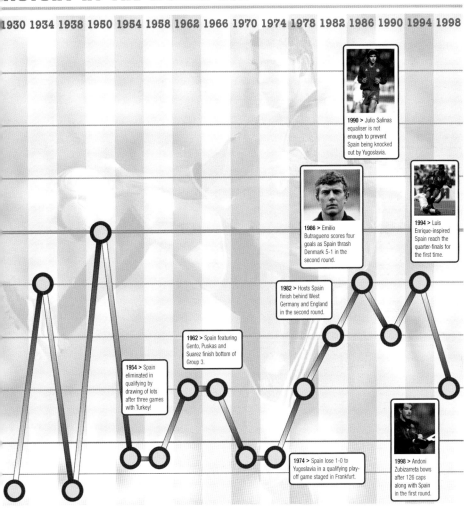

1990 > Julio Salinas equaliser is not enough to prevent Spain being knocked out by Yugoslavia.

1986 > Emilio Butragueno scores four goals as Spain thrash Denmark 5-1 in the second round.

1994 > Luis Enrique-inspired Spain reach the quarter-finals for the first time.

1982 > Hosts Spain finish behind West Germany and England in the second round.

1962 > Spain featuring Gento, Puskas and Suarez finish bottom of Group 3.

1954 > Spain eliminated in qualifying by drawing of lots after three games with Turkey!

1974 > Spain lose 1-0 to Yugoslavia in a qualifying play-off game staged in Frankfurt.

1998 > Andoni Zubizarreta bows along with Spain in the first round.

★ WORLD CUP HISTORY

1930 >> Did Not Enter		**1970** >> Did Not Qualify	
1934 >> Quarter-Final		**1974** >> Did Not Qualify	
1938 >> Did Not Enter		**1978** >> First Round	
1950 >> Fourth Place		**1982** >> Second Round	
1954 >> Did Not Qualify		**1986** >> Quarter-Final	
1958 >> Did Not Qualify		**1990** >> Second Round	
1962 >> First Round		**1994** >> Quarter-Final	
1966 >> irst Round		**1998** >> First Round	

★ WORLD CUP RECORDS, STORIES AND WEIRDNESS

MOST GOALS IN A MATCH >> Emilio Butragueño put 4 past Denmark in 1986.

SHOCKING RESULT >> Spain against Denmark 5-1 in 1986: In the first round Denmark had been cruising, winning all their matches, including thrashing South American champions Uruguay 6-1 and West Germany 2-0. They even took the lead in their second round game against Spain, but then the wheels fell off. Butragueño scored four of Spain's five goals in this astonishing game.

OPPONENT	DATE	UK TIME	VENUE
England	**2 June**	**10.30**	**Saitama, Japan**
Nigeria	**7 June**	**07.30**	**Kobe, Japan**
Argentina	**12 June**	**07.30**	**Miyagi, Japan**

"the Swedes, not to everyone's taste"

SWEDEN

★ THE LOWDOWN

Population: 8.8 million

Capital: Stockholm

Leader: Goran Persson

Life Expectancy: Male: 77 yrs
Female: 82 yrs

>> Contrary to popular belief, Sweden is only 21st on the list of heaviest alcohol consumers in industrialised nations. However, it may be traditional to drink only occasionally in Sweden, but it is customary to drink until drunk.

>> Stockholm is known as the "Venice of the north" and is built on 13 small islands.

>> Volvos are designed to fit in 4 people dressed as Abba and 2 flat-packed bookcases from Ikea!

The current Swedish side is arguably short on world class players and is considered a workmanlike side that makes up for a lack of flair with good organisation, hard work, and team play. It's a hard side to beat that ploughed its way, doggedly, through qualifying – topping a group, luckily for Sweden, devoid of any of the more powerful European sides. It was better than Azerbaijan, Macedonia and Moldova, but in no way superior to Slovakia or Turkey.

Sweden have developed a reputation as a cautious, goal-shy outfit that scores few goals but, fortunately, concedes even less. This was evident at Euro 2000 where they failed to win a single game. Top striker Kennet Andersson, who before retiring from the game had run up a tally of 31 goals in 71 appearances, failed to score at the tournament. The Swedes were also reliant on Henrik Larsson who had barely recovered from a long-term injury.

A defeat by Iceland in a friendly – Sweden's first loss to the Icelanders in 49 years – coupled with a narrow World Cup win over Azerbaijan and draws with Turkey and Slovakia, had the Swedish media baying for the heads of joint coaches Tommy Söderberg and Lars Lagerbäck. Under Söderberg/Lagerbäck Sweden had averaged less than a goal a game and the 0-0 draw with Slovakia meant they'd gone some 14 matches since scoring more than one goal in a game.

Sweden ploughed on beating Macedonia 1-0 by a single Anders Svensson goal. The Southampton player had also scored the winner against Azerbaijan in the opening qualifying game.

Substitute Marcus Allback was the saviour in Moldova. The Heerenveen forward came on in the 81st minute and scored twice in the last two minutes of the match to give Sweden a 2-0 win in a game they had fielded an experimental and disastrous midfield

system. Allback scored both goals in the 2- home win over Slovakia in a game tha Lagerbäck described as Sweden's mos important result yet.

Four days later, and to everyone" amazement, they thrashed Moldova 6-C Henrik Larsson, Europe's Golden Boo Winner with his 53 goals in all competition for Celtic, who had been widely criticised fc his lack of goalscoring at international leve netted four times – albeit with a hat-trick c penalties. The 2-1 victory over Macedoni set up a daunting trip to Istanbul to decid who would automatically qualify and wh would be condemned to the play-offs.

Turkey's Hakan Sukur beat goalkeepe Thomas Hedman in the 51st minute givin Turkey a deserved lead – they'd dominate the game – and the play-offs beckoned fc the Swedes. Henrik Larsson stole an equalise in the 87th minute then, dramatically, Andrea Andersson scored in the dying seconds t snatch a 2-1 win and qualification for th World Cup.

The majority of the current Swedish squa play outside the country and the two bigges names in the side are Celtic's phenomena striker Henrik Larsson and defender an captain Patrik Andersson. Larsson is one c the world's best marksmen. Andersson wo the UEFA Champions League with Bayer Munich in 2001 before moving to Barcelon last summer. The emergence of Zlata Ibrahimovic in the latter stages of qualificatio suggested that he could have an importan role to play in the new side. The 19 year-ol left Malmö FF in 2001 for Dutch giants Aja Amsterdam, becoming the most expensiv Swedish footballer in history.

Sweden's last World Cup appearance wa in 1994 when they reached the semi-finals an ultimately secured third place. Whether th current side can repeat such endeavours wi depend, for the most part, on the performanc of these three players.

- ★ **ASSOCIATION:** Svenska Fotbollfoerbundet
- ★ **JOINED FIFA:** 1904
- ★ **JOINED UEFA:** 1954
- ★ **PLAYERS:** 485,000
- ★ **CLUBS:** 3,250
- ★ **WEBSITE:** www.svenskfotbol.se
- ★ **HONOURS:** Olympics – 1948.

Captain Patrik Andersson steadies the Swedish ship.

★ ROAD TO QUALIFICATION

Sep 00 **Azerbaijan** (a) > (w) 0-**1**
Svensson, A 9

Oct 00 **Turkey** (h) > (d) **1**-1 Larsson 65

Oct 00 **Slovakia** (a) > (d) 0-0

Mar 01 **Macedonia** (h) > (w) **1**-0
Svensson, A 43

Mar 01 **Moldova** (a) > (w) 0-**2**
Allback 89, 90

Jun 01 **Slovakia** (h) > (w) **2**-0
Allback 45, 51

Jun 01 **Moldova** (h) > (w) **6**-0
Larsson 38 pen, 58, 68 pen, 79,
Alexandersson, D 74, Andersson 77

Sep 01 **Macedonia** (a) > (w) 1-**2**
Larsson 28, Andersson, P 33

Sep 01 **Turkey** (a) > (w) 1-**2**
Larsson 87, Andersson, A 90

Oct 01 **Azerbaijan** (h) > (w) **3**-0
Svensson, A 52, Larsson 60 pen,
Ibrahimovic 69

★ FINAL GROUP TABLE

Team	P	W	D	L	F	A	Pts
Sweden	10	8	2	0	20	3	26
Turkey	10	6	3	1	18	8	21
Slovakia	10	5	2	3	16	9	17
Macedonia	10	1	4	5	11	18	7
Moldova	10	1	3	6	6	20	6
Azerbaijan	10	1	2	7	4	17	5

★ RECENT RESULTS

Feb 02 **Greece** (a) > (d) 2-**2**
Svensson, A 31, Selakovic 64

Mar 02 **Switzerland** (h) > (d) **1**-1
Allback 29

173

DID YOU KNOW?

Sweden's first official international was an 11-3 victory over Norway in Gothenburg in July 1908.

Sweden's squad lacks depth and this tends to be reflected in the dour way the team plays. With no real flair players, Sweden are a dogged yet reliable side. Patrik Andersson and Johan Mjallby are the breakwaters of defence with Olaf Mellberg and Teddy Lucic sandwiching them as full backs. Mellberg and Lucic are not creative when moving forward but solid in their defensive duties. Sweden's midfield has undergone enormous change. Tobias Linderoth is the defensive anchor looking to supply the flanks where Niclas Alexandersson and Freddy Ljungberg seek to find ways round defences. Anders Svensson is a lively attack-minded midfielder, but lacks consistency at international level. Celtic's goal-machine Henrik Larsson is still the man the Swedes look to for goals, but in Marcus Allback they might have discovered a new star.

PROBABLE FORMATION 4-4-2

HEDMAN

MELLBERG — LUCIC

P ANDERSSON — MJALLBY

ALEXANDERSSON — LINDEROTH — A SVENSSON — LJUNGBERG

ALLBACK — LARSSON

★ MEN THAT MATTER!

MARCUS ALLBACK

Age>> 28
Club>> Heerenveen
Marcus Allback has stepped out of the shadow of Kennet Andersson and begun finding the net regularly for Sweden. His goals against Moldova and Slovakia were vital in qualifying.

HENRIK LARSSON

Age>> 30
Club>> Celtic
An extraordinary goalscoring machine for his Scottish club with 35 goals in 2001, he scored a hat-trick of penalties against Moldova.

PATRIK ANDERSSON

Age>> 30
Club>> Barcelona
Captain of the national side and a rock in defence. Andersson's transfer to Spanish giants Barcelona from German giants Bayern Munich reflect his reputation as one of Europe's top defenders.

★ PROBABLE SQUAD ★ QUALIFICATION RECORD

NAME	POSITION	CLUB	APS/GOALS	GAMES	MINS	Y/C	R/C	GOALS
Magnus Hedman	Goalkeeper	Coventry, England	42/0	10	900	0	0	0
Mattias Asper	Goalkeeper	Real Sociedad, Spain	0/0	0	0	0	0	0
Magnus Kihlstedt	Goalkeeper	Copenhagen, Denmark	6/0	0	0	0	0	0
Christoffer Andersson	Defender	Helsingborgs, Sweden	12/0	3	169	0	0	0
Patrik Andersson	Defender	Barcelona, Spain	94/3	10	844	1	0	1
Karl Corneliusson	Defender	AIK Stockholm, Sweden	9/1	3	215	1	0	0
Pontus Kamark	Defender	IFK Gothenburg, Sweden	57/0	2	151	0	0	0
Jozo Matovac	Defender	Helsingborg, Sweden	3/0	2	180	0	0	0
Olof Mellberg	Defender	Aston Villa, England	19/0	8	720	0	0	0
Kleber Saarenpaa	Defender	AaB Aalborg, Denmark	12/0	5	311	0	0	0
Niclas Alexandersson	Midfielder	Everton, England	55/6	7	565	0	0	1
Daniel Andersson	Midfielder	Venezia, Italy	32/1	8	228	0	0	1
Tobias Linderoth	Midfielder	Everton, England	15/1	6	512	1	0	0
Fredrik Ljungberg	Midfielder	Arsenal, England	30/2	9	810	1	0	0
Haken Mild	Midfielder	Wimbledon, England	74/8	5	219	0	0	0
Johan Mjallby	Midfielder	Celtic, Scotland	31/4	5	427	0	0	0
Stefan Schwarz	Midfielder	Sunderland, England	69/6	2	170	0	0	0
Anders Svensson	Midfielder	Southampton, England	23/7	9	450	1	0	2
Magnus Svensson	Midfielder	Brondby, Denmark	24/1	3	248	0	0	1
Marcus Allback	Forward	Heerenveen, Holland	15/6	6	433	0	0	4
Zlatan Ibrahimovic	Forward	Ajax, Holland	4/1	1	24	0	0	1
Henrik Larsson	Forward	Celtic, Scotland	64/21	10	900	0	0	8
Yksel Osmanovski	Forward	Bordeaux, France	14/2	3	110	0	0	0

KEY: APPS/GOALS = International Appearances/Goals; GAMES=Qualification Games played; MINS=Minutes played; Y/C= Yellow cards R/C=Red cards

HISTORY AT THE WORLD CUP

1930 1934 1938 1950 1954 1958 1962 1966 1970 1974 1978 1982 1986 1990 1994 1998

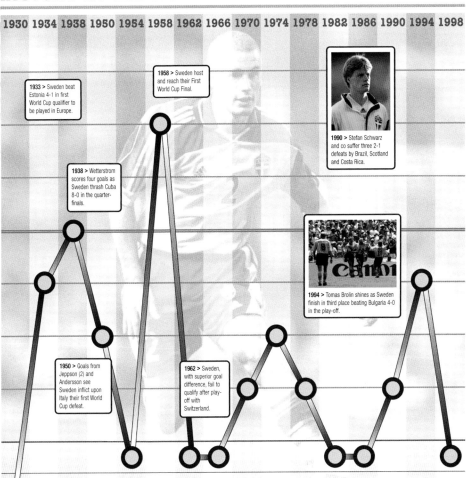

1933 > Sweden beat Estonia 4-1 in first World Cup qualifier to be played in Europe.

1958 > Sweden host and reach their First World Cup Final.

1990 > Stefan Schwarz and co suffer three 2-1 defeats by Brazil, Scotland and Costa Rica.

1938 > Wetterstrom scores four goals as Sweden thrash Cuba 8-0 in the quarter-finals.

1994 > Tomas Brolin shines as Sweden finish in third place beating Bulgaria 4-0 in the play-off.

1950 > Goals from Jeppson (2) and Andersson see Sweden inflict upon Italy their first World Cup defeat.

1962 > Sweden, with superior goal difference, fail to qualify after play-off with Switzerland.

★ WORLD CUP HISTORY

1930 >> Did Not Enter	**1970** >> First Round
1934 >> Quarter-Finals	**1974** >> Second Round
1938 >> Fourth Place	**1978** >> First Round
1950 >> Second Round	**1982** >> Did Not Qualify
1954 >> Did Not Qualify	**1986** >> Did Not Qualify
1958 >> Runners-Up	**1990** >> First Round
1962 >> Did Not Qualify	**1994** >> Third Place
1966 >> Did Not Qualify	**1998** >> Did Not Qualify

★ WORLD CUP RECORDS, STORIES AND WEIRDNESS

MOST GOALS IN A MATCH >> Gustav Wetterström scored 4 against Cuba in 1938.

PENALTY SUCCESS >> Sweden has converted 5 of the 6 penalties it has been awarded at World Cup Finals, a performance bettered only by three other nations.

GROUP H

OPPONENT	DATE	UK TIME	VENUE
Russia	**5 June**	07.30	**Kobe, Japan**
Belgium	**10 June**	10.00	**Oita, Japan**
Japan	**14 June**	07.30	**Osaka, Japan**

"'Les Aigles de Carthage' impress in qualifying"

TUNISIA

Tunisia impressed with the way they qualified for their third appearance at a World Cup Finals. During France 98 they found themselves in a tough group with Colombia, England and Romania – against whom they secured an impressive 1-1 draw. All in all they had generally acquitted themselves well on the world stage. Many of the players at France 98 will be back again to compete at Japan/Korea as the Tunisians have kept the core of a side – originally assembled at under-23 level – to compete at the 1996 Atlanta Olympics.

"Les Aigles de Carthage", who had finished fourth at the 2000 African Nations Cup under Italian coach Francesco Scoglio, dismissed Mauritania 5-1 on aggregate in the preliminary round and kicked off the group stage away against main rivals Ivory Coast.

Midfielder Zoubier Beya was in magnificent form setting up both goals for Imed Mhedhebi and Kais Ghodhbane in the 12th and 19th minutes respectively. What would have been a fantastic start to the group was tempered by poor defensive play that allowed the home side to recover and achieve an unlikely 2-2 draw. The Ivory Coast fans were even less happy with their team than the Tunisian supporters were with theirs and both teams found themselves holed up in the stadium while the police used tear gas to disperse the crowd.

It needed a sterling performance in their next game against Madagascar when Hassan Gabsi was sent off in the first half. Ten-man Tunisia battled on, Beya putting them ahead on the stroke of half time. That was all that was needed as the Tunisians defended well, keeping the Madagascans at arms' length.

Immediately after, Tunisia's qualification hopes were undermined when coach Scoglio quit. The Italian had been offered a job by club side Genoa and wanted to split his time between Italy and Tunisia. The Tunisian FA decided this was not an option and so Scoglio stepped down to be replaced by German Eckhard Krautzen. Krautzen continued Scoglio's good work, winning 2-1 in Congo and thrashing the Democratic Republic of Congo (formerly Zaire) 6-0 at home.

Two goals in the last five minutes from Ali Zitouni and Imed Mhadhebi clinched a 2-0 win in Madagascar followed by a 1-1 draw with Ivory Coast, now the only team who could stop them qualifying.

Tunisia then disposed of Congo 6-0 at home with goals from Badra, Zitouni, Beya (2), Mhadbi and Jelassi, virtually assuring qualification. In their last game, Tunisia travelled to the Stade de Martyrs in the Congo Democratic Republic and, in a brilliantly controlled performance, inflicted upon the home side their worst-ever home defeat. Khaled Badra put Tunisia ahead after 14 minutes with Zoubier Beya netting twice just after the break for a deserved 3-0 win. A result that unfortunately led to rioting among the unhappy Congo Democratic Republic supporters.

However, not all is entirely well with the North Africans. In reality Tunisia are an ageing side who lack sufficient depth in their squad to deal with injuries, as was demonstrated by their poor performance at the 2002 African Nations Cup where they not only failed to win, but failed to score. German coach Krautzen has also gone to be replaced by ex-France and Morocco coach Henri Michel.

★ THE LOWDOWN

Population: 9.7 million

Capital: Tunis

Leader: Mohammed Ghannouchi

Life Expectancy: Male: 72 yrs Female: 75 yrs

>> Agriculture makes up the basis of the Tunisian economy; it accounts for 23% of the labour force.

>> Until 1815 piracy made up a large part of the national income, until, that is, the U.S. Navy attacked Tunis and put a stop to it.

>> In the south the fierce "Sirocco" winds can take the temperatures into the mid-40 degrees centigrade — better wear a hat and take plenty of liquids!

★ **ASSOCIATION:** Federation Tunisienne de Football

★ **JOINED FIFA:** 1960

★ **JOINED CAF:** 1960

★ **PLAYERS:** 18,300

★ **CLUBS:** 215

★ **WEBSITE:** www.ftf.com.tn

★ **HONOURS:** None

★ ROAD TO QUALIFICATION

Apr 00 **Mauritania** (a) > (w) **1**-2
Jaidi 65, Gabsi 76

Apr 00 **Mauritania** (h) > (w) **3**-0 (agg **5**-1)
Bilal 16 og, Jaziri 25, Mhadhebi 49

Jun 00 **Ivory Coast** (a) > (d) 2-2
Imed 13, Kais 20

Jul 00 **Madagascar** (h) > (w) **1**-0 Baya 45

Jan 01 **Congo** (a) > (w) 1-**2**
Zitouni, A 38, Jaziri 58

Feb 01 **Congo DR** (h) > (w) **6**-0
Zitouni, A 8, 90, Jaziri 26, 64, Konzari 30, Baya 84

Apr 01 **Ivory Coast** (h) > (d) **1**-1 Jaziri 49

May 01 **Madagascar** (a) > (w) 0-**2**
Zitouni, A 85, Mhadhebi 90

Jun 01 **Congo** (h) > (w) **6**-0
Badra 28 pen, Zitouni, A 38, Baya 44, 61, Mhadhebi 58, Jelassi 90

Jul 01 **Congo DR** (a) > (w) 0-**3**
Badra 14, Baya 50, 54

★ FINAL GROUP TABLE

Team	P	W	D	L	F	A	Pts
Tunisia	**8**	**6**	**2**	**0**	**23**	**4**	**20**
Ivory Coast	8	4	3	1	18	8	15
Congo DR	8	3	1	4	7	16	10
Madagascar	8	2	0	6	5	15	6
Congo	8	1	2	5	5	15	5

★ RECENT RESULTS

Mar 02 **South Korea** (h) > (d) **0**-0

Mar 02 **Norway** (h) > (d) **0**-0

Genoa's Khaled Badra shows why none shall pass.

DID YOU KNOW?

Tunisia caused a shock in their first World Cup match in 1978 by beating Mexico 3-1 after going a goal down.

Tunisia are reliant upon their first choice strikers Ali Zitouni and Adel Sellimi as became painfully obvious when both were absent from Tunisia's disastrous African Nations Cup – at which Tunisia failed to score a single goal. Sellimi, who has had a falling out with boss Henri Michel, is not guaranteed his place. Considering the current dearth of Tunisian talent, Sellimi's absence could again prove critical. If he does not travel to Japan/Korea then Jamel Zabi is his likely replacement. Tunisia are an ageing team, but age brings wisdom – of a sort. They are a defensively strong side and notoriously difficult to beat. Khaled Badra, Mounir Boukadida, Radhi Jaidi and Hatem Trabelsi are an experienced quartet, three of whom play their club soccer in Europe. The midfield is solid if neither blessed with flair nor an ability to surprise. Watch for Imed Mhadhebi, the player most likely to try and do something special.

PROBABLE FORMATION 4-4-2

EL OUAER

BADRA H TRABELSI

BOUKADIDA JAIDI

BAYA BOUZAIENE NAFTI MHADHEBI

ZITOUNI SELLIMI

★ MEN THAT MATTER!

KHALED BADRA

Age>> 29
Club>> Genoa
Tough, reliable defender who played for Tunisia at France 98 after making his mark at the Atlanta Olympics two years earlier. Highly-rated by ex-Tunisia boss Scoglio who signed him for Genoa.

MHADHEBI

Age>> 26
Club>> Genoa
Featured in all but one of the qualifiers, scoring 4 goals which earned him a move to Genoa from Etoile Sahel at the beginning of the season.

CHOKRI EL OAUER

Age>> 35
Club>> Esperence
El Oauer is a controversial goalkeeper who was banned from club competition after faking injury in an African Champions League. He will captain Tunisia and has played in five African Nations Cups.

★ PROBABLE SQUAD   ★ QUALIFICATION RECORD

NAME	POSITION	CLUB	APS/GOALS	GAMES	MINS	Y/C	R/C	GOALS
Hassen Bejaoui	Goalkeeper	CA Bizerte, Tunisia	0/0	0	0	0	0	0
Chokri al-Ouaer	Goalkeeper	Esperance, Tunisia	101/0	6	540	0	0	0
Ahmed Jaouachi	Goalkeeper	US Monastir, Tunisia	0/0	0	0	0	0	0
Khaled Badra	Defender	Esperance, Tunisia	71/9	8	720	1	0	2
Mounir Boukadida	Defender	Waldhof Mannheim, Germany	51/3	3	149	0	0	0
Raouf Bouzaiene	Defender	Genoa, Italy	40/0	8	586	1	0	0
Radhi Jaidi	Defender	Esperance, Tunisia	41/3	7	630	1	0	0
Hamdi Marzouki	Defender	Africain, Tunisia	4/0	1	22	0	0	0
Emir Mkademi	Defender	Etoile Sahel, Tunisia	6/0	0	0	0	0	0
Hatem Trabelsi	Defender	Ajax, Holland	26/0	3	111	0	0	0
Walid Azaiez	Defender	Esperance, Tunisia	18/2	1	90	0	0	0
Zoubeir Baya	Midfielder	Besiktas, Turkey	76/18	8	692	1	0	6
Slim Ben Achour	Midfielder	Martigues, France	2/0	0	0	0	0	0
Riadh Bouazizi	Midfielder	Bursaspor, Turkey	45/2	3	241	0	0	0
Hassen Gabsi	Midfielder	Genoa, Italy	47/16	6	459	3	1	0
Kaies Ghodhbane	Midfielder	Etoile Sahel, Tunisia	62/3	6	267	1	0	0
Mehdi Nafti	Midfielder	Racing Santander, Spain	2/0	0	0	0	0	0
Bessam Daassi	Forward	Stade Tunisien, Tunisia	4/2	0	0	0	0	0
Ziad Jaziri	Forward	Etoile Sahel, Tunisia	23/8	5	380	1	0	3
Imed Mhadhebi	Forward	Genoa, Italy	30/9	7	228	1	0	2
Adel Sellimi	Forward	Freiberg, Germany	2/0	2	162	0	1	0
Jamel Zabi	Forward	CA Bizerte, Tunisia	4/3	0	0	0	0	0
Ali Zitouni	Forward	Esperance, Tunisia	24/9	8	533	1	0	5

KEY: APPS/GOALS = International Appearances/Goals; GAMES=Qualification Games played; MINS=Minutes played; Y/C= Yellow cards R/C=Red cards

HISTORY AT THE WORLD CUP

1930 1934 1938 1950 1954 1958 1962 1966 1970 1974 1978 1982 1986 1990 1994 1998

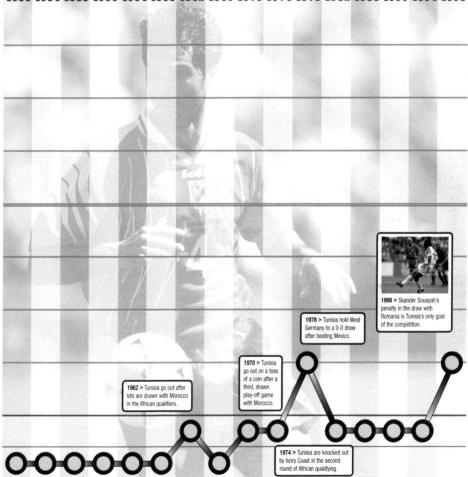

1998 > Skander Souayah's penalty in the draw with Romania is Tunisia's only goal of the competition.

1978 > Tunisia hold West Germany to a 0-0 draw after beating Mexico.

1970 > Tunisia go out on a toss of a coin after a third, drawn play-off game with Morocco.

1962 > Tunisia go out after lots are drawn with Morocco in the African qualifiers.

1974 > Tunisia are knocked out by Ivory Coast in the second round of African qualifying.

★ WORLD CUP HISTORY

1930 >> Did Not Enter		**1970** >> Did Not Qualify	
1934 >> Did Not Enter		**1974** >> Did Not Qualify	
1938 >> Did Not Enter		**1978** >> First Round	
1950 >> Did Not Enter		**1982** >> Did Not Qualify	
1954 >> Did Not Enter		**1986** >> Did Not Qualify	
1958 >> Did Not Enter		**1990** >> Did Not Qualify	
1962 >> Did Not Qualify		**1994** >> Did Not Qualify	
1966 >> Did Not Enter		**1998** >> First Round	

★ WORLD CUP RECORDS, STORIES AND WEIRDNESS

SHORTEST WORLD CUP CAREER >> Tunisia's Khemais Labidi played just two minutes against Mexico in 1978 as they ran out 3-1 winners. He was never seen on the world stage again.

OPPONENT	DATE	UK TIME	VENUE
Brazil	**3 June**	**10.00**	**Ulsan, Korea**
Costa Rica	**9 June**	**10.00**	**Incheon, Korea**
China	**13 June**	**07.30**	**Seoul, Korea**

"will it be Turkish delight in Korea?"

TURKEY

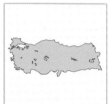

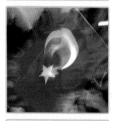

★ THE LOWDOWN

Population: 66.4 million

Capital: Ankara

Leader: Bulent Ecevit

Life Expectancy: Male: 69 yrs
Female: 73 yrs

>> Turkey became a republic in 1923. Its founding father was Mohammed Kamal, who adopted the name Ataturk.

>> Turkey is home to Mount Ararat, the legendary landing place of Noah's Ark.

>> Besides being renowned for Turkish delight, belly dancing and raki (an aniseed flavoured alcoholic drink), Turkish carpets are also world famous. It can take two women over 2 years to make a decent sized one – so careful with those shoes!

Turkey are back at the World Cup after a 48-year absence. Turkish soccer has been improving at international level in recent years; they qualified for both Euro 96 and Euro 2000, and while losing all their group games in England, reached the quarter-final stage in Amsterdam. At club level Galatasaray became the first Turkish club to win a European trophy when they beat Arsenal to lift the UEFA Cup.

The national team has been largely unchanged since Euro 2000 with Inter Milan's Hakan Sukur, who began his career at Galatasaray and is the most accomplished Turkish player of all time, still leading the attack and Fenerbahçe keeper Rüstü Recber in goal with a midfield of Okan Buruk and Tugay Kerimoglu at its heart. New coach Senol Gunes has brought on a significant young talent in German-born Yiliray Basturk. A dynamic and creative player who livens up the Turkish team whenever he is on the field.

Not that coach Senol Gunes has the universal backing of the Turkish media. Turkey's six-team qualifying group came down to a three-horse race between the Turks, Slovakia and Sweden. They started well with wins over Moldova and Azerbaijan sandwiching a dramatic 1-1 draw in Sweden, where Tayfur Havatcu converted an injury time penalty equaliser – an impressive result as they had to field a seriously under strength side owing to injuries, suspensions and Hakan Sukur playing on despite food poisoning.

A 1-1 home draw with rivals Slovakia was followed by wins over Macedonia and Azerbaijan. In the return fixture Turkey were almost blown away by Macedonia in Bursa. Turkey found themselves 2-0 down inside just 20 minutes in front of 25,000 of their own supporters. It needed an unlikely hat-trick from Aston Villa's defender Alpay and the sending off of opponent Krstev to salvage a point in a thrilling 3-3 draw.

Hakan Sukur's first-half winner in Slovakia, however, assured Turkey of at least a play-off place. With a home fixture against Sweden to come, automatic qualification seemed probable. Hakan Sukur gave Turkey a 51st minute lead against the Swedes and they were within two minutes of victory when Henrik Larsson equalised. Andreas Andersson scored the winner for Sweden in the last minute of the game and Turkey were suddenly condemned to the play-offs. Unsurprisingly, coach Senol Gunes was subjected to another barrage of criticism.

In the play-offs Turkey were drawn against Austria. Senol Gunes was able to silence his critics with a 6-0 aggregate win including a 5-0 second leg thrashing in which Basturk netted his first international goal, Hakan Sukur boosted his all-time tally to 35 with Okan and Arif (2) completing the scoring.

Turkey have a realistic chance of progressing to the second round from a group that includes World Cup novices Costa Rica and debutantes China. The Turkish media expect their team to beat both of these sides heaping yet more pressure on Senol Gunes, who is, after all, only the second coach of a Turkish World Cup team.

★ **ASSOCIATION:** Turkiye Futbol Federasyonou
★ **JOINED FIFA:** 1923
★ **JOINED UEFA:** 1962
★ **PLAYERS:** 64,600

★ **CLUBS:** 230
★ **WEBSITE:** www.tff.org
★ **HONOURS:** None.

n Mjallby brings down Hakan Unsal while he's still singing the Turkish National Anthem.

★ ROAD TO QUALIFICATION

Sep 00 **Moldova** (h) > (w) **2-0**
Okan 45, Emre 75

Oct 00 **Sweden** (a) > (d) **1-1**
Havatacu 90

Oct 00 **Azerbaijan** (a) > (w) **0-1**
Hakan Sukur 73

Mar 01 **Slovakia** (h) > (d) **1-1**
Hakan Sukur 53 pen

Mar 01 **Macedonia** (a) > (w) **1-2**
Mitrevski 68 og, Umit Davala 70

Jun 01 **Azerbaijan** (h) > (w) **3-0**
Tayfun 2, Oktay 27, Hakan Sukur 33

Jun 01 **Macedonia** (h) > (d) **3-3**
Alpay 43, 58, 70

Sep 01 **Slovakia** (a) > (w) **0-1**
Hakan Sukur 34

Sep 01 **Sweden** (h) > (l) **1-2**
Hakan Sukur 51

Oct 01 **Moldova** (a) > (w) **0-3**
Emre 8, Nihat 78, Mansiz 82

Nov 01 **Austria** (a) > (w) **0-1** Okan 60

Nov 01 **Austria** (h) > (w) **5-0** (agg **6-0**)
Basturk 24, Hakan Sukur 31, Okan 45,
Arif 70, 84

★ FINAL GROUP TABLE

Team	P	W	D	L	F	A	Pts
Sweden	10	8	2	0	20	3	26
Turkey	10	6	3	1	18	8	21
Slovakia	10	5	2	3	16	9	17
Macedonia	10	1	4	5	11	18	7
Moldova	10	1	3	6	6	20	6
Azerbaijan	10	1	2	7	4	17	5

★ RECENT RESULTS

Feb 02 **Ecuador** (h) > (l) **0-1**
Mar 00 **South Korea** (h) > (d) **0-0**

DID YOU KNOW?

Turkey are back in the World Cup for the first time in 48 years and Senol Gunes is only their second ever World Cup coach.

A serious ankle injury to Aston Villa defender Alpay makes the player doubtful for the World Cup and his probable absence will have a serious effect on Turkey's defensive capabilities. Alpay has been ever present on the left of a back three which includes Emre Asik and Umit Ozat, but Alpay's understudy, Hakan Unsal, has been hovering in the wings and is ready to shine. An exciting midfield, which emphasises attack, mixes the new talent of Yiliray Basturk with the experienced Abdullah, Okan and Tugay, experience which may help to cover any weaknesses at the back. Turkey, though, still rely on goals from Hakan Sukur. In Hasan Sas he has a perfect foil, a player whose movement is an integral part of Turkish attacking play, and who creates the space and chances for marksman Hakan Sukur.

PROBABLE FORMATION 3-4-1-2

RUSTU

EMRE ASIK HAKAN UNSAL

UMIT OZAT

UMIT DAVALA OKAN TUGAY BASTURK

ABDULLAH

HAKAN SUKUR HASAN SAS

★ MEN THAT MATTER!

YILDIRAY BASTURK

Age>> 23
Club>> Bayer Leverkusen

Basturk is a German-born Turkish international playmaker who became the youngest captain in the Bundesliga with Bochum. He later joined Leverkusen for £4 million and has impressed every time he's played for Turkey.

HAKAN SUKUR

Age>> 30
Club>> Parma

Turkey's main striker whose goals have been the reason Turkey have qualified for their first World Cup and two European Championships. Confirmed his status as a top striker in Serie A with Parma.

TUGAY KERIMOGLU

Age>> 31
Club>> Blackburn Rovers

Tugay is Turkey's midfield anchor, a reliable, inventive and experienced player. He has been a consistent performer in the English Premiership with Blackburn.

★ PROBABLE SQUAD ★ QUALIFICATION RECORD

NAME	POSITION	CLUB ?	APS/GOALS	GAMES	MINS	Y/C	R/C	GOALS
Metin Aktas	Goalkeeper	Trabzonspor, Turkey	2/0	0	0	0	0	0
Omer Catkic	Goalkeeper	Gaziantepspor, Turkey	3/0	0	0	0	0	0
Rustu Recber	Goalkeeper	Fenerbahce, Turkey	62/0	12	1080	0	0	0
Fatih Akyel	Defender	Fenerbahce, Turkey	33/0	9	610	1	0	0
Emre Asik	Defender	Galatasaray, Turkey	13/2	1	90	0	0	0
Umit Bozkurt	Defender	Galatasaray, Turkey	2/0	2	180	0	0	0
Bulent Korkmaz	Defender	Galatasaray, Turkey	65/2	7	569	2	0	0
Umit Ozat	Defender	Fenerbahce, Turkey	10/0	7	594	1	0	0
Mehmet Polat	Defender	Gaziantepspor, Turkey	4/0	1	90	0	0	0
Ogun Temizkanoglu	Defender	Fenerbahce, Turkey	74/5	6	482	2	0	0
Emre Belozoglu	Midfielder	Internazionale, Italy	9/1	7	570	3	0	1
Okan Buruk	Midfielder	Internazionale, Italy	25/4	8	585	2	0	3
Umit Davala	Midfielder	Milan, Italy	20/1	6	540	0	0	1
Abdullah Ercan	Midfielder	Fenerbahce, Turkey	67/0	9	730	0	0	0
Tayfur Havutcu	Midfielder	Besiktas, Turkey	37/6	6	333	0	0	1
Tugay Kerimoglu	Midfielder	Blackburn, England	66/2	5	450	1	0	0
Tayfun Korkut	Midfielder	Real Sociedad, Spain	36/1	6	212	0	0	1
Ergun Penbe	Midfielder	Galatasaray, Turkey	18/0	8	316	0	0	0
Hakan Unsal	Midfielder	Blackburn, England	22/0	4	360	0	0	0
Basturk Yildiray	Midfielder	Bayer Leverkusen, Germany	11/1	7	309	0	0	1
Arif Erdem	Forward	Galatasaray, Turkey	48/8	10	513	0	0	2
Hasan Sas	Forward	Galatasaray, Turkey	12/0	11	709	1	0	0
Hakan Sukur	Forward	Parma, Italy	70/34	11	990	1	0	6

KEY: APPS/GOALS = International Appearances/Goals; GAMES=Qualification Games played; MINS=Minutes played; Y/C= Yellow cards R/C=Red cards

HISTORY AT THE WORLD CUP

1930 1934 1938 1950 1954 1958 1962 1966 1970 1974 1978 1982 1986 1990 1994 1998

1954 > Turkey qualify for the World Cup by the drawing of lots after three games with Spain.

1950 > Turkey thrash Syria 7-0 to qualify but then withdraw from the competition.

1958 > Turkey refuse to play Israel in qualifying and withdraw from the World Cup.

1970 > Turkey lose all four qualifying matches to USSR and Northern Ireland.

★ WORLD CUP HISTORY

1930 >> Did Not Enter		**1970** >> Did Not Qualify	
1934 >> Did Not Enter		**1974** >> Did Not Qualify	
1938 >> Did Not Enter		**1978** >> Did Not Qualify	
1950 >> Withdrew		**1982** >> Did Not Qualify	
1954 >> First Round		**1986** >> Did Not Qualify	
1958 >> Did Not Enter		**1990** >> Did Not Qualify	
1962 >> Did Not Qualify		**1994** >> Did Not Qualify	
1966 >> Did Not Qualify		**1998** >> Did Not Qualify	

★ WORLD CUP RECORDS, STORIES AND WEIRDNESS

TOP SCORER >> Turkey's best international goalscorer is Hakan Sükür with 16 to date.

WORLD CUP PERFORMANCE >> Turkey have played a total of 87 matches (including qualifying) winning 28, drawing 12 and losing 47.

GROUP D

OPPONENT	DATE	UK TIME	VENUE
Portugal	**5 June**	10.00	**Suwon, Korea**
South Korea	**10 June**	07.30	**Daegu, Korea**
Poland	**14 June**	12.30	**Daejeon, Korea**

"they will play for honour"

UNITED STATES

★ THE LOWDOWN

Population: 278 million

Capital: Washington D.C.

Leader: George W. Bush

Life Expectancy: Male: 74 yrs Female: 80 yrs

>> The United States spends 277 billion dollars on its military forces every year, which is more than most of us earn in a lifetime.

>> Although the U.S. is 2.5 times the size of Western Europe it is only half the area of Russia.

>> Mount McKinley is the highest point in America and Death Valley the lowest (-86m below sea level).

Events of September 11 have had a profound effect on America and the nation's footballers are by no means immune. On the day the USA played their crucial qualifying match against Jamaica at the Foxboro Stadium in Boston, the US bombing of Afghanistan began. "We knew we were at war so it was pretty emotional during the national anthem, but after that we just focused on the game," admitted forward Joe Max-Moore.

And America's footballers needed to focus on the game – after three dreadful performances (losing, in the process, to Mexico, Honduras and Costa Rica), a victory over Jamaica was crucial to the country's World Cup qualifying hopes. The USA got off to an ideal start when Moore scored after just four minutes with a diving header from Claudio Reyna's free-kick. Ten minutes later Jamaica equalised through Jamie Lawrence, but the USA were dominating the game. Frustratingly, they seemed incapable of creating meaningful chances when, in the 81st minute, teenage star Landon Donovan was brought down in the penalty area. Moore stepped up to send the goalkeeper the wrong way for a 2-1 win which, combined with Honduras's shock defeat by Trinidad & Tobago, meant the USA had qualified for the World Cup on a day of high emotion.

With all they've been through the USA will be a more united squad than they were four years ago when internal disputes between players and staff badly affected the squad and led to the USA finishing with the worst record of the 32 teams at France 98.

After the huge disappointment of the last World Cup, the USA brought in new manager Bruce Arena, America's most successful club and college coach who has won an international cap as a goalkeeper.

So far their Japan/Korea preparations have been good. The USA won the 2002 Gold Cup beating Costa Rica 2-0 in the final in Pasadena. The goals came from Josh Wolff, who missed most of the qualifiers through injury and defender Jeff Agoos, who was ever present throughout the qualifying campaign.

Success at the Gold Cup was helped enormously by a 35-day pre-tournament training camp and coach Bruce Arena hopes to reproduce the camp ahead of the World Cup.

Eight years after hosting the World Cup, America has an estimated 18 million soccer players, but the game can still only be considered a minority sport in the US. There are only ten professional teams in the Major Soccer League after two teams recently went out of business. The Gold Cup attracted an average crowd of 18,500 (compared to the 90,000 spectators who watched the USA women's soccer stars win the World Cup Final in Pasadena, California). Indeed, at home matches against Mexico and Honduras, away support outnumbered the home side's fans – leading to the observation that it was easier for the US to play Mexico in Mexico City rather than Los Angeles.

America goes into the World Cup Finals with justifiable ambition. Under coach Arena they have become a side that can win matches – as the third ever win over Mexico during the qualifiers demonstrated.

★ **ASSOCIATION:** United States Soccer Federation
★ **JOINED FIFA:** 1913
★ **JOINED FOOTBALL CONFEDERATION:** 1961
★ **PLAYERS:** 1,411,500

★ **CLUBS:** 7,000
★ **WEBSITE:** www.us-soccer.com
★ **HONOURS:** CONCACAF Gold Cup – 1991, 2002

Captain America remembers he's left the gas on.

★ ROAD TO QUALIFICATION

Jul 00 **Guatemala** (a) > (d) 1-1 Razov 45

Jul 00 **Costa Rica** (a) > (l) 2-1 Stewart 65

Aug 00 **Barbados** (h) > (w) **7**-0
Pope 14, McBride 28, Moore 45, 82,
O'Brien 46, Ramos 72, Stewart 74

Sep 00 **Guatemala** (h) > (w) **1**-0
McBride 72

Oct 00 **Costa Rica** (h) > (d) 0-0

Nov 00 **Barbados** (a) > (w) 0-**4**
Mathis 63, Stewart 73, Jones 77, Razov 90

Feb 01 **Mexico** (h) > (w) **2**-0
Wolff 47, Stewart 87

Mar 01 **Honduras** (a) > (w) 1-**2**
Stewart 32, Mathis 87

Apr 01 **Costa Rica** (h) > (w) **1**-0 Wolff 69

Jun 01 **Jamaica** (a) > (d) 0-0

Jun 01 **Trinidad & Tobago** (h) > (w) **2**-0
Razov 2, Stewart 20

Jun 01 **Mexico** (a) > (l) 1-**0**

Sep 01 **Honduras** (h) > (l) **2**-3
Stewart 7, 83

Sep 01 **Costa Rica** (a) > (l) 2-**0**

Oct 01 **Jamaica** (h) > (w) **2**-1
Moore 3, 80

Nov 01 **Trinidad & Tobago** (a) > (d) 0-0

★ FINAL GROUP TABLE

Team	P	W	D	L	F	A	Pts
Costa Rica	10	7	2	1	17	7	23
Mexico	10	5	2	3	16	9	17
United States	10	5	2	3	11	8	17
Honduras	10	4	2	4	17	17	14
Jamaica	10	2	2	6	7	14	8
Trinidad & Tob	10	1	2	7	5	18	5

★ SEMI-FINAL GROUP TABLE

Team	P	W	D	L	F	A	Pts
United States	6	3	2	1	14	3	11
Costa Rica	6	3	1	2	9	6	10
Guatemala	6	3	1	2	9	6	10
Barbados	6	1	0	5	3	20	3

★ RECENT RESULTS

Feb 02 **Italy** (a) > (l) **1**-0

Mar 02 **Honduras** (h) > (w) **4**-0
Mathis 14, 59, Donovan 44, 67

Mar 02 **Ecuador** (h) > (w) **1**-0 Lewis 21

Mar 02 **Germany** (a) > (l) 4-**2** Mathis 17,71

Apr 02 **Mexico** (h) > (w) **1**-0 Mathis 65

DID YOU KNOW?

When the USA famously beat England 1-0 at the 1950 World Cup, Haiti-born Larry Gaetjens scored the historic winning goal.

Captain Claudio Reyna is still the USA's key player in a side that, in recent years, has switched from 3-5-2 to 4-4-2. Reyna remains the heart of midfield from which so many American moves begin. The whole system is designed to supply America's twin strike force of Joe Max-Moore and new wonder boy Landon Donovan through Reyna's superb passing which release an attacking midfield of Chris Armas, John O'Brien and Ernie Stewart. Moore is an established member of the side while Landon, a relative newcomer, has made himself an automatic first choice. No mean feat considering the highly rated Josh Wolff is waiting in the wings. Reyna must also deal with the less spectacular but vital defensive work in front of a back four headed by Jeff Agoos. Who will start in goal? It is difficult to choose between Brad Friedel and Kasey Keller.

PROBABLE FORMATION 4-4-2

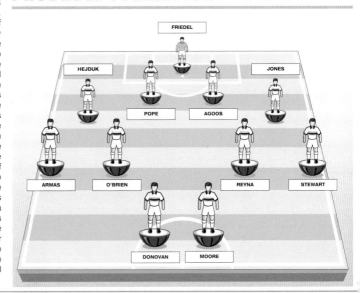

FRIEDEL
HEJDUK
JONES
POPE
AGOOS
ARMAS
O'BRIEN
REYNA
STEWART
DONOVAN
MOORE

★ MEN THAT MATTER!

CLAUDIO REYNA

Age>> 28
Club>> Sunderland
Regarded as America's best player, he missed USA 94 through injury and was considered a big danger at France 98 and marked out of games. He is America's most expensive player at £4.5 million.

LANDON DONOVAN

Age>> 21
Club>> San Jose Earthquakes
Landon Donovan is America's latest bright young soccer star. He has gelled superbly alongside Joe Max-Moore in attack. The MLS signed him back for £145,000 after an unhappy spell with Bayer Leverkusen.

JOE-MAX MOORE

Age>> Everton
Club>> 31
Long serving forward who has been given a boost with the arrival of Landon Donovan. Moore was a squad member at USA 94 and played in midfield at France 98.

★ PROBABLE SQUAD   ★ QUALIFICATION RECORD

NAME	POSITION	CLUB	APS/GOALS	GAMES	MINS	Y/C	R/C	GOALS
Brad Friedel	Goalkeeper	Blackburn, England	73/0	6	540	1	0	0
Tim Howard	Goalkeeper	MetroStars, USA	0/0	0	0	0	0	0
Kasey Keller	Goalkeeper	Tottenham, England	56/0	8	720	0	0	0
Jeff Agoos	Defender	San Jose Earthquakes, USA	125/4	12	1080	0	0	0
Gregg Berhalter	Defender	Crystal Palace, England	22/0	7	454	1	0	0
Steve Cherundolo	Defender	Hannover 96, Germany	9/0	7	606	1	0	0
Frankie Hejduk	Defender	Bayer Leverkusen, Germany	36/5	2	29	0	0	0
Carlos Llamosa	Defender	New England Revolution, USA	25/0	9	653	3	0	0
Eddie Pope	Defender	DC United, USA	44/4	9	764	0	0.	1
David Regis	Defender	Metz, France	24/0	12	1067	2	0	0
Tony Sanneh	Defender	Hertha Berlin, Germany	27/1	14	1205	1	0	0
Greg Vanney	Defender	Bastia, France	12/0	4	249	1	0	0
Chris Armas	Midfielder	Chicago Fire, USA	43/2	14	1216	2	0	0
Cobi Jones	Midfielder	Los Angeles Galaxy, USA	151/14	13	767	0	0	1
Jovan Kirovski	Midfielder	Crystal Palace, England	53/7	8	562	0	0	0
Eddie Lewis	Midfielder	Fulham, England	-	6	301	0	1	0
John O'Brien	Midfielder	Ajax, Holland	12/1	6	337	0	0	1
Claudio Reyna	Midfielder	Sunderland, England	85/8	9	711	2	0	0
Earnie Stewart	Midfielder	NAC Breda, Holland	75/15	15	1301	4	0	8
Landon Donovan	Forward	San Jose Earthquakes, United States	15/2	4	273	0	0	0
Brian McBride	Forward	Columbus Crew, United States	57/18	5	293	0	0	2
Joe-Max Moore	Forward	Everton, England	93/24	12	784	1	0	4
Josh Wolff	Forward	Chicago Fire, United States	14/4	5	259	1	0	2

KEY: APPS/GOALS = International Appearances/Goals; GAMES=Qualification Games played; MINS=Minutes played; Y/C= Yellow cards R/C=Red cards

HISTORY AT THE WORLD CUP

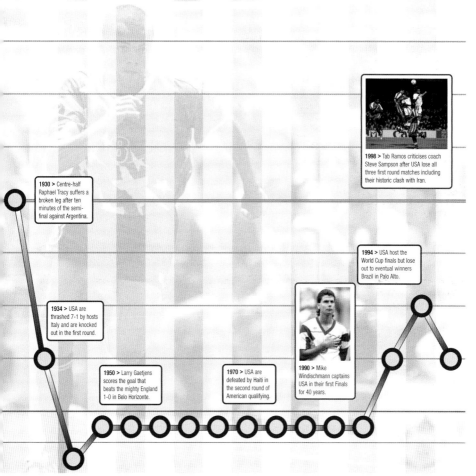

1998 > Tab Ramos criticises coach Steve Sampson after USA lose all three first round matches including their historic clash with Iran.

1930 > Centre-half Raphael Tracy suffers a broken leg after ten minutes of the semi-final against Argentina.

1994 > USA host the World Cup finals but lose out to eventual winners Brazil in Palo Alto.

1934 > USA are thrashed 7-1 by hosts Italy and are knocked out in the first round.

1950 > Larry Gaetjens scores the goal that beats the mighty England 1-0 in Belo Horizonte.

1970 > USA are defeated by Haiti in the second round of American qualifying.

1990 > Mike Windischmann captains USA in their first Finals for 40 years.

★ WORLD CUP HISTORY

1930 >> Fourth Place	1970 >> Did Not Qualify
1934 >> First Round	1974 >> Did Not Qualify
1938 >> Did Not Enter	1978 >> Did Not Qualify
1950 >> Did Not Qualify	1982 >> Did Not Qualify
1954 >> Did Not Qualify	1986 >> Did Not Qualify
1958 >> Did Not Qualify	1990 >> First Round
1962 >> Did Not Qualify	1994 >> Second Round
1966 >> Did Not Qualify	1998 >> First Round

★ WORLD CUP RECORDS, STORIES AND WEIRDNESS

FIRST PLAYER TO SCORE A HAT-TRICK >> American Bert Patenaude scored the first ever World Cup hat-trick against Paraguay in 1930.

UNLIKELIEST RESULT >> When news about the USA's 1-0 defeat of England reached England, people thought it was a misprint in the newspaper. England, with legends Billy Wright and Tom Finney in the side, wasted lots of chances and couldn't prevent the American part-timers from winning.

OPPONENT	DATE	UK TIME	VENUE
Denmark	**1 June**	10.00	**Ulsan, Korea**
France	**6 June**	12.30	**Busan, Korea**
Senegal	**11 June**	07.30	**Suwon, Korea**

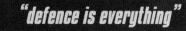
"defence is everything"

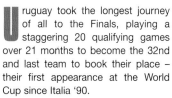

URUGUAY

Uruguay took the longest journey of all to the Finals, playing a staggering 20 qualifying games over 21 months to become the 32nd and last team to book their place – their first appearance at the World Cup since Italia '90.

For Uruguay it's been a tough, long haul made especially difficult by the problems of recalling players from their European clubs and aggravated by the country's leading club, Nacional, refusing to release its players too! In the end, Nacional reluctance to play the national squad game, withholding their players for a sixth time, caused coach Daniel Passarella, and former Argentine international, to quit midway through the qualifiers.

His successor was assistant Victor Pua. It was a natural transition causing the minimum of disruption to the squad and style of play. Pua continued with Passarella's ultra defensive approach making Uruguay very difficult to beat. Uruguay are a team that know how to defend a slender lead, but this also means that they're not at all suited to chasing games.

So the first goal in any Uruguayan international is vitally important and this factor has contributed to the team's inconsistent results. They beat Brazil at home with a first half Federicio Magallanes penalty but were also beaten 2-0 by South America's worst team, Venezuela. The Venezuelan defeat effectively ended their hopes of automatic qualification and Uruguay were left to battle for a play-off place with Colombia in the last round of matches.

Uruguay, with a two-point advantage needed to beat South America's in form team and group winners Argentina to be certain of qualification. In turn Colombia had to win away to Paraguay and see Uruguay lose. Dario Silva, who has been a revelation in attack, gave Uruguay the lead after 19 minutes. It was only Uruguay's 19th goal in 18 matches. However, just before the break Claudio Lopez equalised for Argentina. Meanwhile Colombia had torn apart a lacklustre Paraguayan side and led 4-0. This meant a goal for either Argentina or Colombia would knock out Uruguay. Fortunately, the scores remained unchanged and Uruguay had earned a two-legged play off with Australia.

In the away first leg Uruguay lost 1-0. Now the normally goal-shy Uruguayans would have to score at least twice to qualify. In Centenario, Dario Silva provided the equaliser after 14 minutes. Chances were few and far between but the match was decided ironically, by a Nacional player Richard Morales, who scored twice for a 3-0 win – the first time in 14 months Uruguay had scored three goals in a game.

Uruguay probably won't be the most exciting team to watch at the Finals, although striker Dario Silva is one to watch. Their game is all about stopping the opposition scoring. Captain Paolo Montero marshals one of the best defences in international football – they conceded just 13 goals in qualifying, less than any other side on the South American continent.

★ THE LOWDOWN

Population: 3.3 million

Capital: Montevideo

Leader: Jorge Batlle

Life Expectancy: Male: 72 yrs Female: 79 yrs

>> Freezing temperatures are almost unknown in Uruguay.

>> Three-quarters of the country is grassland used for cattle and sheep grazing.

>> The biggest industries in the country are food processing and textiles.

★ **ASSOCIATION:** Asociacion Uruguaya de Futbol
★ **JOINED FIFA:** 1923
★ **JOINED CONEMBOL:** 1916
★ **PLAYERS:** 134,400

★ **CLUBS:** 1,091
★ **WEBSITE:** www.auf.org.uy
★ **HONOURS:** World Cup 19/50; Copa America 1916/17/20/23/24/26/42/56/59/67/83/87/95; Olympics – 1924/28.

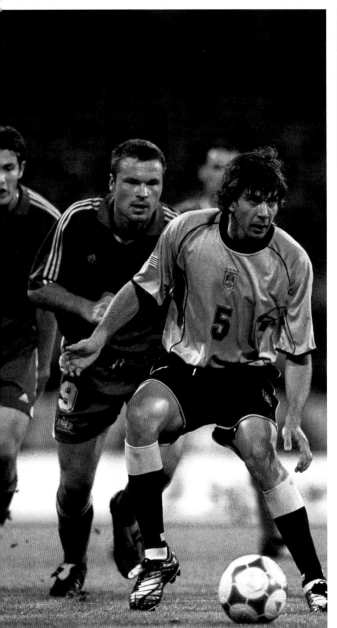

Pablo Garcia hears the patter of Australian Mark Viduka's tiny feet approaching.

★ ROAD TO QUALIFICATION

Mar 00 **Bolivia** (a) > (w) **1**-0 Garcia 26

Apr 00 **Paraguay** (a) > (l) 1-**0**

Jun 00 **Chile** (h) > (w) **2**-1
Silva 34, Ortero Larzabal 42

Jun 00 **Brazil** (a) > (d) 1-**1** Silva 6

Jul 00 **Venezuela** (h) > (w) **3**-1
Olivera, Nic 30, 90, Rodriguez 53

Jul 00 **Peru** (h) > (d) **0**-0

Aug 00 **Colombia** (a) > (l) 1-**0**

Sep 00 **Ecuador** (h) > (w) **4**-0
Magallanes 15, Silva 37, Olivera, Nic 55, Cedres Vera 87

Oct 00 **Argentina** (a) > (l) 2-**1** Ayala 48 og

Nov 00 **Bolivia** (a) > (d) **0**-0

Mar 01 **Paraguay** (h) > (l) **0**-1

Apr 01 **Chile** (a) > (w) 0-**1** Munoz 12 og

Jun 01 **Brazil** (h) > (w) **1**-0
Magallanes 33 pen

Aug 01 **Venezuela** (a) > (l) 2-**0**

Sep 01 **Peru** (a) > (w) 0-**2**
Silva 11, Recoba 45

Oct 01 **Colombia** (h) > (d) **1**-1
Magallanes 34 pen

Nov 01 **Ecuador** (a) > (d) **1**-1
Olivera, Nic 34 pen

Nov 01 **Argentina** (h) > (d) **1**-1 Silva 19

Nov 01 **Australia** (a) > (l) 1-**0**

Nov 01 **Australia** (h) > (w) **3**-0 (agg **3**-0)
Silva 14, Morales 70, 90

★ FINAL GROUP TABLE

Team	P	W	D	L	F	A	Pts
Argentina	18	13	4	1	42	15	43
Ecuador	18	9	4	5	23	20	31
Brazil	18	9	3	6	31	17	30
Paraguay	18	9	3	6	29	23	30
Uruguay	**18**	**7**	**6**	**5**	**19**	**13**	**27**
Colombia	18	7	6	5	20	15	27
Bolivia	18	4	6	8	21	33	18
Peru	18	4	4	10	14	25	16
Venezuela	18	5	1	12	18	44	16
Chile	18	3	3	12	15	27	12

★ RECENT RESULTS

Feb 02 **South Korea** (h) > (w) **2**-1
Abreu 6, 54

Mar 02 **Saudi Arabia** (a) > (l) 3-**2**
Forlan 4, O'Neill 58

189

DID YOU KNOW?

The only World Cup winners never to have defended their title are Uruguay wh
after their 1930 triumph, refused to travel to Europe in 1934.

Great at defending, not so good at scoring goals – that, in short, sums up Uruguay. A solid defence has been the key to their success. Their preferred 3-4-2-1 formation can easily switch to a 5-4-1 when defending a lead and in Fabian Carini, Uruguay have one of South America's most reliable goalkeepers. He is well protected by the three central defenders – Lembo, Montero and Rodriguez – and if the need arises both Tais and Guigou can be pulled back from the flanks, while De Los Santos and Garcia can also form another formidable layer of defence. Frederico Magallenes, the team's penalty taker, and Alvaro Recoba, are the only two midfielders with an attacking brief in support of Dario Silva – who has proved to be an excellent lone striker taking the few chances that come his way. Once Silva has scored, Uruguay will invariably shut up shop.

PROBABLE FORMATION   3-4-2-1

CARINI

LEMBO   RODRIGUEZ

MONTERO

TAIS   DE LOS SANTOS   GARCIA   GUIGOU

MAGALLANES   RECOBA

SILVA

★ MEN THAT MATTER!

DARIO SILVA

Age>> 29
Club>> Malaga
Dario Silva has been a revelation for Uruguay. Cast as the lone striker in a defence-minded team, he scored crucial World Cup qualification goals.

FABIAN CARINI

Age>> 21
Club>> Juventus
Young goalkeeper who played in all but one of the qualifiers and the main reason Uruguay had the best defensive record of South America. Deservedly assumed the mantel as Uruguay's number one.

PABLO GARCIA

Age>> 25
Club>> Venezia
When Pablo Garcia was absent for two games the midfielder was sorely missed — Uruguay were awful. He is an influential player playing in front of the back four instigating many of Uruguay's moves.

★ PROBABLE SQUAD   ★ QUALIFICATION RECORD

NAME	POSITION	CLUB	APS/GOALS	GAMES	MINS	Y/C	R/C	GOALS
Fabian Carini	Goalkeeper	Juventus, Italy	32/0	18	1620	4	0	0
Adrian Berbia	Goalkeeper	Penarol, Uruguay	0/0	0	0	0	0	0
Gustavo Munua	Goalkeeper	Nacional, Uruguay	7/0	1	90	0	0	0
Alejandro Lembo	Defender	Nacional, Uruguay	28/1	16	1365	2	0	0
Gustavo Mendez	Defender	Cagliari, Italy	42/0	8	720	6	1	0
Paolo Montero	Defender	Juventus, Italy	45/3	12	1071	5	0	0
Dario Rodriguez	Defender	Penarol, Uruguay	18/2	11	990	4	0	0
Gonzalo Sorondo	Defender	Internazionale, Italy	15/0	8	638	1	0	0
Washington Tais	Defender	Real Betis, Spain	19/0	9	783	0	0	0
Pablo Garcia	Midfielder	Venezia, Italy	33/1	17	1521	4	0	1
Guill'mo Giacomazzi	Midfielder	Lecce, Italy	6/0	5	115	1	0	0
Gianni Guigou	Midfielder	Roma, Italy	32/0	17	1352	1	0	0
Nicolas Olivera	Midfielder	Sevilla, Spain	22/8	13	1006	3	0	4
Diego Perez	Midfielder	Defensor, Uruguay	8/0	2	8	0	0	0
Gonzalo D L Santos	Midfielder	Valencia, Spain	25/0	9	810	2	1	0
Gustavo Varela	Midfielder	Nacional, Uruguay	5/0	3	193	0	0	0
Sebastian Abreu	Forward	Cruz Azul, Mexico	9/4	2	47	0	0	0
Federico Magallanes	Forward	Venezia, Italy	22/4	11	689	3	0	4
Richard Morales	Forward	Nacional, Uruguay	9/3	2	51	1	0	2
Alvaro Recoba	Forward	Internazionale, Italy	40/8	17	1349	1	0	1
Mario Regueiro	Forward	Racing Santander, Spain	10/0	8	305	1	0	0
Dario Silva	Forward	Malaga, Spain	36/12	8	613	1	1	4
Javier Chevanton	Forward	Lecce, Italy	4/1	3	187	0	0	0

KEY: APPS/GOALS = International Appearances/Goals; **GAMES**=Qualification Games played; **MINS**=Minutes played; **Y/C**= Yellow cards **R/C**=Red cards

HISTORY AT THE WORLD CUP

1930 1934 1938 1950 1954 1958 1962 1966 1970 1974 1978 1982 1986 1990 1994 1998

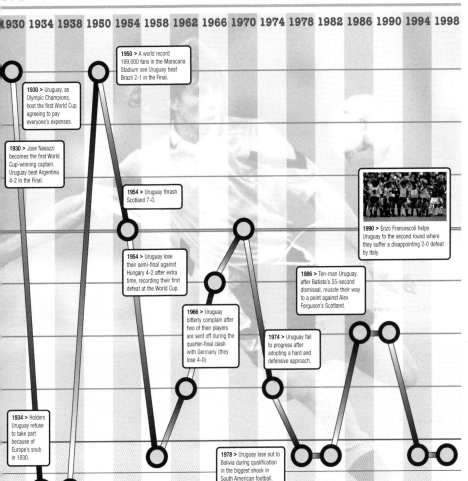

1930 > Uruguay, as Olympic Champions, host the first World Cup agreeing to pay everyone's expenses.

1930 > Jose Nasazzi becomes the first World Cup-winning captain. Uruguay beat Argentina 4-2 in the Final.

1950 > A world record 199,000 fans in the Maracana Stadium see Uruguay beat Brazil 2-1 in the Final.

1954 > Uruguay thrash Scotland 7-0.

1954 > Uruguay lose their semi-final against Hungary 4-2 after extra time, recording their first defeat at the World Cup.

1966 > Uruguay bitterly complain after two of their players are sent off during the quarter-final clash with Germany (they lose 4-0).

1974 > Uruguay fail to progress after adopting a hard and defensive approach.

1986 > Ten-man Uruguay, after Batista's 55-second dismissal, muscle their way to a point against Alex Ferguson's Scotland.

1990 > Enzo Francescoli helps Uruguay to the second round where they suffer a disappointing 2-0 defeat by Italy.

1934 > Holders Uruguay refuse to take part because of Europe's snub in 1930.

1978 > Uruguay lose out to Bolivia during qualification in the biggest shock in South American football.

★ WORLD CUP HISTORY

1930 >> Winners	1970 >> Fourth Place
1934 >> Did Not Enter	1974 >> First Round
1938 >> Did Not Enter	1978 >> Did Not Qualify
1950 >> Winners	1982 >> Did Not Qualify
1954 >> Fourth Place	1986 >> Second Round
1958 >> Did Not Qualify	1990 >> Second Round
1962 >> First Round	1994 >> Did Not Qualify
1966 >> Quarter-Finals	1998 >> Did Not Qualify

★ WORLD CUP RECORDS, STORIES AND WEIRDNESS

MOST GOALS IN ONE MATCH >> Juan Sciaffino scored 4 against Bolivia in 1950.

ONLY PLAYERS TO SCORE IN EVERY MATCH >> Only two player have managed to score in every game of a tournament including the final, one being Alcide Ghiggia of Uruguay in 1950. The other was Brazilian Jairzino.